CW00671554

COLLABORATION ARTISTS

CONVENERS
AND
CONNECTORS
ON

HARNESSING SERENDIPITY

DAVID ADLER
JAMES CORNEHLSEN
ANDREW FROTHINGHAM

CONTENTS

An Invitation   xi
Introduction   xiii

SAFE SPACES FOR REAL TALK . . . TRUST

Jason Alexander   3
Collaborating on Stage, Screen, and Beyond

Richard Attias   8
Global Impressario Engineers Intimate Interactions

Mary Boone   11
Innovator Designs Meeting Experiences That Stimulate High-Performance Collaboration

Paul Bulencea and Claus Raasted   15
Creating Immersive Learning At the College of Extraordinary Experiences

Esther Coopersmith   23
Behind-the-Scenes Diplomat Leverages Spouses for Peace

Edie Fraser   28
Networking Ninja Creates Opportunities for Women

Natalie Jones Hallahan   32
Statecraft Expert Sets the Stage for Diplomatic Results

Coach Kathy Kemper   36
Tennis Teacher to the Powerful Exerts Unique Power Off the Court

Wynton Marsalis   40
Musical Superstar On Improvising Together

Seth Moulton   44
Military-Trained Congressional Leader On The Democracy Of Collaboration

Hervé Sedky   49
The Ultimate Connector Uses Trust to Reshape Communities

Xavier Mufraggi   53
At The Epicenter of the Powerful, Exclusive YPO, The Corporate Leadership Community

David Stark   59
Event Visionary Builds Moving Moments

ATTUNE TO THE NEEDS OF OTHERS . . . AWARENESS

Felice Axelrod   65
Fundraising Dynamo on the Changing Philanthropy Environment

Erica Boeke   68
Unlocking Collaborative Energy By Democratizing Experiences

Taylor Buonocore-Guthrie and Mollie Khine   72
Expanding Jeffersonian Dinners to Align Participants to Solve Problems

Gianna Gaudini   77
Tech-Savvy Event Planning Pro On Purpose

Joe Goldblatt   80
Professor Emeritus of Events on Turbocharging Collaboration With Mindfulness

Mo Husseini   83
Experience Design Leader on Establishing Common Ground

David Isaacs   86
Co-Founder of the World Café, a Transformative Collaboration Format

Amanda Ma   91
A Practiced Expert on Understanding the Role Of Cultural Differences

Capricia Marshall   94
Outspoken Advocate for Soft and Smart Power Roads to Success

Leslie McGuirk   99
Star Uses Astrology to Bring People Together ... and It Actually Works

Holly Peterson   103
Pace-Setting Hostess Shortcuts Path to Successful Collaborative Gatherings

Andrea Sullivan   106
Organizational Psychologist on Understanding Brains and Bodies In Collaboration

FOSTER COMMUNITY . . . BELONGING

Bernie Banks   115
Former General, Now Professor, on Diverse Teams for Ultimate Effectiveness

Steven Clemons   119
Newsperson Uses Real-Time Collaboration to Solve Real Problems

Arthur Pearson   124
Veteran Outward Bound Icon on Collaboration in Learning

Nick Sakellariadis   129
Minor League Team Owner in Continuing Major Success With Communities

Angela Scalpello   133
Communications Consultant on Catalyzing Serendipitous Conversations

Adrian Segar   138
Advocator-in-Chief of the Unconference on Collaborative Environments That People Love

Amanda Slavin 142
Collaboration Wizard on the Progression of Levels of Engagement

Jonathan Steffert 146
New Zealand's Cultural Attaché in D.C. Can't Afford to Tell a Typical Story or Have a So-so Party

Deborah Szekely 151
Life Lessons on Collaboration From Rancho La Puerta Retreat

Ian Ziskin 155
Guru on Collaborations of All Sizes

DREAM THE OUTRAGOUS . . . CREATIVITY

Cheryl Cecchetto 161
Hollywood Events Producer Casts Her Collaborations

Michael Cirino 164
Novel Experience Creator Pushes Boundaries and Raises the Bars

Chris and Jill Drury 168
Duo Leads a Company That's Pioneering New Models of Event Interaction

Tahira Endean 172
People-Centric, Purpose-Driven, Intentional Design Inspires Involvement

Steve Gottlieb 176
Platform Creator Increases Participation By Using Tech to Allow Collaborators to Choose Their Own Journeys

Francisco J. Núñez 180
Choirmaster Leverages Diversity and Mentorship to Create Harmony

Bryan Rafanelli 184
Event Maestro Creates Opportunity for Serendipity By Planning Every Moment

Sandy Safi 187
Connecting the World By Creating FOMO Phenomenon

Sarah Shewey 191
Making Trained Talent on Demand a Reality

John Woo 195
Connecting Physical and Virtual Audiences By Breaking the "Fifth Wall" in Hybrid Gatherings

LET WONDER LEAD . . . CURIOSITY

Lisa Belzberg 201
Conscious Connector Breaks Down Barriers to Create Larger Caring Communities

Sarah Brown 204
Quiet Activist, Spouse of Former British Prime Minister, Takes Deliberate Steps to Create Change

Colin Cowie 208
Celebrity Event Professional Intersects Hospitality and Entertainment to Motivate Action

Lauren Kotkin   211
Philanthropic Specialist Helps Unlock the Riches and Energy of the World
Through Conferences

Anita McBride   215
D.C. Insider Shines Spotlight on the Power Of First Ladies

Roger Nierenberg   220
Teaching Businesspeople Collaboration Through Immersion in the
Orchestra Experience

Charlie Palmer   223
Chef and Host Cooks Up Collaborative Experiences

Ben Parr   227
Entrepreneur, Influencer, and Writer Pays Attention to Attention

Dr. Wayne Pernell   230
Exponential Success Coach With a Doctorate in Clinical Psychology
Applies Principles of Couples Therapy to Get Big Business Results

ALLOW PEOPLE TO FEEL ... EMPATHY

Marc Friedland   237
Inviting Participation and Pushing the Envelope for Stimulating Details

Joanna Stone Herman   240
Dealmaker Births New Collaborations Destined for Success

Ruud Janssen   244
Event Canvas Artist Who Envisions the Success Journey

Mark Johnson   247
Uniting the World By Making it Possible for People To Sing Together
Virtually

Andrew Lacanienta   252
Strategically Designing Transformations With an Understanding of the
Types of Experiences

J. B. Miller   256
Go-To Resource for Next Level Collaborations With Greater Impact

Barry Ross Rinehart   259
Leverage Emotions for Impact

Brian Solis   264
Global Innovation Evangelist Combines Digital and Real-World
Experiences to Reach More People

Caitlin Walker   269
Pioneer of Using Clean Questions Movement for More Effective
Collaborations

Going Forward: Collaboration Is Contagious   277
About the Authors   279
Our Collaborators   281

This book is dedicated to all those who have been under-appreciated for their hard work to get people to work together. Your skills and accomplishments have been minimized over the years, and it's time to change that. You have artfully advanced collaboration in unique ways, so that today—just when we need it most—we have new understanding and abilities in using soft power for positive progress. In a world where humans and human interactions are still too complex, unpredictable, and varied to be coded into programs, you have piloted new kinds of people-based fusion.

You have found ways to harness serendipity.

A warm Thank You to all who have collaborated on this book.

Adrian Segar, Adrienne Fontaine, Alex Plaxen, Amanda Ma, Amanda Slavin, Andrea Sullivan, Andrew Lacanienta, Angela Scalpello, Anita McBride, Arthur Pearson, Barry Ross Rinehart, Beka Troutman, Ben Parr, Bernie Banks, Brian Solis, Bryan Rafanelli, Caitlin Walker, Capricia Marshall, Charlie Palmer, Cheryl Cecchetto, Chris Drury, Christian Conner, Claire Hoffman, Claus Raasted, Coach Kathy Kemper, Colin Cowie, David Isaacs, David Stark, Deborah Szekely, Dr. Wayne Pernell, Edie Fraser, Erica Boeke, Esther Coppersmith, Felice Axelrod, Gianna Gaudini, Hervé Sedky, Gregory Newton Brown, Holly Peterson, Ian Ziskin, J.B. Miller, Francisco J. Núñez, Jason Alexander, Jacob Adler, Jill Taub Drury, Joanna Stone Herman, Joe Goldblatt, John Woo, Jonathan Adler, Jonathan Steffert, Lauren Kotkin, Leslie McGuirk, Lisa Belzberg, Marc Friedland, Mark Johnson, Mary Boone, Michael Adler, Michael Cirino, Mo Husseini, Mollie Khine, Natalie Jones Hallahan, Nicholas Sakellariadis, Paul Bulencea, Rachel Curran, Richard Attias, Roger Nierenberg, Ruud Janssen, Sandy Safi, Sarah Brown, Sarah Shewey, Seth Mouton, Shaun Loftus, Steve Gottlieb, Steven Clemons, Taylor Buonocore-Guthrie, Wynton Marsalis, Xavier Mufraggi

AN INVITATION

The biggest challenges we face will only be solved by artful collaboration. Artful collaboration might be the most critical resource for our successful future. It is in the boundaries of artful collaboration that serendipity turns into solutions.

A "Collaboration Artist" knows how to bring people together, enroll them in a common mission, create idea flow, and translate ideas into new solutions to solve problems and drive achievement of important goals. From modest challenges like moving a small corporate initiative forward, to eradicating a disease, whether in small or large endeavors ... collaboration equals success!

Our culture is full of celebrated individual achievers: the home run hitter in baseball, the pop artist in music, the hot designer in fashion, the company founder, or the inventor. But *imagine* if we celebrated the greatest collaborators, the conveners, facilitators, co-creators, negotiators, consensus builders, and more—the most collaborative filmmakers, event producers, corporate project managers, legislators, community and NGO organizers, civic catalysts, and more.

If we listened to stories of their collaboration virtuosity and noted their philosophies, methods, behaviors, habits, and favorite tools—and emulated them—the benefits would spread across neighborhoods, communities,   charities,   companies,   industries,   governments, geographic populations, and the world.

Imagine if we centered collaboration in our culture, creating places for people to go to learn about the practical tools, techniques, and best practices to build a community of like-minded enablers of collaboration.

Imagine if we elevated the very idea of collaboration, teaching it to children in our schools so that artful collaboration became seen by them as one of the most important skills to have.

In the world they would create for themselves and future generations, innovations would come to life faster, problems would get solved faster, agreements would be reached with less rancor, solutions would be made stronger, and the world of possibilities would be bigger.

This book provides an opportunity for you to learn from some of the greatest collaborators of our generation. Our intention in putting it together is nothing less than launching what may turn out to be the most important collaboration in history … the collaboration to teach, enable, and celebrate collaboration as a universal ideal.

Join us. Help us create the new era of high-impact collaboration and make it a hallmark of mankind to carry us into a brighter future— a future with more people than ever before motivated and empowered to work together to solve problems, invent the new, and improve the lives of people around the world.

INTRODUCTION
IT STARTS WITH "LET'S"

When you rub elbows with people in unexpected ways, magical things happen.

It has been suggested that the most powerful phrase in the English language is "Let's." When people meet and connect, the word can invite and initiate action and results, as in "Let's go to lunch," or "Let's study that," or even "Let's start a revolution."

Together, we can be more powerful than we are individually.

But while new ideas, breakthrough thinking, and progress are most often the product of collective interaction, intelligence, and initiative, the talent for getting a group of people to "Let's" isn't distributed evenly among the population. It never has been. Some people are just naturally more adept at getting people to connect and work together. Others have studied and learned to be effective catalysts of human interaction.

What can we learn from those special people who are masters at facilitating connections? How do they work their magic? What makes them so good at bringing people together? They have been among our best teachers, lawyers, politicians, marketers, event organizers, impresarios, restaurateurs, non-profit leaders, entrepreneurs, innovators, matchmakers, community leaders, medical researchers, engineers, and artists. You recognize these rare individuals when you encounter them.

They are the ones who others rely on for inspiration, ideas, and assistance on everything under the sun.

Sometimes it's easy to forget that collaboration is a skill we can all better learn, develop, and share. There are so many different ways that humans can come together. So many, in fact, that the act of convening often seems random. But when you talk to people who have spent their lives energizing group efforts, patterns start to emerge. The stage has often been set for success in specific ways. There is usually some orchestration—a structure, a community, or a person—involved. The resulting serendipity, it turns out, often isn't totally serendipitous: it's just waiting to be harnessed by you and your fellow collaborators.

"Harnessing Serendipity" might seem like an oxymoron, a phrase that contradicts itself. Like "jumbo shrimp," *harnessing* and *serendipity* seem to clash. Harnessing evokes the idea of designing, controlling, and directing. Meanwhile serendipity hints at surprise and randomness. But we don't see the phase as having an internal conflict. We think "Harnessing Serendipity" aptly describes something that happens whenever people collaborate.

X-rays were discovered by accident. In 1895, German physicist Wilhelm Roentgen saw evidence of something unseen while he was experimenting. This accident ultimately exposed X-rays, which have become fundamental to medical diagnosis and treatments.

Penicillin grew from serendipity. In 1928, Scottish biologist Alexander Fleming noticed an unexpected phenomenon during a laboratory experiment. Looking for an explanation, he discovered penicillin, the world's first antibiotic drug.

During World War II, the technology that became the microwave oven bubbled up when people were looking to create something for warfare, not for the kitchen. The story, possibly accurate, is that American engineer Percy Spencer discovered the potential of microwaves to cook food when he was surprised to find that a chocolate bar he had been saving for a snack had melted.

Individually, we're wired to experience serendipity when we notice something surprising and promising in our environment. When two or more individuals discover each other, the potential for energy, innovation, and power is exponential. Of course, people don't always mesh and move forward—but when they do, the results can be stunning.

You know those stories of people experiencing love at first sight? Or how a couple can magically seem to have complementary strengths that "complete each other?" That's serendipity, harnessed by a couple for the benefit of a partnership. It happens in non-romantic situations all the time, as well.

Think of the harmonies created by Paul Simon and Art Garfunkel. Consider the chemistry of Abbott and Costello and other comic teams. How about Jordan and Pippen in sports? The legends of business are many: from Harley and Davidson to Shelby and Ford.

Those are just some of the more famous examples. Consider the teams we don't hear as much about because one partner is the public face, while their counterpart stays behind the scenes (editor and author, promoter and performer, producer and musician). Serendipitous teams are everywhere.

Academics have started to examine the phenomenal rise and success of the Beatles. Once the band replaced the original drummer with Ringo Starr, it had four members who worked brilliantly together. Those four members were struggling to get a record deal, however. The band was on the verge of breaking up when they met Brian Epstein, who was managing his family's record store in central Liverpool. It was Epstein who worked non-stop to convince the A&R men that the Beatles were worth listening to, helped the group weather another lurry of rejections, and ultimately convinced EMI's George Martin to take a chance on what would become the most famous band in history.

It seems like humans are natural engines of serendipity when they can break through their differences and come together. Unfortunately, individual serendipity does not always lead to progress. While we may be inclined to notice surprises, we also face a society that can condition us to be territorial, competitive, and individualistic.

In the best cases, we find ways to work together. While's there's no formula for harnessing serendipity, it is a skill we can set an intention towards discovering and developing. And it's a bit like a muscle: The more you exercise it, the stronger it gets.

Every collaboration artist, connector, and convener profiled in this book has succeeded in harnessing serendipity. They've continually remained open and dedicated to collaboration with others, with an eye towards surprise. They've leaned into the things they do not know. They've prioritized being surprised. And they've come to have profound insights as to how serendipity, something we equate with fate, can be turned into an actively harnessed practice.

What has your life as a collaboration artist looked like? In the best-case scenarios, the right notes are struck, generating connections and conversations that lead to discovery, risk-taking, and shared awareness that enables progress. In the worst-case collaborative scenarios, we're often left feeling unheard, unfulfilled, and alone. The people profiled have done amazing things in real world circumstances. Often, the approaches that have contributed to their positive results are surprisingly simple. Chances are, they've faced many of the same collaboration challenges as you have. The purpose of this book is to be an album of excellence that we can all draw on in our quest to be stronger collaborators who are better at harnessing serendipitous moments in our own lives.

We spoke with sixty-six individuals who excel at collaboration in various industries. We found that when serendipity is positively harnessed, the results can be amazing. You'll find their advice sorted into six different thematic baskets that, together, attempt to tell the story of collaboration in our ever-changing world.

Look for the stories that sing to you. Create a playlist of approaches you can adapt for your particular collaborative challenges. And share what you learn.

Let's start harnessing serendipity to make our world more collaborative.

SAFE SPACES
FOR REAL TALK...

TRUST

JASON ALEXANDER
COLLABORATING ON STAGE, SCREEN, AND BEYOND

"One of the first things I say at the first day of every rehearsal is that every-body here needs to feel they're working in an environment where they are seen, where they are respected, and where they are safe."

JASON ALEXANDER, COLLABORATION ARTIST

JASON ALEXANDER IS, famously, the actor who—among many other roles—played George Costanza on the iconic TV series *Seinfeld*. Less well-known is his more recent work as a sought-after theater director. His current project? Directing a Broadway-bound adaptation of *The War of the Roses*, a play based on the original novel by Warren Adler (David Adler's late father).

Jason tries to only get involved with projects that have a clear, defined intent. "Sometimes, people have asked me to be a part of something and I say, 'You don't have a clearly defined goal yet other than you just want something to happen,'" he explains. "It doesn't matter if it's a production, an award show, a benefit, or a gala. If it's a production, what is the show truly about? I don't mean what happens from moment to moment. I mean, what is the point, the theme, the moral? Why should anyone care about it?"

Jason continues, "This applies to other, more specific entertainment events too. Yes, award shows give out awards. Benefits and galas raise money and awareness for a cause. That's the given. But if you're creating an 'event'—there are huge gains in understanding what you want that event to specifically be. How does it build? What is the tone? How much 'educating' do you need or want? Do the creative elements work well together? How do you want the participants and audience to resonate with these elements? Specificity is a big, important element in connecting people to do superior work."

Jason has developed his own approaches for bringing a cast and crew together during the short, pressured timespan leading up to a play's presentation. Once involved with a project, he immediately works to establish an environment of trust. "One of the first things I say at the first day of every rehearsal is that everybody here needs to feel they're working in an environment where they are seen, where they are respected, and where they are safe," he says. "I also say that it should be a place where they can experience joy, as well. If any of those things doesn't feel true for you, please come tell me. If I'm not the right person, tell it to someone you trust, tell it to someone who can change things."

He adds that in the entertainment world, it's crucial to begin in a place where everyone feels seen, respected, and safe because intimacies and trust need to be built quickly. "Consider *The War of the Roses*. It features two people who are going to say and do horrific things," Jason says. "An actor has to know that their partner is not going to make assumptions or try actions that could be disrespectful or diminishing or inadvertently make the creation of good work harder. So communication and a sense of community and collaboration is foremost. The actors must trust and support each other to allow the characters they play to do horrible things."

Jason makes it clear that even in the case of a play where everyone starts off with a similar purpose, a lot of careful work needs to be done to get people into productive alignment. "A big thing in directing is acknowledging that everybody is coming to the table to achieve a similar goal, usually the script or the project," he explains—but keep in mind that everybody comes with their own ideas and points of view. "So, how do you encourage everyone's individualized participation?

How do you utilize their life experience and what they bring to the project, and still coordinate something that's a unified effort? How do you get people to care more about the overall project than what they individually bring to it and hope to personally get from it?"

Jason approaches this challenge with deep, conscious humility. "It requires a certain amount of ego to say, 'I can direct this.' Then that same ego has to be able to say, 'But I don't know everything,'" he says. "Unfortunately, what often happens in theater is the assumption by the person in charge (the director) that everybody else is already aware of and committed to you and your vision. But it is not a one-way street. Just because I've cast them doesn't mean I *know* them. I know on paper what their experience is, but that doesn't tell me everything. I don't know their ultimate ability. I don't know what their strengths are. I don't know what their weaknesses are. I don't know what their vision is of the piece."

Jason makes an effort to spend as much time as he can asking people what has brought them to this particular project, along with "what they perceive, what they think it's all going to be about, what their expectations are, what their fears are," he says.

"If an actor says, I really believe that this is what happens in this moment, more often than not, I'll say, 'Try it. Let's see it. Let's see what happens,'" Jason continues. "I do this because they deserve an opportunity to share their point of view. And I may very well learn something from that, even if I don't agree with it. It could illuminate something I've never thought, or confirm something I already believe. Either way, it will inform and possibly elevate my own work."

Sometimes, though, Jason has to point out that the actor's idea may not work as well as they think, or may not be as strong a choice as another alternative. "Most of the time, I'm able to adjust things by going, 'Let me see if I understand what you are advocating for. You believe B, C, and D. But I'm not getting that when I watch you execute your choice. I'm not getting the result you want when you do that. So, I'm advocating for A, B, C, and D, and here's why," Jason explains. "I acknowledge and reflect back what they are saying and doing. That lets them know I have fully taken in their idea and contribution—and then I find they are far more receptive about trying my alternatives."

While Jason wants everyone to contribute to a successful production, he doesn't expect them to coalesce into a big, happy family. "When I start a rehearsal process of a show, my goal is not to make these people the best of friends. My goal is to make them the best of *colleagues*," he says. "I love ensembles. I love the comradeship of ensemble work. And often the working relationships do take on a familial feel. But I also know that if I am able to make one true, lasting friend on a project then that is a true blessing."

Jason clarifies that there's a difference between a healthy, productive, creative working relationship and other more personal relationships. "It is not my job to make people who work together love each other. It is part of my job to make people who work together *respect* and *support* each other," he says. "And working to create that is a privilege. On *Seinfeld*, our four main actors were not social friends. We didn't go and have dinner on the weekends together. We never took a vacation together. We didn't do that stuff. We were work friends. Our stated goal was to make each other brilliant in the workspace. Everything went great. Because we weren't social friends, when things came up in the workplace that could have involved hurt feelings, we were always able to go, 'It's not personal. It's all business.'"

As a director and a performer, Jason's sense of collaboration extends to the audience. "In previews especially, there's a tacit, semi-collaboration between artists and audience. It's very tricky. My experience has shown me that if you talk to audience members individually, you get a hodgepodge of feedback," he notes. "They've been asked to 'critique,' so they look at the piece through that lens and then they do what you asked for—they critique. But opinions are like nostrils. People usually have at least two. So, I don't believe in asking most of them to serve as individual critics."

As *collective* critics, though Jason describes audiences as "brilliant." "If you watch them, they'll tell you everything you need to know. You look for shifting. You listen for coughing. You look for people getting up to go to the bathroom," he says. "Are there intended laughs or unintended laughs? You can feel the energy of a room. You can see when people are leaning forward or sitting back. When the lights come down at the intermission, how quickly are they up and out of their chairs? If they bolt, that means they can't wait to get out of there—but if they sit for even a second, that's generally good."

Jason's commitment to collaboration isn't limited to his artistic work. He actively advocates for ways to get people working together across difficult divides. He has been a prominent public supporter of the OneVoice initiative, which seeks out opinions from moderate Israelis and Palestinians who want to achieve a mutual peace agreement. He's also a founding partner of Starts With Us, a movement to foster curiosity, empathy, and courage as daily habits to overcome the polarization, blind tribalism, and dehumanization threatening the social fabric of our communities.

WHAT WE HEARD AND LEARNED

- A project is more than just what happens—understand its intent and its essence
- Establish an environment of trust and safety
- Listen humbly to your participants
- Align individual choices to the overall production

RICHARD ATTIAS
GLOBAL IMPRESSARIO ENGINEERS INTIMATE INTERACTIONS

"You need to have a purpose."

RICHARD ATTIAS, COLLABORATION ARTIST

RICHARD ATTIAS IS the guru who world leaders, foundations, countries, and companies turn to when they want to have a high-level conference that attracts the top minds in the world—and he creates the greatest chance that they will come together to create significant results. He and his team have been behind the World Economic Forum, the Clinton Global Initiative, and the Nobel Laureate Conference, among other marquee world events.

While he still creates events as part of the foundation of what he does, at this point, he defines his company's focus as "strategic consulting." He says, "We are a catalyst of thinkers, of great minds, of producers, of institutions—all who are transforming the world."

Few in the world get to work on his level, with big budgets, access to the people at the top, commitments to yearly events, and more—but we can still learn from the wisdom that he generously shares. Perhaps by drawing on Richard's approaches, more people in that world can move towards engineering dynamic, collaborative experiences that feel special.

To start with, Richard insists that events need a compelling reason to exist. "You have to build events with deliverables," he says. "You need to have a purpose." This foundational idea defines all that his company does. "We are really trying to put people together to be game-changers and to see some action."

To accomplish that, Richard believes it's essential to design events that include both big plenary sessions and smaller, more intimate sessions. The big sessions can have 2,000 or more people in the room, with even more joining by remote media. These are highly produced performances that draw media attention and often get extensive coverage. He typically schedules them in the mornings.

But the magic that leads to results *really* happens in the smaller sessions of up to 100 people (and in the informal moments when participants socialize and network).

What makes those smaller sessions so transformative is Richard's focus on trust and creating safe spaces for creativity, and environments where collaborators can share honestly and openly without fear of misrepresentation, misappropriation, or judgment. These smaller sessions do that by adhering to the Chatham House Rule, which specifies that participants are free to use the information received—but neither the identity nor the affiliation of the speaker(s), nor that of any other participant, may be revealed. (For the record, Chatham House, also known as the Royal Institute of International Affairs, is an independent policy institute headquartered in London.)

Richard explains that the rule is essential for trust. Having a strict agreement that "what is discussed in this room stays in this room" offsets people's inhibitions about speaking freely due to a fear of their words going public.

While the smaller closed-door sessions, which last between 70 and 90 minutes, are decidedly informal, they are not unguided: They are led by strong moderators. "Good moderators are very direct," Richard says. "They are timekeepers. They know how to build good chemistry and trust. They are able to get the best from people, which results in a conversation that's unique and unexpected."

Appropriately, Richard started out as a civil engineer. He likes to build bridges between categories. Mixing big and small sessions is just the start. He also likes to connect live events with technology. "I'm a strong believer in physical events and face-to-face conversation, but I'm not ignoring at all the impact of social media and the impact of technology. The marriage of these two things will help us to keep the conversation alive," he says.

Increasingly, technology is fostering collaboration by serving as a bridge between the event itself, and all the important things that happen pre- and post-event—a development that excites Richard. "We're trying now to focus more on creating platforms and building an ecosystem around the event," he says. "The ecosystem means that before, during, and after the event, you have different tools which keep you alive, which keep the community alive."

WHAT WE HEARD AND LEARNED

- Have a reason to gather
- Create safe spaces to encourage creative breakthroughs
- Enable strong moderators to keep things on track
- Use the marriage of in-person and digital collaboration to keep conversations alive

MARY BOONE

INNOVATOR DESIGNS MEETING EXPERIENCES THAT STIMULATE HIGH-PERFORMANCE COLLABORATION

"If you haven't created an environment of psychological safety, you're not going to get much collaboration."

MARY BOONE, COLLABORATION ARTIST

MARY BOONE DESCRIBES herself as "fascinated by what makes people want to be together and want to do something together."

That's doubtlessly true, but it understates the depth and strength of her expertise and thought. As the president of Boone Associates in Essex, Connecticut, for several decades, she has specialized in "high-performance collaboration" in everything from leadership retreats to large-scale face-to-face, virtual, and hybrid meetings. Her passion is to harness the power of collaboration to connect people and manage its complexity.

To start with, she believes that several factors need to be in place in order to design an experience that will stimulate collaboration. "You need careful attention to the design elements, the hospitality elements, and the infrastructure elements," Mary explains. "The logistics piece of it has to be in place—because you can have the best design in the world, and it won't work without the logistics really being buttoned up. And you can have the best logistics in the world, and they won't make a single bit of difference if you haven't thought through the design and what the impact is going to be on the participants."

She was a pioneer in defining the term "meeting design" in 2005. "The designer's job is to purposefully integrate the form and the content of the meeting, designing within the constraints of the venue, constraints of the budget, and the constraints of the technology we have available, and more."

Note her earlier use of the word "participants." "I don't like using the word *audience*, because now we are designing meetings so that everybody should have a voice," she says, pointing out how meetings have changed profoundly.

"The microphone is the perfect metaphor for the old style of meeting. It means that 'I have the microphone. I control the message. You are listening to me.' That's why they've been called audiences for so many years," she continues. "Now we are designing meetings so that everybody should have a voice. Everybody should be interacting. We are changing the model from 'tell and sell' to 'ask and engage.' The purpose of meetings is no longer just to broadcast a message. The purpose of meetings is to move people into a space of commitment and engagement where they want to act and they feel ownership. Designers, facilitators, and collaboration artists today are trying to wield power *with*, not power *over*, their participants."

Mary is often asked to design retreats for senior leaders who are working on strategy for their organizations—and the experience she provides can change how the leaders lead their enterprises. "Once I have designed a retreat for them specifically, they start to really understand what it is they could be doing," she explains. "Those retreats include a huge amount of preparation and designed interaction. The participants start to get the notion of how you can design human interaction beyond a one-time event. Then they start to think 'OK, how can I apply this capability in other ways?'"

Designing for human interaction, however, has historically fallen flat of full inclusion—a trend that Mary is seeking to change. She believes that better design and facilitation can make meetings more inclusive and effective. "Most meetings have not been designed in ways that suit people who are more introverted," she points out.

"Somebody who's introverted might not want to be called on in a meeting. A facilitator should have the sensitivity to go up to them privately and ask 'How would this work better for you? Would you prefer small group discussions?' In another example, I facilitated an offsite that included two practicing Muslims. I asked about their prayer schedule, and designed the meals and breaks around it."

Mary stresses that there is no one formula for success. "I can't give you a set design formula because I never, ever have the same elements from one meeting to the next," she says. "It's going to depend on the business objectives, and what the facilities are like at the place where I hold an event. It's going to depend on constraints. You have to have a very intuitive sense of timing, and you've got to be humble enough to mid-course-correct by asking the participants 'How is this working for you?'"

While there is, of course, no formula for these retreats, Mary does have a distinct approach. "Before the meeting starts, I do a significant amount of qualitative research to get those leaders to surface the issues that are most pressing for them—either challenges or opportunities," she says, adding that the entire event is then designed around that research.

"So, we go into it knowing that it's going to be highly relevant to all the people who need to own that meeting and the results," she continues. "I tell the CEO and the leadership team when I have the first meeting, 'This is not my meeting. This is *your* meeting. You own it. You own its success. You own the design. You own the outcomes.'"

Part of the art of facilitation is also knowing how to get out of the way. "Ideally," she says, "you design meetings so that there's a huge amount of self-organization. The meeting participants come up with a set of rules and guidelines for how they want to operate together. Then they largely self-police. It helps to have a good facilitator who knows how to ask the right questions, and to intervene at the right time. If you haven't created an environment of psychological safety, you're not going to get much collaboration."

WHAT WE HEARD AND LEARNED

- There are no audiences anymore—only participants
- Design for self-direction as much as possible
- Consider the collaborative needs of people who are introverted or struggle to feel included for other reasons
- Collaboration can't happen unless psychological safety is established first

PAUL BULENCEA AND CLAUS RAASTED

CREATING IMMERSIVE LEARNING AT THE COLLEGE OF EXTRAORDINARY EXPERIENCES

"A day at the College can have impact equivalent to a year of university."

PAUL BULENCEA, COLLABORATION ARTIST

"With everybody mirroring each other, it only takes a very few individuals to carry a very strong culture."

CLAUS RAASTED, COLLABORATION ARTIST

IF YOU'VE NEVER HEARD of The College of Extraordinary Experiences, a once-a-year, five-day, immersive experience in an exotic location, that's not entirely surprising.

Paul Bulencea, one of the founders, says, "People hear about the College in different ways, but we actually don't market the College. Because a) it's work to do marketing, and b) I don't think great experiences need traditional marketing. People find out about it through a conversation, or people might listen to a podcast in which it's featured, or the College might be mentioned in a book. Sometimes, people come across a project that was born when people met at the College and began to co-create and they ask, 'What is the story? How did you meet?'"

Even if you did find out about the College, fill out and submit an application, and get an interview, neither Paul nor his partner Claus Raasted are likely to try to promote the wonders of the College. "At the interview," Paul says, "there's no selling. Actually, people being interviewed need to demonstrate that they have genuine interest in coming, and that they're coming for the right reason. They need to show that they have openness to experience and an open mindset. The conversation that they have with us is more about us telling them what they're about to step into, because when we're creating, we're taking off some of the guardrails of events. People are not used to these types of immersive events. When you create immersive events, you never know what's going to happen. Some people might be afraid of not knowing what's going to happen."

Another reason they don't tend to get specific when talking about the College is that it's always evolving. Paul and Claus don't know all the specifics of what's going to happen at an upcoming session—because the participants will play a large role in determining them.

Beyond staying mum about many of the details, Claus openly proclaims that he will misdirect participants for strategic purposes. "We tell them straight up that part of what they experience as random will be tightly designed, and part of what they see as being designed will just be random stuff happening. But since they can't tell the difference, and we're going to actively lie to them about what's going on, if they treat everything like a learning experience, then they will get the most out it. I think that simple mindset does a lot for a lot of people because it tells them 'Don't dismiss sitting in the bathroom.' 'Don't dismiss a hallway conversation.' 'Don't dismiss a class.' 'Don't dismiss dinner.'

"Way too often, I go to experiences and part of the experience is *not* part of the experience," he continues. "You go to a conference and think 'Who designed this moment?' Nobody. Physically, yes, you may be there, but you're not part of the conference experience anymore. We don't do that. Everything is part of our design, and some of it isn't … but we lie about that."

The attitude of secrecy—or of leaving room for surprise and

serendipity, if you prefer—even extends to alumni of the program who return for another session. After a participant flies from their home to Poland, they board a bus for a three-hour drive to the College. Claus reports that "a lot of people have no idea what they're getting into. On that bus, people are talking about 'What are we doing?' 'Why are we here?' 'What is this place, even?' Most of the alumni on the bus will have this slightly secretive vibe. They want to tell stuff, but they don't want to say too much—which, of course, only adds to the mystery. They'll address practical concerns. Things like 'Yes you will have a bed to sleep in,' 'Yes the showers have warm water,' 'No the Polish water is not poisonous.' But things like 'What's going to happen?' will be more likely met by 'Well, you'll see.'"

It's a bit surprising that the College is willing to create so much mystery among people whom they plan to have co-operating closely together in an unfamiliar location, but Claus and Paul rely on a number of factors that help make everything work out well. The first of those factors is probably their careful curation of the composition of each class. They carefully and consciously select and balance the people they admit, always aiming for diversity. Claus says, "We have senior people; we also have people who are not senior at all. And people who are from different cultures, different backgrounds, different religions, ethnicities, ages, pursuits, etc. Because if you just get together 50 doctors, that's going to be an interesting meeting … but when the doctor talks to the CEO, who talks to the street magician— that's when things get really interesting."

Bringing diverse people together is part of the College's original DNA. "The whole project started with a couple of questions that Paul and I asked each other. One of those was 'What if you had a table, and at that table sit a Hollywood film producer, a Formula One race car driver, a professional jazz musician, and a surgeon. Would you like to be the fifth person?' Turns out most people say yes with no pause," says Claus.

"The problem is that few people curate that table," he continues. "But even if you do, people are going to look at each other and they're going to think 'You're too old,' 'They're too corporate,' 'You're too artsy,' 'You're too young,' 'You're too silly,' 'You're too serious,' 'You're too French,' 'You're wrong.' And then they're not going to have conversations that are open. So, you need to curate, but you also need to team build—and then the rest flows pretty naturally."

The curation of the College classes for diversity is reflected and reinforced by the College's pricing structure. Claus explains, "We operate with a very transparent structure of tickets. We have several categories of invitation. We'll need to raise the prices because of inflation, but as an example, the full price business invitations were 7,200 euros last time. That tended to attract people who have either businesses or somebody else, some business, paying for them. This is somebody who's at Apple or at Google or at a successful boutique consultancy."

"The next level was the academics, who paid half that. There's a sweet spot for a lot of academic institutions, especially in the western world, that is around there. It's harder to get the institutions to pay for more than 3-and-a-half thousand euros. We want to be able to spread knowledge, so we offer this discount."

"Then we have 20 free, fully subsidized tickets. We get a lot of applications for the free and discounted ones."

"This is the basic structure, but we have some flexibility. We have some that are on an individual discount level. Some will pay 5,000. Some will pay 2,000. Some will pay 800. But, essentially, we have a set amount of each category available that we stick to pretty rigorously, so we don't end up with 40 business tickets, two academics, and 33 scholarships, or vice versa."

While curation of the class is an important step to which they devote a lot of energy, it is not sufficient for success. They work to establish an appropriate, productive culture. At every opportunity— from the initial interview to the opening moments of each session to the workshops—it's about instilling a nourishing ground culture that encourages exploration. "One task," Paul says, "is to move people from 'fear of missing out' to 'love of missing out,' because there's so many things going on every single day."

They also work to allay other concerns. "There might be too much novelty for some people, so we talk about 'brave space.' This is where you explore. Even if you might feel uncomfortable, we encourage you to be aware of that and push."

They also establish a safety valve for their participants. "If it's too much, then just opt out. I think this is really important, and I think this is what some other conferences make weird for people. If I'm at a traditional conference, in a workshop space, or maybe not feeling very well, or I'm down, or I'm tired, or I'm not interested ... it can be really hard to leave without creating some social unrest for the organizers or for the person that's leading the workshop. But at the College, you just say, 'I've got to go.'"

Another way that the College tees up its participants to collaborate is by establishing nesting circles of trust. "On the first days, the participants get split into groups of about 15. Each group has two prefects, one male and one female, who are previous participants. They get to know each other intimately, and that creates a smaller circle of trust within a bigger circle of trust of about 150 people. You always have your small group that you can relate to, talk to, and exchange ideas."

The presence of the prefects in each small group relates to a powerful social dynamic that is behind much of the College experience: herd competence. Claus says, "We take advantage of the concept of herd competence. Basically, we all mirror each other socially. If you walk into a room with 50 people and you think, 'Oh my God, they're all friendly, smiling, open-minded, vulnerable' ... then you think, 'I'd better be that as well.'

"With everybody mirroring each other, it only takes a very few individuals to carry a very strong culture. You walk into the room and somebody says, 'Let's all just share one thing.' If the first thing that is heard is somebody saying 'I'm Bob. I'm a mechanic' ... that's going to give a different atmosphere than the first one saying 'I'm Robert and my daughter died and that shaped my life, but I tried to find peace within.' Then the next person thinks, 'Whoa, I was just going to say I was a mechanic, too. But, apparently, here we're sharing in a deeper way.' Then that person shares. Then the third one thinks, 'Oh, this is how we do it here.' Suddenly you've got 50 people being extremely emotionally vulnerable.

"We mirror. So, if you have a few key people in the right places, you can create incredibly strong culture. The people who come back are automatically culture bearers. We also place a certain number of people who are part of our team."

Paul tends to talk on a high level about the College as a sandbox or a container where they have set up some basic rules to encourage co-creation. And Claus is quick to point out just how remarkable their particular 'sandbox' is. "The first thing people see on arrival is a magnificent medieval castle. A beautiful 13ᵗʰ-century castle with original parts from 1241. It's been modernized over the years, but it still looks like something straight out of *Harry Potter*.

"Soon after they're welcomed and checked into rooms by us and our staff (we handle that, not the hotel staff), it's exploration time. There are some preset experiences waiting for them in the castle. People just start discovering the castle. They start exploring secret passageways. They start exploring the different rooms. They start finding different activities. They find our non-alcoholic bar.

"It's a huge advantage. For a lot of people, the castle is pretty interesting as it is, even if we don't do anything. If we were doing this at a classic conference center, we would have to do a lot more spatial design, but here a lot of it is given. There's already a secret dungeon, so we don't have to build one."

The five-day experience is life-changing for many of the participants. Paul notes, "For the 150 or so people that participate in different roles, either as a traditional participant, or as someone from the backstage team, or as a co-creator, as a professor, as a supplier ... each journey of transformation (or not transformation) is unique and different. But if I imagine that most people experience deeper openness to life. They feel a very strong sense of belonging. They develop and maintain very strong bonds with the people who join them in this experience."

"It's a condensed experience. A day at the College can have impact equivalent to a year of university. That's how condensed it is. Insights emerge that are unique for each individual. Insights, professional insights, personal insights, metaphysical insights. There's a sense of awe. There's a deeper sense of interconnection and interrelatedness and having a renewed sense of wonder for the world."

Claus, as usual, makes similar points in slightly plainer terms. "There's so much talk still, even though it's shifting, about business versus personal, business versus private. Yet, when you break down those barriers, that's when the interesting stuff happens in both spaces. We have people who have gone home and changed their business, but we also have people who've gone home and changed their parenting. And we don't see one as necessarily more valuable than the other."

While the basic College experience may be time-limited and happen in a special, remote location, it has lasting impact in the many projects that arise out of co-creative efforts started at the castle.

Paul mentions Stone Soup as an example. "It's an open source cookbook for creating immersive events that are democratic. Anyone can do it. No one is charged. No one is organizing them; everyone is an organizer and everyone is a co-creator. It has been unleashed in the world and it has had, I don't know, seven, eight, nine editions by now. And last year it debuted in Australia and in Europe."

Claus describes a project that impressed him. "This was a big Las Vegas initiative. I don't know where it landed, because we only talked with them in some of the early stages. But those early stages were thrilling and full of potential. A scrappy street magician hooked up with some high-level event guys and an Oscar-winning, very emotionally intelligent filmmaker, and there were some escape room people involved. Together, they created a concept about regenerative life, and pitched that to some high-level Las Vegas people. The chances of those people meeting and trusting each other just rise exponentially at the College.

Paul mentions other outcomes. "New books, new podcasts, people teaching at each other's universities, or having guest lecturers take over courses. A lot of non-profit initiatives, as well. Also, people getting married and having babies. That's the ultimate type of project."

WHAT WE HEARD AND LEARNED

- Curate your crowd
- Create small circles of trust within larger ones
- Team build

- Take advantage of herd competence
- If at all possible, have a castle

ESTHER COOPERSMITH

BEHIND-THE-SCENES DIPLOMAT LEVERAGES SPOUSES FOR PEACE

"I want everyone to get to know each other and spend time together and speak to each other."

ESTHER COOPERSMITH, COLLABORATION ARTIST

ESTHER COOPERSMITH IS A LEGEND, particularly in the Washington, D.C., area. She has had many titles, and has won awards ranging from the United Nations Peace Prize in 1984 and the United Nations Education & Science Organization Award in 2008. She's still a Goodwill Ambassador.

Even these high honors understate the huge role she has played, often unofficially and behind the scenes, for decades. Her stories start with FDR, and they continue today. While she has never been called shy, she doesn't tend to speak of her own accomplishments. Her daughter Connie, however, is eager to join the conversation and illuminate her mother's history and contributions.

For decades, Esther has been a hard-working player in D.C. and beyond, helping move good candidates and causes forward. She evolved from an astute political fundraiser to a community and international activist, raising money and the profile for a bevy of causes including preserving the King Tut collection at the Cairo Museum, the Hermitage Museum in St. Petersburg, and Washington's famed Union Station as well as arts groups and programs for under-privileged children. She was appointed Special Ambassador to the United Nations during the Iranian hostage crisis, a job that entailed public facing and private diplomatic efforts. She has a remarkable ability to get things done—most often providing a good time in the process.

She was born and raised in the Midwest. While there, her daughter recalls that she did political dinners and found out she was really good at raising money—perhaps because she hadn't come from money, and realized its importance in getting tasks accomplished. Estes Kefauver, who had run for vice president and led famous crime hearings, noticed her unique energy, and said, "Come to Washington; you'll get a job"— not thinking Esther would actually show up.

Esther partly just wanted to get out of Wisconsin. Instead of dreaming about, say, Hollywood, she dreamed about Washington, D.C. She wanted to be Eleanor Roosevelt. But when she arrived in D.C, along with her brother and sister, there was no job offer.

Esther, characteristically, landed on her feet. Connie says, "She wound up hanging out in all these offices and learned so much that she became the first female lobbyist. She represented the railroads, which in the 1950s were incredibly powerful. While she was working on a fundraiser at the Mayflower hotel for Harry Truman, a friend of hers took her to a synagogue tea dance where she met my dad, Jack Coopersmith. They seemed to click. She came to his office a couple days later and sold him a ticket to the big dinner."

Ironically, while Jack Coopersmith grew up in Washington, he was oblivious to politics. The high dollar event she had sold him a ticket to was the first fundraiser he had attended. Since it was at the haute Mayflower Hotel, he assumed he would be getting pheasant under glass, not rubber chicken. Still, he proposed to her a few months later.

Jack loved to watch her use her magnificent, innate social skills. "I'm interested in what you're doing," Esther says to people. Connie chimes in, "I think that's why she and President Clinton got along so well. They're both interested in you as a person. There's energy around her. She has what they would now call emotional intelligence. She can read people faster than other people [can]. If we're standing in a line, she'll pick the right line to stand in for the customer service. She'll know from observing who will be the best person. She knows instinctively how to connect people. She just has that kind of gift."

While Jack often played a role behind the scenes, he insisted that Esther get all the credit. He was delighted to underwrite her activities, which gave Esther an unusual edge in her efforts to get people to collaborate: She wasn't personally out for profit. Her gatherings, therefore, felt like safer spaces.

Looking at just a few of her many accomplishments, it's evident that Esther was one of the first to use many approaches that are alive and well today in the world of gatherings. She practiced what we call 'branding' and 'event marketing' before those fields were named.

When fundraising for President Lyndon B. Johnson (LBJ), she noted that he used a style of "barbecue diplomacy" at his West Texas ranch. It involved his chef, Walter Jetton, known as the "Barbecue King," cooking whole animals over open pits. Esther set out to bring this experience to more of the country.

"Back then, you didn't see Texas barbecue anywhere but Texas. It was a novelty," Connie explains. "My mom had Walter Jetton travel around the country. He'd do the whole show, complete with wagons. It wasn't just the food—she made sure the events were really fun. She got Paul Newman to show up. And this was back when there weren't as many celebrities doing political stuff. They had started a little bit with civil rights … but to have Paul Newman there was huge."

For every state that LBJ went to, Esther found out who the richest person was, or who had the best house, Connie explains. "She'd approach them and say, 'Would you like to have the president come to your house?' No matter whether they were Republican or Democrat, everybody was excited by it. She sold a ton more tickets because people would want to see, say, Henry Ford's house in Michigan. It was a big deal. She'd tell aspiring politicians, 'This is an important moment in American history. If you want to be part of this history (and if you want to become a senator), you have a chance to really prove yourself. Get on the phone and sell tickets.'"

The events were memorable, as Esther was essentially practicing branding before that term gained traction. She was also practicing a level of collaborative awareness and inclusion that many before her had failed to grasp. "My mom had a great relationship with Ladybird Johnson and their daughters," Connie says, as an example. "Most people didn't pay attention to anybody's spouses."

Esther went on to do heroic backchannel work while Jimmy Carter was working on the Camp David Accords with Anwar Sadat of Egypt and Menachem Begin of Israel. She had been involved with projects in Egypt and already knew Sadat's wife, Jehan. "The wives met and bonded before their spouses really met," Connie remembers. "We had our own event. We had the first-ever barbecue and meeting of Egyptian press and Israeli press and staff. We invited their kids. People got in the pool, and it just broke all the ice. Egyptians and Israelis actually talked to one another."

At another point in time, Esther organized a special group of Senate wives—Democrats and Republicans—that went on missions to countries such as Thailand, India, Jordan, Saudi Arabia, and Taiwan which benefited the United States' soft diplomacy efforts. And it fostered enduring friendships, even amongst the senators. And that in turn led to tangible, bipartisan collaboration in Congress.

While Esther has created and produced many events and contributed in many different ways to many important causes, she is best known for the parties she has hosted. For many years, she did a lot of her hosting at other people's places because she didn't want to fundraise in her own home. The basic proposition is simple, according to Connie: "You sit down. You have the meal. You get to know each other."

But the execution is a bit more nuanced—even though it all seemed to come so naturally for extroverted Esther. To start with, she is laser-focused on inviting "a mix of people who have a similar interest in whatever the topic is. She hand-selects the people who we think should be there," says Connie. "She wants to have both Republicans and Democrats. And, of course, their spouses. She often identifies younger people who are up and coming, staffers, people she just likes, and invites them. Some of them grow to be big stars."

Having the right invitees is just the start. Next, Esther concentrates on the seating plan. "She is a genius at seating, so people really get to know one another," says Connie.

As carefully thought-out as her seating plans are, Esther still insists on starting things off right. "She will say, 'I want everyone to get to know each other and spend time together and speak to each other," Connie explains. "Then she'll literally go around to each guest and say something about them. It is pretty efficient. She just says something quick and fun about everyone. It could be light. She can be funny and say stuff most other people couldn't get away with."

Then, before the dessert is served, before the speeches typically begin, she will go around the room, interacting with people and encouraging conversation.

Esther's ability to catalyze gatherings decade after decade is probably related to her natural optimism. "Her kind-of theme in life is 'Life is Good,'" says Connie. "She actually believes that. She has an ability to block out terrible stuff. I've always thought that she saw one too many Judy Garland and Mickey Rooney movies. She's got that 'Hey, let's put on a show' attitude."

Esther's optimism has, for the most part, been justified. "Over the years, she has found that a lot of people, particularly men, were either willing to help or underestimated her, not understanding her power and how much she could absorb."

And the rewards for Esther's long career have been many.

WHAT WE HEARD AND LEARNED

- To create trust, avoid letting profit drive your motives
- Seating matters
- Get guests talking to each other with introductions and ice breakers
- Life is good. Believe it. Reflect it back.

EDIE FRASER

NETWORKING NINJA CREATES OPPORTUNITIES FOR WOMEN

"I believe there is no 'I' in 'we.' It's all about we."

EDIE FRASER, COLLABORATION ARTIST

EDIE FRASER LIKES to cite Madeleine Albright, who famously said, "There's a special place in hell for women who don't help other women." Then she adds, "And men who don't, too." Then, ever-positive, she comments, "We're supporting each other in this movement, so I think we all can hope to go to heaven."

Edie is the Women Business Collaborative, a non-profit that is driving progress toward equal position, pay, and power for all businesswomen. Prior to this, she achieved a long list of accomplishments, including building three companies, nurturing several movements, authoring books, issuing influential reports, serving on numerous boards, and receiving over 50 major leadership awards. However, she's much less interested in talking about her track record than about noting both recent progress and the promise of the future.

In short, Edie is quick to give credit to other individuals and organizations who are helping drive positive change. "I believe," she says, "there is no 'I' in 'we.' It's all about we." Consistent with that, the WBC is a massive coalition. "Actually," she says, "It's an alliance, a collaboration, and a movement."

WBC is also an accelerator. It has only been around a short while, and there has already been significant progress in some of its areas of focus. "Before we started, the data said it would take over 150 years for women to get to parity. We knew that we only had so many years where we could drive change, so we needed a more expedient way to give back, to be transformative and leave a legacy of change. The answer was to build a major collaboration and invite all the major women's business organizations to collaborate—and not compete—with each other, for the first time in history," Edie says. "As long as we committed to organizing around action initiatives for equal position, pay, and power, we could drive action, results, and impact. In May 2019, we pulled the first 22 women's business organizations together. We formed a non-profit board in March and agreed on the theme 'faster together.' Today, we have 76+ women's business organizations working together."

The WBC is pursuing nine major initiatives simultaneously. On each initiative, Edie explains, "We have probably eight organizations working together to really drive data and change towards 2025 and 2030." A logical question is how WBC gets the leaders of these organizations to be collaborative rather than competitive. "What we have been able to do is find what niche they were interested in and where we could propel their leadership," she says.

A perfect example of this is the Women CEO initiative that was jointly sponsored by Catalyst and Ascend and WBC. "Catalyst looked at the Fortune 500 framework," Edie explains. "C200 provided focus on small and mid-sized (SMB) companies as well as private companies. Ascend delved into diversity."

Edie continues: "We now have 24 organizations working on our board initiative. We put out a monthly report on all women joining public boards, and the results have been significant. For the last 15 months, an average of 43 percent of those joining public boards have been women—a third of those women of color. That's double what it was three years ago. And now we're beginning to do the same on private boards."

The monthly reports list the names of those who have joined boards and the companies involved, in part to direct positive attention to them. "We do recognition and celebration every day, in every way we can," says Edie, including on social media and with honors like the Trailblazers Award. "We're pleased to honor people like Judy Woodruff of PBS and Geena Davis, and so many others. We single out those who are embracing collective leadership to drive change."

The board initiative is just one example of the related areas that Edie has been working in for years. "I started Diversity Best Practices 22 years ago," she recalls, "to start working with diversity officers and CEOs. We went from Diversity to Equity to Inclusion, or DEI—and now that we've added the word Engagement, it has grown to DEIE. The leadership in this movement is very inclusive and engaging, and they give each other leadership positions. There is no way that WBC could make the progress we're making without our 76+ organizations, all those we call champions, our advisory board and leaders, and, of course, all our companies."

Publishing regular reports is consistent with the belief at WBC that transparency and sharing of information is crucial to engagement and results. "We believe that transparent data is now critical to all CEOs and boards. The Business Round Table, particularly after George Floyd, went after diversity as never before," says Edie. The group also took the approach of providing positive recognition, and have published a report of hundred companies that are standing up and disclosing DEI data. "It's not mandatory, but all the best companies are doing it," she says. "We're working on an effort to pull the DEI annual reports for 800 companies. With the help of alliances with universities, we'll have the DEI annual reports of those companies on our website soon."

Edie thinks a lot about how to foster talent that will carry the gains that WBC makes today into the future. "We all need to learn from young people. I think COVID taught so many CEOs that it's a new ballgame, as they were on screens every day with women and dogs and children. It's a new world of flexibility at work. It's a new world of innovation," says Edie. "The younger generation has skills in tech that so many of us that are older need to learn about and need to respect. I think this inter-generation, the intersectionality is changing us totally."

This will provide real benefits for younger people too, says Edie. "Whether it's mentorships, sponsorships, internships, apprenticeships, or even online support … we should do whatever we can do to support their emerging leadership so they can have a fruitful and satisfying career pathway."

WHAT WE HEARD AND LEARNED

- Find niches where coalition members can best contribute
- Elevate and celebrate successes
- Seek to elevate underrepresented voices to positions of power
- Create a talent pipeline

NATALIE JONES HALLAHAN
STATECRAFT EXPERT SETS THE STAGE FOR DIPLOMATIC RESULTS

"Technology allows those kinds of private moments to take place unseen."

NATALIE JONES HALLAHAN, COLLABORATION ARTIST

NATALIE JONES HALLAHAN is executive vice president at the nonpartisan diplomacy center called Meridian International Center in Washington, D.C. It is, literally, her job to get some of the most powerful decision-makers in the world to play nicely together.

In her previous role at the State Department, Natalie has led large teams in planning and executing high-level international summits and diplomatic events, serving as the central interlocutor between foreign governments, the United States Department of State, and the White House through complex processes. She has innovated, pioneering programs such as the Diplomatic Culinary Partnership and the American Chef Corps, where she inducted one-hundred chefs to be ambassadors.

The need for diplomacy continues no matter what is happening in the world of public health and safety measures. That's why it's been essential for Natalie to explore how to emulate high-touch events such as the G8 World Leader Summit, and study how other tools of diplomacy can work in the virtual and hybrid world.

"The marker of our success at Meridian House," she reports, "is whether we're able to connect people from different backgrounds to work on a global issue together."

Today, that will sometimes require the deft use of technology. "We changed our events from being passive events and one-dimensional to being active, multi-dimensional, nuanced events where the participants are in the driver's seat as to who they want to converse with," she says about the use of technology.

"Higher-level diplomacy still requires larger engineered group conversations," she continues. "But to get to that engineered group conversation, you need a lot of side conversations to happen. You need a lot of that relationship-building and trust-building on the side to be able to get to a place where you can have open, constructive back and forth. Those elements are the same, whether it's a G8 or whether it's a staff meeting."

This general idea is not new. "For each summit we did, we almost always had the main plenary room, and then we had a series of rooms you would reserve for leader-to-leader meetings," Natalie says. "And we had lounge space that allowed those very impromptu, kind of candid interactions to take place. Those pull-aside moments can be much more powerful sometimes than the facilitated, engineered conversation."

What's new is being able to make those moments happen virtually, which can be superior to having them happen in person. "Sometimes you just don't want the world to see you say, 'Senator, can you take a step aside so I can talk to you about this or that.' Technology allows those kinds of private moments to take place unseen."

The world of diplomacy can be secretive and insular, and some players have been alarmed at the prospect of everybody being potentially able to talk to everybody, Natalie explains. But the overriding value quickly became apparent. As did the need to scaffold the technology with extensive human support. "In this new space," she adds, "you can judge an event not by how many people attend, but how many conversations you're curating."

Natalie says the first time they used new technology was for their Meridian Ball and Global Leadership Summit, which was completely virtual. "The magic of that event had always been the connections that were formed. So, we used technology for a networking reception. We looked at our guest list, and we assigned staff hosts because we knew people were encountering this for their first time. We made sure that when folks joined, they were personally welcomed by a staff member, and asked if all their tech was working," she explains.

Natalie continues, "Next, we looked at our guest list and told the team things like 'we want everyone to make sure that this ambassador is not alone.' We also looked at strategic connections that people wanted to make. We had a number of our corporate partners who wanted to meet certain ambassadors or certain government officials, so we made sure as hosts that we brought those initial connections together. And then we stepped away."

Natalie has found that the new virtual context solves a number of etiquette challenges. "We told our guests they could put some social norms aside in this virtual reception. You're able to delicately and quietly enter a conversation or delicately remove yourself from a conversation. Just drop in and drop out—that's OK. You can go from one group to another, and don't feel like you have to be locked into one group," she says. "We gave permission for people to do that."

Natalie sees technology as creating new possibilities—but also making some things harder. "Event planners are going to face harder decisions. People are going to have greater choice now. They're going to feel greater permission to say no to in-person events," she points out. "You have to make sure if you're having an in-person event, that there's a *reason* that it's an in-person event—that it's not just the content that you're getting, it's the connections. And you've really got to wow people to bring them out."

Hybrid events need intense consideration too, she warns. "You really have to think, 'Is this going to augment my event? Is this going to help make it better or is it going to dilute it? Because I could see if you have a hybrid event, people may feel like they can stay home. You'll need to be intentional about it.'"

Natalie's decision matrix is simple: "Virtual makes sense when it lets you consume the content in a more timely and convenient way." She is also particularly interested in technology's ability to achieve a broader reach. "We want to get a global audience, including people who would never have been able to make it to an event in person."

WHAT WE HEARD AND LEARNED

- Make your events active, multi-dimensional, nuanced
- Plan for meaningful pull-aside moments
- Take advantage of the privacy of virtual interactions
- Use connections over content to help wow people

COACH KATHY KEMPER

TENNIS TEACHER TO THE POWERFUL EXERTS UNIQUE POWER OFF THE COURT

"It's always the people. Whether it's a big conversation with many people or just two people talking, trust and humor are essential. That's the tone you want. When it's present, everybody just relaxes and enjoys."

COACH KATHY KEMPER, COLLABORATION
ARTIST

ASSOCIATE SUPREME COURT Justice Stephen Breyer once paid tribute to Coach Kathy Kemper and her organization—the Institute for Education (IFE)—in a toast where he cited its 30-year track record of working to break through the social paralysis in Washington, D.C., to help good people have good relationships so they can solve real problems. He reflected, "Just think how bad it would be if you hadn't been doing this."

Coach Kathy's current status as an op-ed writer, columnist, regular Huffington Post blogger, as well as master connector and convener, grew out of her more than 30 years of teaching tennis to movie stars, monarchs, Supreme Court justices, business moguls, and the movers and shakers at all levels of the U.S. government. When she began to bring the people whom she taught—her "team"—together socially, the relationship she had developed with them as a coach allowed her to speak directly and openly to this powerful group.

"When I was teaching the CIA director or a king or a queen," she says, "they all had loads of security. At first the security people always wanted to come out and start helping you pick up the tennis balls. I didn't want that to happen. Because when you pick up balls, that's when you actually start talking to the person. You do that with people month after month, a few times a week, and you develop a real rapport. You learn about their lives. You learn about their marriages, their kids, their families.

"Plus," she adds, "a coach can tell a king to move his feet and get his racket back. You can instruct them—whereas in real normal life, you could never say anything like that to a president of the United States. They're not running the show on that tennis court at that particular time. They're the student. That's a very different dynamic."

Coach was primed for success as a hostess and convener because she had been entertained by some of the best. Early in her coaching career, she had taught the author, journalist, and socialite Nina Gore Auchincloss Straight, who invited her to fancy dinners and seated her between, for example, a senator and a national security advisor. Coach taught Katherine Graham, the publisher of *The Washington Post*, who would invite her to dinners attended by "everybody that ran the world."

When her husband, Jim Valentine, suggested that she bring some of her higher echelon students together with some of his associates from the world of finance, she was at first reluctant. "I thought that was the worst idea I'd ever heard. I thought, 'I'm not like a mover and shaker, I'm a tennis coach,'" she recalls. "I was in the press all the time because I was coaching all these big shots, but I was just a tennis coach. I just said it would be an imposition to ask them to come and I didn't feel comfortable at all."

But then she vetted the idea with her friend, then Secretary of Defense Les Aspin, who said, "That sounds like a great idea. I'd love to hear what's going on in the finance world."

"At first, we invited six people," Coach explains. "Then people started to want to get invited again. It grew to 10 people." Then, a tennis contact of hers from coaching at the White House suggested a new tack. "I had invited Wolf Blitzer to join a doubles game. We were talking about my gatherings, when Wolf said, 'Coach, that sounds really great. How come you don't invite me to any of these things?' I said, 'You're part of the press.' He replied, 'You can trust me. If it's off the record, it's off the record.'"

Wolf not only participated in several gatherings in the early 1990s—he encouraged Coach and Jim to create the non-profit Institute for Education.

Coach is clear about what makes or breaks a gathering: the people that you have around the table. "Of course, you want to have nice food, nice flowers, and have everything look great, but people won't come away talking about the flowers or the food," she says. "They'll come away thinking, 'I really liked meeting that person,' and, 'She was so interesting.' They'll repeat the conversation because they connected with a few people there, and that's what is a treasure. It's *always* the people, in the room, at the table."

Coach adds, "Whether it's a big conversation with many people or just two people talking, trust and humor are essential. That's the tone you want. When it's present, everybody just relaxes and enjoys."

In her early days as a convener, it probably didn't hurt that in a city where almost everyone had multiple agendas, Coach was motivated mainly by pure curiosity, and emanated sunny optimism. But over time, she and the brilliant colleagues she attracted to the Institute for Education became a bit more directed and purposeful in what they did. She evolved a format for the gatherings.

"I welcome people. Once we started getting contributors and sponsors for programs, I would also thank them for their support. Then I introduce the special guest speaker—or if somebody else has invited the special guests, they do that introduction," she says. "Next, before the speaker speaks, we go around the table and everybody says who they are and what they do. That's always fun. Then we have a really lively, rigorous Q&A, moderated by me. A lot of times, it will turn into not just a Q&A but a conversation, because the speaker then will ask questions. It is always heavy on substance, respect, and humor."

While the format stayed the same, the venues changed. Early on, she held many events at her own house, but as events grew bigger they took place at hotels and clubs. And when market changes dried up most of the support that paid for those venues, her tennis connections came into play again. "I had coached a lot at embassy courts, so I had relationships with several ambassadors. The Belgian ambassador said to me, 'Why don't you have your gathering at my residence?' I thought, 'This is a great idea. Everybody likes to go to embassies,'" Coach remembers. "That changed the whole paradigm. Now, we almost *only* go to embassies. There's really no reason not to, because every embassy is eager to host a salon or a dinner or a breakfast with the people that we can bring there to them."

The focus of Coach's events also evolved when she met up with the former White House Office of Science and Technology Policy's senior advisor for innovation, John Paul Farmer, and former U.S. Chief Technology Officer, Todd Park. Park said to her, "I hear you do all these amazing things. How come you're not doing much on technology?" Coach's response was to say to them, "Let's do it." And the Institute for Education pivoted to tech issues.

"In 2012," she explains, "nobody knew what coding was. No one knew what an algorithm was. Certainly, nobody knew what AI or machine learning was. That just wasn't part of the conversation. To me, that was what all the future is going to be.

"I'm a lay person," she adds, "so it's not easy for me—but I want to be in the conversation. So, I just kept saying, 'You have to dumb it down.' Then, 'You guys got to dumb it down more.' We had a panel that did a great job of dumbing down the Internet of Things (IoT). They said, 'Wouldn't it be great if stoplights could talk to each other and, if no one's there, they would turn green?' Then the lights clicked for all the lay people at the salon."

WHAT WE HEARD AND LEARNED

- Curate the people around the table
- Relax people with humor and trust
- Pull "coach rank" when needed
- Dumb down high tech so lay people get it

WYNTON MARSALIS
MUSICAL SUPERSTAR ON
IMPROVISING TOGETHER

"Most times, when people finish playing in a jam session, they always shake hands with or hug—even the people they didn't know before the session. That's a sign of respect, and of co-creation."

WYNTON MARSALIS, COLLABORATION ARTIST

HAVING A CONVERSATION WITH WYNTON MARSALIS, famous musician and the managing and artistic director of Jazz at Lincoln Center (JALC), is—appropriately enough—like listening to great jazz music. His voice rises, falls, and takes off in delightful directions as he thinks about the experience of creating and appreciating music.

He loves the endless potential and the traditions of jazz. "Most times," he says, "when people finish playing in a jam session, they always shake hands with or hug—even the people they didn't know before the session. That's a sign of respect, and of co-creation. I always thought that was a beautiful part of our music."

Wynton didn't set out to create JALC. Like some of his music, it evolved. Its origins trace back to a few "classical jazz" (Wynton never liked that term) concerts that he programmed and played in the 1980s. He played them for free, having been asked by Dorthaan Roland Kirk, the widow of jazz legend Rahsaan Roland Kirk, who was associated with the concerts' sponsor, WBGO, the jazz radio station based in Newark, New Jersey.

Wynton, who had been comfortable with his professional life, wasn't looking for a new challenge. "At that time, I was actually on the road playing a lot of concerts every year as well as going into schools and teaching," he recalls. "Essentially, I was doing things I had seen my father do when I was growing up in New Orleans."

But he spotted a new opportunity when the classical jazz summer series became successful and started happening year after year. "I saw then that we could use the program to develop rehearsal techniques and a type of music that I and other musicians in my generation would never otherwise get a chance to play. We started to add the music of Duke Ellington."

Soon, he found himself talking with a board and various members of the business community. "I had never worked with that broad kind of swatch of citizenry," he says. "I didn't know how to pull together constituents for Lincoln Center. But with their guidance and leadership, I began to see the value and beginning of a program."

He continues, "The biggest challenge for me was to give up doing the things I had been doing with my own music and my own career—and making the type of money I was used to making—to make much less money and be more involved in the community. I got involved with more people and began to do more for the benefit of jazz and music as a whole. Then we embarked upon the journey that became Jazz at Lincoln Center."

Ramping up to the full schedule that JALC presents today has required Wynton to work with a greater and broader array of performers. In order to better do so, he has developed criteria for them. "There's a range of different voices, different perspectives, that you need to comprise an orchestra," he explains. "You don't want everybody to be the same in their style, but you *need* them to have the same intention; a knowledge of the music; the ability to bring past, present, and future of the music to bear in a moment; a seriousness about the overall mission; a belief in what we're trying to play. And the willingness to pursue that creativity, no matter what, to go through all the things you have to go through to develop a first-class group and make the sacrifices that you have to make."

The quality of his collaborators matters, in part, because of 'the freedom' of jazz. "You're given choice. So, you always try to edit and choose things that will allow you to assert your individuality, but that also will allow for a good feeling in the momentum of the group," Wynton says. "Many times, those two things are at odds. You're always on a ledge where your intelligence is always challenged. You can make the mistake of being too giving, of not asserting yourself enough, but the mistakes that we most often make are those of being too self-involved.

"Jazz provides the ability to combine with other people to create new things," he adds. "The way it's set up is ingenious. It has a light framework. There are many possibilities in the form for changing tempos, changing grooves, collaborating, integrating with other art forms. Jazz makes it easy to collaborate with most other forms of music, especially most other forms of Western music."

Wynton notes there are some things that are dictated like the form. "But in other things, your sense of taste, your manners … all of that … determines how things will go. And, a lot of times, they don't go as well as they could go. You have things you have to know: harmonies, forms, rhythms. Of course, the more you know about a subject, the more eloquent you will be. And the easier it's going to be to converse with others, even if they don't have the same level of eloquence or information. But the less others know, the more manners you have to possess. Jazz is a music that requires good manners."

Wynton and his associates at JALC mostly get to teach kids who are already into jazz. But, he notes, "When we give classes where we don't have jazz students, we always try to talk about the music and expose people to it, and get them excited about listening to it. I give them a listening list with blues, Anglo and Afro-American hymns, spirituals, country, New Orleans music, Afro-Latin music, and American popular songs. It's maybe 80 songs or so that I've compiled. I find that often they don't really know too much about roots music."

For Wynton, teaching is a very two-way process that speaks to the heart of collaboration—and to the same community energy that the greatest jam session thrives on. He says that his students often start sending artists and articles his way. He'll send others back in response, and the loop continues. "It's a great symbiotic relationship," he says.

"A student of mine at Juilliard spoke about what he liked about jazz. He said, 'When you came into it, you had the feeling it was already going on,'" Wynton continues. "That got me thinking. So, you just jump into the stream of what is going on, and you become a part of this thing that's already there. And it doesn't demand that you be the whole stream; it just demands you to be swimming in there. We don't know the future ... but we can envision a future. We do what we can to work with our time towards that future."

WHAT WE HEARD AND LEARNED

- Seek mentors and mentor-mentee relationships that are reciprocal
- Embrace different voices and balance individuals and the group
- Trust that shifting how you're operating will lead to new avenues
- Jump into the stream of what's going on, trusting you'll find your fit

SETH MOULTON

MILITARY-TRAINED CONGRESSIONAL LEADER ON THE DEMOCRACY OF COLLABORATION

"I want to be the dumbest person in the room. I want to surround myself with the smartest people."

SETH MOULTON, COLLABORATION ARTIST

SETH MOULTON IS a graduate of Harvard University and Harvard Business School, a Marine veteran, and currently the U.S. Representative for Massachusetts's 6th congressional district. He is successful, driven, and brilliant. He's the kind of person who's often called a natural leader. A big part of his brilliance and success may, however, come from his preference to seek wisdom from the various members of the teams that he's on, and to encourage collaboration to the fullest extent possible. Given his military training, he won't hesitate to make critical decisions in times of crisis—but his whole approach and attitude involve working with his teams *not* to have those crises arise.

"I do not like being the smartest person in the room," he says. "I think a lot of people are the exact opposite. They love being the smartest person, especially in Washington. They don't want anyone to challenge their authority or their intellectual prowess or whatever else. I want to be the dumbest person in the room. I want to surround myself with the smartest people. By doing that, I'm saying, in effect, 'I'm probably not going to be the one who figures this out. I have to be committed to being a collaborator if this is all going to work.'"

Seth starts with the attitude that he can learn something from everyone. "I certainly found that in the Marines. I served with people from all over the country who had very different educational backgrounds than I had. I can't tell you how much I learned from them," he says.

He continues, "You need to develop trust with someone you need to work together with. You have to start by just being able to relate to them, and they need to relate to you. How do you do that? You find common ground. You might have very different backgrounds, very different perspectives on things, but you find some common ground. A very random thing can be the basis for starting a conversation and, hopefully, a relationship."

Being able to relate to people is how you start to develop trust, Seth says. "A practical example of this comes from my time in the Marines. The 18- and 19-year-old enlisted guys often felt a real divide between themselves and the officers. I was only a few years older, but I'd been to college while they'd come into the Marines straight out of high school. Their experience was very different. They liked to sit around, smoke cigarettes, and shoot the shit. I would sometimes go and join them," he explains. "They were surprised that an officer would come have a cigarette with them. It put me on an equal footing with them, and it put them on an equal footing with me. So, we were able to have a conversation. They'd expect an officer with my background to give them a lecture about not smoking. I didn't do that. I just came over, smoked a cigarette, and started a conversation. That's fundamentally how you build trust."

Once trust was created and a relationship established, Seth would start to look for common ground around the work that needed to be done. "Just like how you establish common ground to start a relationship, you then try to find common ground in your shared goals," he says. "It might not be where you expect. It might not be the way the mission was presented to you. You've got to figure out why it's in their interests to do it. And, sometimes, it's frankly *not* in their interests. In the Marines, you're asking young Americans to literally put their lives on the line. There are times when I'd say, 'Honestly, guys, I don't want to do this either … but we have to do it so no one else has to do it in our place.' That, sometimes, was enough. That's why we showed up. I would try to find better reasons than that, but sometimes that's what it came down to. That was the place where we could find common ground in the mission. It's not about convincing people of your point of view. It's about finding places where you already agree. If you go in from the get-go saying, 'I'm going to change that person's mind' … that just won't work."

Seth says he would tell his Marine team: "If you believe we should be doing something differently, then I want to hear your idea. That doesn't mean that in the heat of combat we can always have debate. But, otherwise, I want to hear your idea … but there are two rules. The first is you have to give me a reason for why you want to do something differently. The second rule is that the only reason you cannot give is 'Because that's the way we've always done it, sir.'"

As challenging as it could be to foster collaboration in the military, Seth finds it equally daunting to work across the aisle in government. "Congress, at least today, is an environment which is almost built on distrust," he explains.

Still, he has been able to deploy what he learned in the Marines to get things done. "There are obviously differences [between] combat and Congress. But I think there are a lot more similarities than there are differences. I'm a Democrat, but I was able to work effectively with a conservative Republican from Oklahoma, Steve Russell, for many years while he was in Congress," Seth says. "We started with the simple fact that we were both Iraq war veterans. That was our point of common ground, even though we had a lot of different perspectives, not only on politics and on that war. That was the start of our relationship. We became friends. He's still a friend. And because of that personal trust, we were able to do some politically contentious things like advocate for Syrian refugees. That was unpopular on my side of the aisle at the time, and it was extremely unpopular on his side of the aisle."

In keeping with his sense of not wanting to be the smartest guy in the room, Seth surrounds himself with team members who are ready, willing, and able to push back. "Once you establish a basic trusting relationship, then you have to push people to disagree with you, to challenge you. When I'm interviewing people to join my team, one of the critical questions I ask is, 'How would you approach me if you disagreed with the position I was taking?'" he explains. "Interestingly, a lot of my colleagues in politics do not want anybody to disagree with them, especially staff that work for them. They want them to get in line. Some people will answer that question by being very conciliatory and saying, look, 'You're the boss, we do what you want.' Those are not people I hire. I want people who will challenge me, who are going to push me intellectually.

"You get pushed intellectually by people who disagree with you," he continues. "I have to set that expectation very explicitly for my junior staff. I have to pull that out of them. I don't have to pull it out of the senior members of my team. They know that they're expected to do it."

Seth has a clear, stated commitment to being innovative; his office has even won awards for being the most innovative office on Capitol Hill. He puts that in context, saying, "If I were to join a highly successful company, it would be quite arrogant for me to come into that organization and immediately say we should do everything differently. On the other hand, if I join a pretty low-performing institution like Congress, it would be quite naive to simply do what everyone else has already been doing."

Seth lives by a well-worn Marine Corps maxim about diligence, consistency, and reinforcement. "The first time that you walk by someone doing something below the standard, and don't correct them, you've just set a new, lower standard." He feels that this is a point that some of his peers miss. "Most know to first establish their mission and values as something that's central to your organization. But a lot of people ignore the second, essential step: continually reinforce them."

An example of this philosophy in action is his insistence on his staff being open about the naps he takes in order to stay sharp and focused, despite the potential for wisecracks about "sleeping on the job." He explains, "I actually don't sleep that much at night, so I usually need a nap in the afternoon. I discovered that when I was taking a nap, my team didn't want to say, 'The congressman is sleeping' so they would say 'He is on a phone call' or 'He is in a meeting.' As soon as I figured this out, I said, 'No. Absolutely not. Because you're lying. We do not lie in this office. Now you don't have to say, "He's sound asleep and snoring like a banshee". But do not ever lie, because integrity is one of our core values.' The first time that you say, 'I know we're committed to honesty, but we can just be dishonest this one time,' you've just set a new standard that actually honesty doesn't matter."

WHAT WE HEARD AND LEARNED

- Learn from everyone
- Become OK with *not* being the smartest person in the room
- Find common ground in your mission
- Vigilantly reinforce your shared values

HERVÉ SEDKY

THE ULTIMATE CONNECTOR USES TRUST TO RESHAPE COMMUNITIES

"We even celebrate failures. There's nothing wrong with failing. We all fail."

HERVE SEDKY, COLLABORATION ARTIST

HERVÉ SEDKY HAS LONG PLAYED a significant part in the events industry. In January 2021, he took on the roles of president and CEO of Emerald, a company that provides platforms that integrate live events and media into rich experiences. They are the company behind brands in industries like action sports (Outdoor Retailer, Surf); home and gift (ASD, NYNOW); design (BDNY, HCD, ICFF); luxury (Couture); residential (KBIS, Cedia); cannabis (Mybis); advertising and media (Advertising Week, Rice); food (Pizza); and many other forums.

Emerald serves an extraordinary range of clients and industries. Hervé, for whom trust is extremely important, sees joint problem-solving as one of the many productive ways to bring the company together. "We have many people on a call once a week," he says of managing such a sweeping enterprise. "When there's a problem, we try to solve the problem together. Many of the people on the call will have a role to play in addressing that particular problem. Doing this requires a culture of trust, and it also helps create that culture. We have to trust each other, because we have to be vulnerable. We have to be able to talk about when we're not successful, when we're not achieving things, when we're a little behind. That hasn't always been comfortable for people. I feel like we've made significant progress. Now we have a culture where it's perfectly okay to actually say, 'I'm not doing well' or 'I'm behind.'"

Ultimately, Hervé is seeking to have Emerald evolve to have a unique culture in several ways. "I think it's critical to have an entire organization that is extraordinarily curious. You drive change through curiosity: by questioning, by asking, by really fighting the status quo, by not getting too comfortable. Intellectual curiosity is something I look for in the people that I'll work with all the time."

He sets high standards for himself and his senior team in order to establish the conditions needed for Emerald's culture. "We have to have leaders that genuinely care. I have seen leaders conflate caring with bio data. 'I know that this guy has five kids and I know that one is going to college,'" he says. "That, to me, is not what's important. It doesn't really make a difference. What makes a difference is that the person you're interacting with knows that you authentically care about them."

He looks for "people who are outwardly focused. I think it's so easy for people in organizations to start thinking in very internal ways. But often, business is actually not that difficult if you have the right attitude. When you have a problem, you go talk to customers, you educate yourself on what's going on in the industry and the market."

Hervé, despite being the president and CEO, does not think that financial results should be the first focus for the company. "Organizations that succeed don't make the shareholders the primary concern. They think about their people. They think about their customers. An organization maniacally focused on delivering financial results typically fails," he says. "Organizations that are successful have great people who love working with each other. They trust each other. They succeed together. They fail together, too. They're places where you trust that someone else has your back. When they do that, by the way, their shareholders get handsomely rewarded."

Hervé believes that part of his job is to set the stage for risk-taking. "I take our obligations to our people, our customers, and our shareholders very seriously … but I also keep perspective. If I screw something up today, there is no patient on the operating table that's going to die. We actually celebrate risk-takers. We even celebrate failures. There's nothing wrong with failing. We all fail. We value the ones who have the courage to admit failures and also have the courage to learn and share. After something didn't go as hoped, I told the leader responsible for it 'You're going to get our Biggest Loser award this year.' By the way, that comes with real compensation, just as if the winner were the top revenue producer. But it has one condition: You have to share what you've learned with the entire organization to get it," he says.

Hervé gave back to his industry by leading SISO, the Society of Independent Show Organizers, through challenging times. "Initially, technology seemed to promise to bring us much closer together. Ironically, I think people began feeling more isolated and craving contact more than ever before," he says. "Then the pandemic really accentuated that trend. Social media is not really anywhere close to the real face-to-face experience. People have resorted way too much to communicating by email, even with someone down the hall. They're Zooming instead of having lunch together."

Hervé's sense of the nature of the problem? "The bottom line is that there's actually a trust issue. People are not trusting each other as much as they used to. We had to confront that problem to bring back the in-person contact that we need."

When the pandemic blasted the businesses of the members of SISO, Hervé responded. "At that point, I went with collaboration. Given the magnitude of the disaster for the industry, I felt that no one leader and not one company would be able to solve it on their own. For me, collaboration was the only way to go."

This was a tall order because it involved "bringing competitors together to try to solve the issue so we could all survive. Luckily, the members turned out to be "wonderful individuals. We started looking at our standards, making sure we didn't all have our own, different standards. No one was saying 'My standards were better than your standards.' That wasn't going to help the industry. It was about creating the best standards for the entire industry so that we could give people renewed confidence that attending an event was not a dangerous thing."

Hervé is adamant that the technology involved has to be done right. "I do think that we have to make things really easy for people. People use apps that are easy to use. They want a very simple way to interact with the content and the people and the companies that they interact with. We should focus on making those experiences really easy."

Hervé looks forward to a greatly changed and much stronger event industry. "I don't stay awake at night wondering, 'Oh my gosh, are we going to have events in the future? It's a waste of time to think about that. We will always have events. We've had them for thousands of years and we'll continue to have them," he says.

He actually sees it as an amazing opportunity to reignite the industry. "We've had more headwinds than almost anyone else; now all we have are tailwinds. We're coming back," he says. "Do we have some issues? Of course we do. But I really feel that our industry today is in a great position to continue to grow. You're already seeing companies doing things that they never would've done before. Relationships and the level of trust have grown dramatically. We're coming out of this crisis stronger."

WHAT WE HEARD AND LEARNED

- Have leaders who genuinely care
- Celebrate risk-taking and failure
- Use technology to enhance trust and curiosity
- Make your technology easy-to-use

XAVIER MUFRAGGI

AT THE EPICENTER OF THE POWERFUL, EXCLUSIVE YPO, THE CORPORATE LEADERSHIP COMMUNITY

"'My mother is bipolar'—that's an example of something a member could share in their forum. How often do CEOs tell each other something like that? Never. But the moment someone says it, the next person's going to go even deeper."

XAVIER MUFRAGGI, COLLABORATION ARTIST

THE COMBINED asset value of the companies whose leaders are involved with YPO is equivalent to the third largest economy in the world. The organization is powerful and nimble enough to be able to address some of the stickiest world problems—in part because of the unique nature of its membership. YPO is a global community of chief executives driven by the shared belief that the world needs better leaders.

"We have 33,000 members," notes Xavier Mufraggi, who became the CEO of YPO in December 2020. The member CEOs tend to be highly involved—as well as highly influential. "Some members, for example, have just sold their family business or put somebody in charge of operations. When people are 50, and they sell their first business, they still want to be in the game. They have some time available, so they dedicate two years or even more to YPO, perhaps giving 50 percent of their time. Now, more and more entrepreneurs are selling their first business when they're 30. At 30, most don't want to retire. I've got around 900 employees, but I also have 2,000 of the most talented CEOs in the world ready and eager to work to keep making YPO better and better."

The range and depth of involvements that members have with YPO is impressive. "You are likely to enter YPO via your local chapter of perhaps about a hundred people and participate in a chapter-level event once a month," Xavier explains. "Then you are likely to be part of smaller groups called forums that meet once a month. Plus, network activities. You might do numerous virtual events and occasional in-person meet-ups once or twice a year. Then there are national and international events. We have Edge, which is the biggest gathering of CEOs in the world. It starts with a plenary session, but quickly breaks down into smaller groups, sometimes as small as just seven people, that focus on topics that have emerged."

Xavier thinks this is the future model for all big conferences. "The big group moments should be limited as much as possible. Then you go in smaller presentations and work groups," he suggests. "What I want to do next year is, instead of doing a huge party at night, have people work in groups of seven and present something from the group the next morning. Have them work like they were students for the night. They're going to have a blast."

Take a moment to imagine how difficult it could be to get groups composed exclusively of alpha types accustomed to leading their organizations to work together, and you have an idea of the challenges that Xavier faces. Fortunately, he brought to this daunting task the irrepressible optimism that had been a hallmark of his time at Club Med, where he was CEO of Club Med Europe/Middle East/Africa markets and before that CEO of Club Med North America. At both Club Med and at YPO, he has relentlessly focused on "the experience" of the participants.

"At Club Med, the rooms were not best-in-class. The buildings were never new. But we would overcompensate for that by delivering a spectacular experience," he says. "Our guests would arrive stressed. We would get them together as fast as possible and help them create connections. Put kids together with potential friends. Introduce fellow tennis enthusiasts. Later, we brought everybody back to family tables where we had moments together. Everybody will come back to Club Med because it is a deep, positive, emotional experience for the family."

He got a big clue about getting CEOs to work together the first time he moderated a forum when a member told him, "As CEOs, we like to lead or to be led." Xavier likes to use shared activities as a way to increase a team's focus. "When I use Zoom, I'll sometimes say, 'Let's walk and talk virtually.' When you walk, you cannot text at the same time." At Club Med, he reports, he took this even farther. "I brought 10 bikes in for a meeting."

Now that he's working at YPO, he, true to form, works to shift the conversation. "People have been spending too much of their time saying, 'We're going to be in a five-star hotel and the food will be great' before talking with the team about creating the right content. What's the objective? What will we try to achieve? How do we create emotions?"

Xavier understands the value of having great speakers. YPO uses its massive prestige to attract speakers for large meetings that local chapters of YPO couldn't afford. But he understands that, ultimately, the audience is more important to the experience than the speaker. "Speakers might be a reason you come, but the experience depends on who is sitting next to you. You're rarely going to talk to the speaker," he points out. "The question is, are you going to check your emails during the session, or are you going to be really there? That's where the quality of the audience comes in. It's better to be very selective, to have fewer people in a room, as long as they are able to connect with each other because they really want to listen."

He continues, "The members of YPO are extraordinarily motivated to connect. Some of them have big egos—to be a CEO, you need to have a certain level of ego—but they're really able to listen. There's an interesting dynamic that happens. You start to realize that you're not the smartest when you're surrounded by equally successful people. Your level of ego starts to decrease. And when you're in a forum with people from different industries, you start to realize the power of diversity."

To get 'magic' to happen, and channel true serendipity among collaborators, Xavier believes there needs to be vulnerability. In smaller gatherings, he creates the right kind of atmosphere with icebreaking activities and by setting an example. "At smaller YPO gatherings, we often start things off by asking people to reveal things they might not even tell their spouses," he says. "It helps if an experienced participator is able to set the tone on a deeply personal level. 'My mother is bipolar.' How often do CEOs tell each other something like that? Never. But the moment someone says it, the next person's going to go even deeper. Within 30 minutes, people who were complete strangers have shared something it took them years to tell their best friends. They have a pure connection, extremely tight. Then they build that relationship over months and months of contact with this small group."

Xavier sees his job is to "scale trust." "When somebody who looks like the most amazing person in the newspaper arrives in a Tesla, everything seems great. Then he tells you, 'I've got a problem with alcohol,' or 'I just saw my kids taking drugs.' They have put their shield to the side. You can talk person-to-person."

While the executives are eager and the dynamics can be beneficial, YPO still relies on specific procedures and rules to keep everything on track. "It's hard, for example, to tell a CEO, 'You've exceeded your allotted time.' I try to tell my moderator that we need to stick with the timing. You need to have somebody in the forum to be very strict on the rules."

One of the fundamental tenets of YPO is "You don't come for business. There's no solicitation. You come to be a better leader, a better businessman for your employees and your company, a better dad or mother, and better for yourself. The whole foundation is that if you don't feel as good as you can, you're not going to be able to do your job. We're very strong on that pillar."

For the record, "You can still do business, but you need to be introduced by a third party," he continues. "An unwritten rule is that any time you meet a new member, you need to introduce them to at least two members who can have an impact for them. The number-one rule is if somebody asks you something, you need to get back to them in 24 hours.

"Forums can have very strict rules. We tell people, 'If you don't follow the rules by the book, the forum won't be of optimum quality.' You get expelled from a forum if you violate strict confidentiality rules. You can't even share what you've heard with your spouse. If you don't attend twice, you can be kicked out of the forum or re-voted on by the rest of the members. If you don't respond in 24 hours, you can be kicked out. If you are late by even just three minutes, in some chapters, people ask you to pay for the next dinner and so on. People are very respectful of all the rules. It's part of our culture."

Xavier points to tools in YPO that can be exported into other areas, as well. "When we have an online meeting, we start with something positive," he says. "It takes two minutes. You connect, you learn something new about somebody. I do that with all my teams."

Another useful tool is asking, "Is there something that will take your mind out of the discussion? Did you experience something just before the meeting that's still in your head? We say, 'clear the air.' Is there anything that happened at the last meeting that you didn't feel good about? Are we good to move on? This is extremely powerful because sometimes there's friction between people for prior stuff that could be resolved just this easily."

To get some perspective on the statement about YPO's financial impact at the start of this chapter, consider this: "If you want to raise money, we have a business platform. There are $50 billion in deals every year between members from the network."

The financial impact is matched by accomplishments that can't be measured in dollars. "Businessmen and members know they share values, despite the polarization of the world, and this can contribute to a new kind of diplomacy," he says. "For example, there are a lot of Israelis who would love to visit Saudi Arabia. Except they can't, unless YPO members are able to arrange for it. If we really want to resolve the Arab and Israeli situation, we need to connect. We need to understand each other. And the best way to do it is for people in Israel to go to Saudi Arabia and people in Saudi Arabia to go to Israel."

He adds, "What energizes me is the potential ripple effect of the organization. When you add up our members and their families and their employees, you get to the point where we can impact 200 million people."

WHAT WE HEARD AND LEARNED

- Focus on relationships and the experience
- Coach people to listen
- Encourage vulnerability to build trust
- Respond within 24 hours

DAVID STARK
EVENT VISIONARY BUILDS
MOVING MOMENTS

"Fine artists have to set up their own problem that they answer. As a designer, I am answering problems that somebody else has set. If you said to me, 'Do whatever you want,' I wouldn't have a single idea."

DAVID STARK, COLLABORATION ARTIST

DAVID STARK, the chief creative director of New York-based David Stark Design and Production, has evolved during his time in the event industry. So have his clients, which range from high-profile charities to financial services companies to significant retail operations. And his comments about the business, like his events, deliver some surprises.

David started out as a fine artist, and initially got into events as a way of supporting his painting. "It was a really good, flexible side job that also used some of the principles of painting, color, and texture," he explains. "It was a more creative solution than waiting tables, which I also did. When I started, I worked with flowers. It was during a time period in the events industry that if you had an event, you had flowers. Then, somewhere along the way, I realized that flowers were just one of the tools in the toolbox.

"I also realized I was a better designer than I am a fine artist," he continues. "Fine artists have to set up their own problem that they answer. As a designer, I am answering problems that somebody else has set. If you said to me, 'Do whatever you want,' I wouldn't have a single idea. I'm actually a better reactor. There are many times where somebody comes to the table with something for me to react to. There are also many times where I have to dig and find that thing."

David sees not-for-profit events as a particularly strong example of the trend toward more purposeful design. "We spend a lot of time thinking about how the people in the room can have the experience that they're having, but also how people that are *not* in the room can share the experience. The answer is a combination of social media, word of mouth, and traditional PR," he says. "Back in the day, not-for-profit events were often simply a glamorous opportunity for people to dress up, buy a table, buy a ticket, and that money went to the organization. Today, they are incredible platforms in which an organization can share its message, tell its story, make new friends, reinforce the friends that they already have, and put into three dimensions who they are as an organization in an experiential way."

David cites a recent event for one of the nation's leading not-for-profit charitable organizations as an example of strategic integration. "Everything that happened on stage during the presentation and throughout dinner was married to the overarching theme. All of those things were really connected in a way that the decor functioned as it should, which is to set the stage for the content that's going to transpire within that environment.

"It was a truly lovely experience," he adds. "Everybody was aligned with the same goal, which was to make the best darn thing that they possibly could for the sake of doing the most good that could be done. Every single penny of what it took to create that gala and to run that organization was underwritten by the board, so every single dollar raised went to the people that needed it. It's a very empowering thing to know that what you're doing can have so much weight and can have so much impact."

David also sees a change in events for financial service enterprises. "Some clients come to us because the traditional financial conference is just boring. They go to events that we do, and they realize that their events don't have to be boring. They like the idea that we can create interactive art experiences that tell the story of what the financial conterence is about, or what the hedge fund is about, or what the consortium of funds is focused on.

"We're asked to tell some really difficult stories that are hard to tell. I find this extremely engaging and exciting. In some ways, it's as close to making art as anything is that we do," he explains. "The folks who work at these hedge funds are often extraordinarily forward-thinking, so it's the greatest pleasure to collaborate with them. They are delivering content to us that we've got to really work hard to wrap our heads around. Together we make these content nuggets that are beyond decorating in any way, shape, or form."

David's clients tend to follow him from sector to sector. "We live in this funny spot where we actually create relationships with people. We really enjoy going back and forth between all of it," he says. "Over the years, I've worked with a notable mass retailer. They have evolved incredibly. It's not like they're always the same company. It's my job to be constantly checking the heartbeat and listening and feeling. I have an ear to the pavement and understand that balancing act between the brand, its design ambitions, and the brand that they're partnering with. A really important aspect of being a service provider is listening. Not just listening, but hearing."

You might not see the difference between a David Stark Design project that has a large budget versus a relatively small budget. That's good design—though the projects with smaller budgets further his belief that constraints can be hugely beneficial to creativity. "We're always looking at, 'Where do you get the most bang for your buck?'" he says. "I'd always rather do one amazing, great thing than seven watered-down, measly things. Some of the best projects that we've done have come out of having many limitations."

WHAT WE HEARD AND LEARNED

- Bring your artistry to more purposeful design

- Combine gatherings with social media, word of mouth, and traditional PR
- Have an overarching theme
- Embrace limitations

ATTUNE TO THE
NEEDS OF OTHERS...

AWARENESS

FELICE AXELROD
FUNDRAISING DYNAMO ON THE CHANGING PHILANTHROPY ENVIRONMENT

"If I can recommend something to you that is something that's going to enhance your life, or improve your life, or just make your life easier—that makes me feel good."

FELICE AXELROD, COLLABORATION ARTIST

FELICE AXELROD IS Special Projects Consultant to Bloomberg Philanthropies and Bloomberg LP. She has expertise in strategy, innovative partnerships, and employee engagement and has overseen strategic development and management of corporate donor programs and community engagement. She serves on many non-profit boards and advises on fundraising, event production, marketing, and strategy.

Felice believes that benefits have changed during COVID, and will continue to evolve in the years to come. "We have had three years of not going to events, and they are now beginning to come back. Some people are still not comfortable attending these events, and we have to respect their decision. But hybrid events have allowed those donors to participate on their own terms, which to me is a win-win."

She points out that one can be engaged in other collaborative ways. "It could be volunteer initiatives where employees support the non-profit's programming or attend their performances. Volunteering can be a win-win-win! For the company, for the employees, and for the non-profit. In-person volunteering is coming back, but the ability to participate virtually is a terrific option."

Felice continues, "I have been tutoring virtually for two years, and it works for both me and my mentee. I also volunteer in person where I meet people that I would otherwise not have the opportunity to interact with, and at the same time learn about the non-profit's programming and mission."

Felice points out that the pandemic may have changed expectations about the length of events. "We got used to going to 45-minute virtual events. The first event I attended virtually, I thought, 'I just went to an entire event in 45 minutes! And I didn't miss much!' I do think that going forward, hybrid events will allow guests to have a choice about their participation while still financially supporting the organization. And since so many people have relocated, the organizations can keep those donors engaged."

"Events have become condensed over the years, and now 9 p.m. seems to be the magic departure time. Cocktails, speeches/programming, and auctions are all shorter now but still work. People seem to have no hesitation about leaving in the middle of an event. I attended a benefit dinner recently, and guests started to depart after the main course was served. It was pouring rain that evening, but come on!"

She continues, "Recently I planned a weekday benefit luncheon, and we did not have a reception, served a one-course, one-plate (room temp) entrée, and had a dessert buffet. It allowed the guests to comfortably leave when they wished to in the middle of a workday. And I have attended a few benefit galas where they had a short cocktail 'hour,' followed by a buffet seated dinner, and back to the cocktail area for a dessert buffet. I like these formats where guests aren't stuck at a table for several hours. And I believe that if the programming is done correctly, guests can have an enjoyable experience while learning about the non-profit's mission.

"My main focus is to put myself in the shoes of the attendees. I 'walk through' the event in my mind while planning it. I think about how the guests experience the event. And my little trick is: How do they leave the event? What is their last experience? Are they waiting in line for coats/cars/swag? At that point, they just want to leave, and my motto is: Leave them with chocolate! (Literally and figuratively.)"

Fundraising will become more targeted and strategic. "I always say you should ask a donor to give to something that *they* want to support, not what you want them to support. For example, you might be raising funds for a new building, but the donor is only interested in children's programming. A lot of fundraisers make that mistake. I would try to figure out a way that both sides benefit."

Another win-win!

"And I believe that fundraising will become more creative, interactive, and collaborative to allow for more meaningful and lasting relationships," she adds. "Isn't that the point?!"

WHAT WE HEARD AND LEARNED

- Walk through the planned event through the eyes (and shoes) of both the donor/attendee and the planner/nonprofit
- Keep it as personal as possible
- Keep things short

ERICA BOEKE

UNLOCKING COLLABORATIVE ENERGY BY DEMOCRATIZING EXPERIENCES

"Artists are just getting so cool. There's been a creative Renaissance. While some people were hitting pause, others have blossomed. The creativity is going to be off the hook."

ERICA BOEKE, COLLABORATION ARTIST

ERICA BOEKE RAN Condé Nast's experiential division prior to founding Liberty & Co., a fundamentally new and different kind of company in the events and experiences space.

"I launched Liberty & Co.," she says, "to focus on creating experiences that matter. Many experiential agencies can build the stage for you. We are focused on experiential strategy and programming—all with an editorial lens. Where should your event be, what should it be? Who should be on stage? What should they be doing on stage? Should there even be a stage? Who should be in the audience? How can you create community and content before/during/after? How do you push culture forward through events that truly transform people? And the all-important—how do you generate revenue?

"My team and I," Erica explains, "have created experiences where connections are being made and lives are being changed right in front of you, including the Fast Company Creativity Conference and Innovation Festival as well as the Teen Vogue Summit. Those events stay with you. Those events stand apart from the rest because they actually make your audience feel something and, in many ways, transform them."

Liberty & Co.'s forte is helping brands find their editorial voice. "That's our specialty," Erica says. "We love finding that editorial voice. It starts with their end users. Some brands have a cult following, they have the passion. They already have permission to use their editorial voice. Some brands don't have it. They need a partner to help them find it."

Liberty & Co. is built around a model involving a small core team of 10 people, who pull together specialists to create a dream team for each event. And the company is built around a foundation of awareness and listening—not only to its clients, but to its employees. "We have this incredible talent pool we can call on," Erica says. "Experiential editors, strategists, designers, producers, PR gurus, content creators, and more who can do anything. We do a ton of virtual, so we've discovered some really great technical producers. The company is called Liberty because I want people to work in the way that they want. We have one woman who doesn't want to work in July and August. Great. We work around her. We have moms who want to work in the middle of the night."

Erica insists on being transparent about how she builds her teams, even to the point of encouraging contact between clients and the partners who have been brought on board for a particular project. "In one instance, a client asked why we had three different leads on a call. I answered, 'We could have one main project manager, but it doesn't make sense. It would be a game of telephone with me talking to a fabricator—and I guarantee you, that's not my expertise.' The client thought the change was refreshing."

While Erica is generally quick to laud all the resources she relies on, she does have a pet peeve. "I actually hate writing big checks to venues before a chair or a morsel of food is in the space. It kills me. When you start at a deficit from writing a check to a hotel for half a million or a million dollars, that's a lot to dig out of." It's not the venues she minds; it's the expense. "I had a really smart woman who was opening a new hotel come to me and say, 'How about *I* pay *you* to do an event there?'"

Erica has succeeded in finding new venues for a variety of events. "When I was at *Fast Company*, I went to one of our partners with gorgeous offices and said, 'We're planning a creativity conference with CMOs from all over the world. How'd you like to have 350 of them on your campus? P.S.: Many of them are not your clients, but maybe they could be. I'm doing it on a weekend. It's not going to disrupt much.' Tech companies have such gorgeous offices. If you find one that's not conflicting with what your content is and you want it, it's a great opportunity for them to open their doors and show off."

Erica is optimistic about the future of the experiential industry, and about how clients have become more aware of what goes into all aspects of events and how much impact they can have. "As long as everyone's safe and healthy, these times of massive disruption excite me," she says.

She sees opportunity and advantage where others see disaster. "I think there were two recent pivotal moments for our industry. Number one was the Fyre Festival documentary in 2019. It showed people how difficult what we do is. Before that, people just showed up and expected perfection. I thought that was the best thing that could've happened to those of us who have integrity and produce excellent events."

The second thing she cites is, of course, the COVID pandemic. "After COVID hit, we no longer had to explain the importance of people gathering together," Erica points out. "I remember when I would go into a pitch to a client, and I would have 10 slides about why experiential matters. Now I don't even need it. Everyone gets it."

Erica cites a recent business-to-business (B2B) event as an example of the pent-up demand for gatherings. "The people in the audience were as interesting as the people on stage," she remembers. "They wanted to get together and do deals. We did an immersive artists' dinner and then we had people choose their own adventure. It was colorful. It was loud. It was sexy. It was *people*. That's what we have all missed about being together."

Ultimately, Erica sees fun times ahead. "Artists are just getting so cool. There's been a creative Renaissance," she says. "While some people were hitting pause, others have blossomed. The creativity is going to be off the hook."

WHAT WE HEARD AND LEARNED

- Create experiences that matter
- Find your editorial voice
- Satisfy the pent-up desire for gatherings
- Be colorful, loud, sexy. Be *people*.

TAYLOR BUONOCORE-GUTHRIE AND MOLLIE KHINE

EXPANDING JEFFERSONIAN DINNERS TO ALIGN PARTICIPANTS TO SOLVE PROBLEMS

"This is a memorable, meaningful experience."

TAYLOR BUONOCORE-GUTHRIE AND MOLLIE KHINE, COLLABORATION ARTISTS

TAYLOR BUONOCORE-GUTHRIE and Mollie Khine facilitate group conversations in a host of business areas, including sales training, focus groups, and corporate team building.

They specialize in the Jeffersonian dinner format—and believe so strongly in this approach that they have created a game to help people facilitate conversations in all aspects of their lives. Named after Thomas Jefferson's gatherings at Monticello, a Jeffersonian dinner is basically a curated conversation where you give people permission and the supporting structure to have one conversation around the table at a dinner party.

"It's essentially a way to gather people for meaningful dialogue," Taylor explains. "Everybody gets together around a table. You share a table, you share a meal, and you share a single conversation. History says that Jefferson was known to gather people from around the region at his personal dinner table as a way to share ideas and exchange knowledge. He moderated and facilitated these conversations."

"I actually stumbled upon the format before realizing there was a name for it," Mollie adds. "In attending all kinds of happy hour-style networking events, I found myself desiring more conversational depth, so I started hosting small groups in my New York City apartment. Each time, I would choose a conversation topic in advance, and that would inform who I invited. Folks didn't leave those parties raving about my food—I'm a terrible cook!—but they deeply enjoyed the conversation and often shared that they learned something. They were always eager for the next dinner, and I began to grow a list of future invitees as guests had asked to bring along friends or partners next time."

"I learned about the format from Jennifer McCrea and Jeff Walker, in our roles supporting the UN Millennium Development Goals," Taylor shares. "I first used the dinner formats when hiring a team of people that did not know each other. We needed to ramp up exceptionally quickly to tackle a very big problem. I hosted a Jeffersonian dinner during their first week as a team that laid the foundation for trust and fluid collaboration."

Because they have now created and facilitated so many Jeffersonian dinners, Mollie and Taylor are able to provide practical, step-by-step guidance about them. They suggest that the first step is to define the purpose of the gathering. This often means choosing a topic that will guide discussion and setting guests' expectations. For example, Taylor talks about invitations: "My invitations are very specific and start to answer a number of questions in advance. What is a Jeffersonian dinner? How does this work? What's expected of you? What are we here to talk about?" she explains. "Setting expectations is important."

Mollie shares how to start things off. "A welcome by the host is such a critical part that's often missed. I like to introduce the history of a Jeffersonian dinner and anchor the group in the purpose," she notes, while Taylor adds, "There's something really special about recognizing that this is something that never goes out of style."

Mollie prefers a family-style meal and advises, "A great moment to set the tone is when you invite your guests to take a seat at the table.

I'll say, 'Please help yourself and enjoy the food. While we have a bit more structure to the conversation than a typical dinner party, let's keep this fun! Feel free at any point to top up your plate or step away as needed.' People look to the host for how to show up, and the simple act of permission in that moment to enjoy the food as the conversation ensues is small, but important."

Mollie continues, "Then the first question is an icebreaker—something that, without being cheesy, is just easy to answer. It doesn't require a lot of self-vulnerability and thought—but, importantly, the icebreaker gets everyone speaking at least once. Once you've spoken, you're more likely to speak again, and you're more comfortable doing so. Our favorite type of icebreaker is one that encourages a sharing of an experience and that levels any hierarchy or power imbalances. For example, you might simply be asked to share a memory."

Taylor adds, "One of our favorite opening questions is, 'What's something small or unexpected that brings you joy?' We've also used, 'Who's your favorite person to call when you have good news?' These questions set a positive tone. Often, I'm looking for a question that speaks to the topic of the dinner. For example, "Who is someone in your life who inspires you to be a lifelong learner?"

Then, Taylor and Mollie suggest asking a "big question." Mollie says, "Let's say our topic is 'meaningful work.' The first question might be, 'What does meaningful work mean to you?' to make sure we're all speaking about the same thing."

When asked how they keep everyone involved and prevent people from dominating the conversation, Mollie and Taylor mention various techniques. "A 'Round Robin' approach," Mollie says, "works well to draw in the full group. Most of the time, however, you can just ask people to jump in."

Taylor notes that different formats work for different groups. "If you have a smaller group, it's easier to take turns in the Round Robin format. In fact, a lot of groups find the structure reassuring. Some people don't feel comfortable jumping in. They like to wait for their turn, and then speak."

"If one person seems to dominate the conversation," Taylor adds, "it is important to gently wrestle the conversation away from that person." Mollie uses a simple tool to keep the conversation balanced, "I often call on specific people." Taylor expands on the idea. "That's actually a great way to tackle that moment. It serves as a signal to everyone else at the table that we want to hear from everyone."

Taylor is ready to redirect as needed. "I see my role as a facilitator to ensure everyone can be heard so I'm not afraid to interrupt. I think everyone appreciates a productive interruption."

Asked about the ideal size of a Jeffersonian dinner, Taylor answers, "I think the sweet spot is at about 12 at a table." Mollie adds, "We've done corporate groups with 300 people, divided into tables of 10, with a dedicated facilitator for each table. That's critical. We've also designed for larger events where you empower an individual at each table to become the dedicated facilitator."

The duo has also created a product called Convers(-ate) to enable people to host their own Jeffersonian dinners. Taylor says, "We felt like this format was so powerful and we wished that everybody had access to a how-to. People shared common challenges to making the conversations work. Some people weren't sure what to talk about. Some didn't feel comfortable facilitating. So we decided to package our know-how into a box so that anybody who was interested in creating this kind of dialogue would have all the tools that they needed. We packed everything that we know into this thing."

Mollie provides more details. "It's got a pocket guide for the facilitator. There's a series of conversation cards. We have the obvious, big topics like family and friendship, spirituality, parenthood," she says. Taylor adds, "We also have some a little bit more off the beaten path, like survival, bravery, and endurance. We choose topics that will speak to everyone, in some way. By virtue of being alive, you have something to say about this topic."

They like the product so much they often use it themselves. "A fun thing to do is to actually hand the conversation card stack to someone and let them flip through and see what they're interested in."

Commenting on the versatility of the Jeffersonian dinner format, Mollie notes, "It's completely up to the host to decide on the level of formality and the level of sophistication. This can be done around a campfire with some s'mores and a facilitator mom who wants to engage her children. It can be used to engage an organization's funders or board members in a way that brings them back to their own reasons for being a supporter."

Taylor was also an early pioneer of hosting *virtual* gatherings inspired by the Jeffersonian dinner format. By using the foundational elements of the Jeffersonian dinner—a specific topic, a clear invitation, and question prompts that she prepared in advance—she was able to gather strangers for meaningful conversation online during the pandemic lockdown. "I was skeptical about whether a virtual platform could lead to the same kind of intimacy people feel at a dinner table. To my surprise and delight, it still worked."

Taylor sees the Jeffersonian dinner as providing something that is in increasing demand. "This is a memorable, meaningful experience."

WHAT WE HEARD AND LEARNED

- Set expectations in the invitation
- Welcome and introduce the guests
- Make icebreakers easy to answer
- Moderate, facilitate, and enjoy

GIANNA GAUDINI

TECH-SAVVY EVENT PLANNING
PRO ON PURPOSE

"As event planners, we're also storytellers. We're creators of memories."

GIANNA GAUDINI, COLLABORATION ARTIST

GIANNA GAUDINI DREW on her long career—including 10 years of producing events at Google—when writing the book *The Art of Event Planning: Pro Tips From an Industry Insider*. The book is her way of giving back. She reveals not just how to create an effective event, but also what event planners can do to stay healthier and happier.

"As event planners," she says, "we're also storytellers. We're creators of memories, and those memories drive actions that ultimately drive business revenue. We have to break through to attendees. People are inspired to act when they feel an emotion."

Events, in Gianna's view, need to really begin with their intention. "There's a tendency to think 'design first' when it comes to planning events," she explains. "Especially with the rise of platforms. It's fun. Everybody likes making a pinboard and starting with the style and the design. But I encourage people to start with the goals and objectives before diving into the weeds."

Gianna shares how she establishes the purpose of an event. "One of the exercises that I take my stakeholders and my agencies and team through is asking three basic questions: What do you want your atten-dees to think? What do you want them to do? And what do you want them to feel? That gets to the heart of what your goals are, and ulti-mately puts the attendee experience first and foremost—which is why we have events.

"If we're stumbling," she advises, "one way to take a step back and get to the bottom of what you want to accomplish is to ask yourselves, 'If there was going to be a headline written about this event, what would it be?' It's actually a hard exercise. It really makes you focus in on, 'What is that thing that has to happen at this event?' Then you can ask, 'How are we going to get that headline? Who's coming and how are we going to make them feel that way?' The headline also helps you figure out what you *don't* want to have happen. It even helps you home in on your resources. There's always a budget, and there's always going to be the need to prioritize."

Gianna is frank about the rising requirements for a successful event "There's more substance behind a basic event. We're in a world where everybody wants everything to be relevant to them, to have meaning. It's expected that if you have an entertainer at an event, it's not enough for them to be a great world-class performer. There's an expectation now that they're also going to tell you what inspired them to write the songs," she says. "People want to walk away with important learnings and messaging, even at social events. Having a narrative that weaves through your event is really important. You can have all the bells and whistles and great food and entertainment, but if your content falls flat, people are going to remember that—and not in a good way."

Gianna also stresses the importance of the event team. "Planning events is definitely a team sport. I would not be able to have built a career where I developed and produced the types of events I've produced without an incredible team behind me." She has advice about how to assemble and manage an event team, as well: "You have to hire people that you inherently trust, and that trust you. I'm a huge fan of not micro-managing. I've got brilliant team members. I fully entrust them to do their job."

She recognizes that many event planners don't have the scale or budget for a large team. "If you're working at a smaller company with a smaller events team, you're going to have to be more of a generalist and wear a lot of hats," she advises.

Gianna believes that the best qualification for joining an events team is experience. "A lot of the things that have to do with event planning come with experience. The more on-the-job experience you have, the more types of events you work on, the more types of people you work with and teams that you're working on. Getting more experience under your belt is going to make you better."

Beyond the purpose of an event and the team orchestrating it, Gianna has thoughts on mood and mindset as well—particularly when deliverables such as good press coverage are involved. She talks about friends who work in the press and are expected to attend events and write glowing reviews of product lines. "But they are stuck in a room with no food and beverage, no power. They're pissed off. Offer them healthy food options, really good juices with vitamins in them for immunity, really good caffeine, robust food, lots of power, really good internet with hard lines to plug into so they can upload large files."

As much as she nurtures reporters, Gianna is even more concerned about the well-being of the members of the event team. "As an event planner, you've got crazy hours. You travel a lot. It's hard to give sleep, eating, and exercise priority," she points out. "But it's essential. Sleep is my secret weapon. If you can get a good night of sleep, that is going to put you leagues above anyone else. Studies have shown what sleep can do to enhance your ability to think and react, and really do everything from metabolizing food to reacting in a crisis to handling interpersonal relationships. You also need a plan to recuperate afterwards. There's a phrase that I really like to live by: 'Stress plus rest equals growth.' You have to build in rest after great effort. Otherwise, it's just 'stress equals burnout.'"

WHAT WE HEARD AND LEARNED

- Make planning a gathering a team sport
- Start with the purpose, not the design
- Weave a narrative through your event
- Build in exercise and rest

JOE GOLDBLATT

PROFESSOR EMERITUS OF EVENTS ON TURBOCHARGING COLLABORATION WITH MINDFULNESS

"I've never had a student say to me, 'I loved your PowerPoint.'"

JOE GOLDBLATT, COLLABORATION ARTIST

JOE GOLDBLATT IS Emeritus Professor of Planned Events at Queen Margaret University in Edinburgh, Scotland. He has been called "the foremost authority in the world of events." He is the author, co-author, and editor of 40 books in the field of event management; is the founding president of the International Special Events Society (ISES) (now known as the International Live Events Association, or ILEA); and was the developer of the original Certified Special Events Professional (CSEP) international qualification program. The list could go on and on.

Joe is a true believer in the value of personal interaction. "I taught for 47 years," he explains. "I've never had a student say to me, 'I loved your PowerPoint.' I've never had a student say to me, 'That was a great video you showed.' But I've had *hundreds* of letters saying things like, 'Thank you for taking the time to meet with me in the library,' or 'Thank you for being there when I was struggling to finish my dissertation.' It's that face-to-face encounter that creates deeply meaningful, long-lasting experiences for an event."

Joe is a repository of practical wisdom. He can go in-depth on a topic like safety and liability issues, making it fascinating with crazy stories—like the time there was a lion attack on a trade show floor. He can answer questions like, 'Who's responsible if someone slips on our dance floor?'

But he also understands that the industry is about something much bigger than practical details. And his latest suggestion for events has an interesting backstory.

"Before I finished my teaching career, I was asked by the head of our university if I would volunteer to learn the practice of mindfulness," he explains. "I thought, well, maybe he's singling me out because I'm starting to lose it a little bit and he thinks it might help me to meditate. But in fact, he had selected me because he thought this might be another tool to help my students learn. For one year, every Wednesday afternoon, I sat with a facilitator to learn to practice mindfulness. I then brought that into the classroom. By the way, I would only do this for about 10 minutes at the beginning of each lecture. By the end of the term, the initially skeptical students absolutely insisted that it be continued in future years. It began to spread to other faculty members.

"Best of all, not only was the students' concentration improved, the questions they asked were deeper, sharper," he continues. "The scores at the end of the semester on their exams and projects were much higher. It definitely had a positive effect."

So what does mindfulness have to do with live events? "In the future, there may be an opportunity for event planners to create a mindfulness transition room where you could go before you enter the general session and practice mindfulness to tune your listening, to tune your breathing so that you're fully ready to concentrate and absorb," he suggests. "I think the use of mindfulness will grow in the future in event settings."

While Joe is the ultimate event guru, even he doesn't have the answer to the age-old question of how to measure an event's return on investment (ROI). "The reason there is no easy answer," he notes, "is because events are attended by *people*, and people's motivations, their history, and their experience changes dramatically between the time you first contact them and the time the event has ended.

He explains, "For example, if you conduct an evaluation during a session at an event, you usually have an inflated set of numbers: People are excited, they're thrilled with the speaker, motivated, et cetera. If you conduct the same evaluation two weeks later, you may have lower numbers. That doesn't mean much. It's just a more reasonable assessment because they've had time to think about it. So, the question is: Do you survey before, during, or after in terms of evaluating ROI? And my answer is you do, where possible, all three—and then you compare, because people's attitudes and their impressions change over time."

Joe believes that any studying of events management needs to be complemented by practical experience. "I tell students from day one of any undergraduate program that you must be involved with events as a volunteer or part-time employee so you can show an employer that progressively, you've been given greater and greater responsibility. Then, when you graduate, you can really seize the world."

Setting high standards for those involved in events makes sense when you have as lofty a sense of events as Joe does.

"You could start off with people who might not ever wish to work together when your event is announced. Then, when a committee is formed, they come together—and if it's successful, they form a team. And if it's remarkably successful, they form enduring, lifelong friendships as a result of delivering the Olympic games, the Commonwealth games, the Tony awards, the Grammy awards, working on any event," he says. "I've always believed that what we do in the events industry is the most noble profession of all—because we bring people together for a common benefit."

WHAT WE HEARD AND LEARNED

- Focus on face-to-face encounters
- Integrate mindfulness
- Survey before, during, and after an event
- Use all your soft skills (actually the hardest skills)

MO HUSSEINI

EXPERIENCE DESIGN LEADER ON ESTABLISHING COMMON GROUND

"I think it's really important to remember that not everyone is one thing all the time."

MO HUSSEINI, COLLABORATION ARTIST

MO HUSSEINI IS NOW the Chief Design Officer at Gen City Labs, a startup focused on building and energizing communities. When we spoke, he was SVP, Design, at the Freeman Company—the world's largest event producer based in Dallas—heading up the design and creative teams across all Freeman accounts. But that understates his actual assignment. Actually, his job was to look at and manage the entire complex Freedman ecosystem in a whole different way—and he did that with design-led thinking.

Mo's design group was somewhere around 400 people before the pandemic, and it's on track to grow back to that size. "There's a lot of demand for the work Freeman does," he explains. "We are engaged in conversations with clients who are focused more than they ever have been around design and business goals."

His team had breadth as well as depth. He reels off some of the roles: "We've got environmental designers. We've got brand designers. We've got creative strategists. We've got creative technologists. We've got UI/UX people. We've got motion graphics people. We've got print people, video people." And in addition to depth and breadth, his team had *quality*. "One of the great things about being at Freeman is we've been a beacon for some of the best talent out there."

Mo has been dedicated to storytelling ever since his days at UC Berkeley, where he had a side gig translating clips from Arabic and French into English for independent documentary films. The same background that positioned him for translation also led him to realize the need to use segmentation and personalization to make event experiences, whether digital or in-person, more effective than ever.

Mo has a lot of tips to share, including: "I think it's really important to remember that not everyone is one thing all the time." His design team needs to effectively code-switch to deliver the right experience for who each participant is in the moment.

He's happy to expand on that thought. "You have to speak and engage in very different ways, depending on where you are and who you are at that moment. Using myself as an example: I'm a husband, a father, a Palestinian. I may not be all of those things at every moment. I may not be thinking in that way at every moment. And that's true for everybody, right?"

Mo, ever the storyteller, further illustrates his point. "Sometimes I'm engaging with you as the knucklehead sitting next to you on the plane. Sometimes I'm engaging with you as your best friend's dad, right? And I have to talk in a different way." Code switching design thinking is essential because, Mo says, "no customer is a monolith."

Mo shares how he first became aware of code switching. "My first lesson in code switching was going from an English boarding school to college in the U.S., where I realized that if you're brown and have a plummy English accent, people treat you differently. I learned very quickly that I needed to switch my accent to sound more American, because that's what people expected here."

Mo stresses that code switching is actually a positive technique. "I see it as a way of making people feel comfortable. I don't see it as being deceptive. We're a Texas-based company. I'll go to meetings and within two days, I'm y'all-ing all over and saying 'bless your heart.' It's the natural result of empathy."

Mo's wife, whose background is in the digital world, inspires him to understand what technology can do for events. "When we talk about live events and stuff like that," he says, "she's always talking to me about all the kinds of data that they have in the digital world and how that relates to how they design things. They are ahead of the events industry.

"Technology will bring us a lot of excitement in the near future," he continues. "I see a world where we start to get to a place where we have great, actionable metrics on engagement. I've seen some really interesting stuff around tracking people's attentions and their sentiments. Just imagine being able to fine-tune an event in real time. With the right technology, you could have an opportunity to say, 'Hey, this thing that's happening in the back corner of the convention hall is not really working. Let's get something over there to perk it up.' Having good data could also help us create the shorter events and interactions that some customers are starting to ask for."

Ultimately, Mo sees virtual technology helping make events more inclusive. "Currently, lots of people don't necessarily have either the means or the ability to engage. They can't be there at a convention center for an event. There are now options for that. With data, you can even create bespoke events for them."

WHAT WE HEARD AND LEARNED

- Manage complex challenges with design-led thinking
- Deliver the right experience for who each participant is at the moment
- Code-switch to make people comfortable
- Make events more inclusive with virtual technology

DAVID ISAACS

CO-FOUNDER OF THE WORLD CAFÉ, A TRANSFORMATIVE COLLABORATION FORMAT

"I don't believe that humans create anything. I think we tap into creation."

DAVID ISAACS, COLLABORATION ARTIST

DAVID ISAACS IS careful to clarify that he did not invent The World Café. In fact, he goes a giant step beyond that and believes that we really don't create anything.

"In contrast, we believe we tap into creation," he says. "Picasso tapped into creation. Mozart tapped into creation. We don't create intelligence; we awaken and remember collaborative wisdom that already exists." This distinction is critical to David because "evoking an awakening collaborative wisdom already has infinite creative possibilities."

It's understandable that David feels this way. After all, The World Café, a social innovation that has spread around the world, basically appeared in 1995 when he and Juanita Brown hosted a small group of business and academic leaders at their home in Mill Valley, California.

"It was raining, and we couldn't be outside on the deck as we had been previously," he remembers. "We set up TV tables. There were 24 people, so we had six tables each with four plastic chairs around them. We just did that so we could have coffee.

"All of a sudden, the meeting started. Nobody called the meeting to order. We were talking and it was a buzz like you wouldn't believe. I said to Juanita, 'Let's let this go. Let's see what happens.' And we did.

"About half an hour later, somebody raised his hand and said, 'I really am enjoying this. Why don't we shift tables? Why don't we have one person stay at each table as a host, and three people go to three other tables and continue the dialogue having to do with ways we resource intellectual capital?'"

David continues, "Then we did another round, moving people from table to table. We had three rounds of conversation of about half-an-hour each, recording their insights on makeshift paper tablecloths. After three rounds of conversation, we led a process that asked, 'What happened here? What did we learn? What was possible?' The place lit up."

The meeting was so inspiring that the participants took the time to look at what they had harvested together. They had uncovered what soon became The World Café. The experience the participants had was so unusual and so rewarding that they later told others in various countries about it, encouraging them to experiment and expand on what they had found.

"We were with a person who advised us to open-source the process immediately," David recalls. "This is not something that you're wanting to sell."

The organization published a book, *The World Café, Shaping Our Futures Through Conversations That Matter*, that hit a nerve and sold over 100,000 copies and was translated into 15 languages.

A set of seven The World Café design principles were soon identified and articulated in a book. After that, a world-wide practice using The World Café methodology and flexible format for group dialogue grew. The design principles are:

1. Clarify the Context
2. Create Hospitable Space
3. Explore Questions That Matter
4. Encourage Everyone's Contribution
5. Connect Diverse Perspectives

6. Listen Together for Patterns and Insights
7. Share Collective Discoveries

It's important to note that these practices are not confining. Specifics of context, numbers, purpose, location, and other circumstances are factored into each event's unique invitation, design, and more. As a result, The World Café can be modified to meet a wide variety of diologic inquiry needs.

David tells a story about a cherished colleague to illustrate the importance of having the right people in the room. "Our friend started doing The World Cafés all over Denmark. He got a call from a small town asking, 'Would you come and work with us on the future of education?' Before committing, he asked, 'Who are you going to invite to this The World Café?' They replied, 'All the regular people: the head of the town, the wise people in the community, business leaders, teachers, and parents.' Our friend responded, 'I think you've neglected an important demographic: the children. Aren't they what education is about?' The people arranging the meeting agreed reluctantly, although they believed in their hearts that children needed to be taught. They invited the children to participate in three days of The World Café. It was really successful. The children said that they had never before been treated as equal human beings, even in an egalitarian society. The adults were impressed by how wise the children really were."

The World Café is based in the fundamental belief that "the capacity to dialogue is in every one of us because our ancestors, in order to survive the night, had to be able to be in dialogue," David says. "They couldn't survive the night individually."

David stresses that while the process starts with individual input, it focuses on the group rather than the individual. "It's not 'what did *you* learn?' but 'what did *we* come forward with and experience?' Everyone contributes," he explains. "But at the end, we feel that we are in a field of consciousness that just comes through us. The more people who are there, the faster that happens. In other words, the more diversity of consciousness we weave together, the better."

David has a deep respect for what happens in The World Café. "In addition to our left brain and our right brain, our heart is inextricably involved." He instinctively questions anything that might limit the process and the results. "When some people tried to productize intellectual capital as 'knowledge management,' they inhibited much of the potential because what evolved is traditionally measured by accountants. But intellectual capital is very difficult to measure. If we need you to measure it, we lose some of the quality." David makes a distinction: "This is dialogue, not just talk following the scientific method."

David speaks with deep humility, expressing gratitude to the many people who have contributed to the evolution of The World Café process over the years. The list is long and impressive, including everyone from mystics to ancient poets to astronauts to pivotal psychological theorists, as well as his own powerful therapist. David's story touches ground around the world, everywhere from the Esalen Institute in Big Sur to MIT. But listening to him, there's no question that he and Juanita have been significant guiding angels in the amazing saga of The World Café. Listening to many other collaboration artists, there's also no question that they have been generously mentored, influenced, and inspired as well.

David spent much of his early career consulting with big, influential corporations and organizations. Later in his odyssey, he has moved away from that work to focus on a mission of using the processes revealed by The World Café to try to co-evolve the future. "We've started to do this work around awakening collaborative wisdom. We're not teaching anything. We're just giving people an experience in awakening collaborative wisdom arising from the dialogue.

'The biggest challenge is helping people, even our own team, transition out of the cultural meme of teaching to remembering and awakening," he adds. "There is much to *un*-discover. We often see something deeper and higher and wiser emerging in the harvest and final reflection of the awakening collaborative wisdom dialogue.

"Our culture is really challenged," he continues. "If we want to find a way past the separation that splits us, we can consider co-evolving and remembering collaborative wisdom that's already present.

"We don't have to make it up. It's there for us to un-discover. It's not about solving problems; it's about generating possibilities beyond measure."

WHAT WE HEARD AND LEARNED

- Focus on group insights
- Harvest and awaken collaborative wisdom
- Share wisdom as an open-source model—not everything is supposed to be transactional

AMANDA MA

A PRACTICED EXPERT ON UNDERSTANDING THE ROLE OF CULTURAL DIFFERENCES

"We do a lot of multicultural events. We are aware of many cultural sensitivities, etiquettes, and protocols. We make sure we ask about these things, from language barriers to incorporating historical references to food preparation to something as simple as the starting time."

AMANDA MA, COLLABORATION ARTIST

AT THE CENTER of Amanda Ma's work as chief experience officer at Innovate Marketing Group—an event management and experience agency in Pasadena, California—is a fervent focus on understanding collaborators from a cultural perspective. "The Asian population in the U.S. is growing," she says. "Marketers are very smart. They want to tap into the Asian market, and also tap into their disposable income."

Amanda helps them understand this audience and avoid cultural pitfalls. "My background is Chinese," she says. "We do a lot of multi-cultural events. We are aware of many cultural sensitivities, etiquettes, and protocols. Some clients don't care, but a lot of them do. We make sure we ask about these things, from language barriers to incorporating historical references to food preparation to something as simple as the starting time. We get into symbols, colors, and numbers. We know all the major culture celebrations. For example, we don't want to be doing an event for Chinese people when it's Lunar New Year, because nobody would attend—they're all busy with their families."

Amanda supplies a very practical example of why it can be essential to understand the audience. "Once we were doing a 2,000-person corporate retreat. When we were negotiating with the hotel on the venue contract, they said, 'We want you to bring your group here. Let us throw in a cheese platter or cheese station for you.' We replied, 'Did we mention that these are 2,000 *Asian* people? Most Asians are actually lactose-intolerant. Instead of cheese, can we get fruit instead? We don't want them to spend all afternoon in the restroom.' The hotel people laughed and said, 'We did not know that.'"

There are sensitivities around color as well. "In American culture, today, we see a lot of white decor," Amanda points out. "That is a bad thing in Chinese culture, where white is usually reserved for funerals. You don't really see a lot of Asian events in all white. On the other hand, they love the color red. Red is often associated with good luck. At events like hotel grand openings, major brand launches or Lunar New Year, you see a lot of people using red or wearing red."

Another note? Amanda strongly suggests that you use round tables for an Asian audience. "A round table is a good symbol. It symbolizes reunion and harmony, wishing you and your family, as well as friends, stay together happily. A round table where everyone sits as equals facilitates easy conversation and eye contact between people. The square is not as nice because it has sharp corners, which is opposite of harmony. We'd love to do long tables because it just has a very striking look. We'd like to change it up with round, square, and rectangle. But when it comes to an Asian client or people marketing to Asians, that's usually something we'll bring up and say, 'Hey, is this a concern?' Usually, they'll tell us, 'We want round tables because we want the good luck.'"

Amanda also details the implications of *face*. "We always want to save face. We never want to lose face. Also, you want to give people face. That sounds a little bit funny. Basically, you want to pay attention to the elders and the higher ranking, especially when it comes to government officials," she explains. "If someone older than you is speaking, you should make eye contact and listen to them. If you're speaking to more than one person, you need to be looking at the person who has the highest rank, out of respect.

"Western culture is a little bit more casual than Asian culture," she continues. "Here, we like using first names. But if you're doing business in China, you would address a person using a title and their last name until you knew them well." Similarly, she notes, "If you're doing business in Japan or if you have Japanese customers, dress up versus dress down. They tend to dress up a little bit more. Here, we love sneakers. But over there, I would recommend you wear loafers. It's just more respectful."

Amanda identifies a cultural difference that can lead to misunderstandings. "When a Westerner says no, they are very direct. If you are dealing with someone Chinese, their no will be softer and less direct so that no one loses face. It's not a direct no, but they're telling you no. You need to listen for this."

WHAT WE HEARD AND LEARNED

- Embrace the importance of culture and diversity
- Determine the cultural composition of your audience
- Heed their sensitivities about numbers, colors and more
- Use the lens of "face"
- Listen for the softer "no"

CAPRICIA MARSHALL
OUTSPOKEN ADVOCATE FOR
SOFT AND SMART POWER
ROADS TO SUCCESS

"A touch point … can change the relationship."

CAPRICIA MARSHALL, COLLABORATION ARTIST

CAPRICIA MARSHALL HAS, quite literally, been behind the scenes of collaborations of global importance: She was the social secretary in the Clinton White House and the chief of protocol in the Obama administration.

In those roles, she had enormous leeway—as well as responsibility—for setting the stage for success. The interactions she fostered were closely scrutinized by the media, but no one paid more attention than she did to every setting and every detail. During collaborative moments, every choice of location, activity, decor, and more was *purposeful.* "My area of expertise," she says, "was using the tools of soft power to assist the foreign policy agenda of the president of the United States and the secretary of state."

Wait. Soft power?

"We all know what hard power is," she explains. "It's when one country declares war or imposes economic sanctions. Soft power involves moving countries to do what you desire them to do. In soft power, what you are attempting is to attract them into your way of thinking and create bridges of understanding by using a whole variety of tools."

Capricia continues, "*Smart* power is a blend of hard and soft. It's the carrot and the stick. So, while I'm possibly sanctioning you, I'm still engaging with you. I still want to pull you into my way of thinking. I'm not giving up. I'm not forfeiting the relationship. For example, today, Russia practices absolute hard power, but China remains a bilateral superpower. We engage with them through people-to-people exchanges while exerting our defenses of democracy."

Capricia learned on the job how vast the opportunities to practice soft power were. "Secretary Clinton prompted us to look at our day-to-day duties and ask, 'What else could we do that would assist in furthering bilateral relationships with our allies and/or creating bridges with countries that we have differences with?'"

Once Capricia started looking, she found opportunity after opportunity. For example, even the simple, time-honored act of gift-giving became more thoughtful and strategic. "When we were selecting and giving a gift, we used every piece of information that was given to us to create a connective tissue," she explains. "When we learned about an engagement that the president or the secretary was going to have, we asked a slew of questions: What is the focus of the meeting? Should the gift reflect a policy issue that the president knew was going to be difficult to discuss? Was this a relationship that's tenuous? Is this a new friendship, a leader we're trying to engage with? Looking at the full-on scope of the relationship, and then also the engagement, how could we—just through the gifting element—create another connection?"

She adds, "If the guest had previously traveled or studied in the United States, we searched for something significant from that time, that place, perhaps a school, that we could use to create that perfect connection. From the moment they opened the gift they were touched that we took the time to learn more about them and create a gift with a beautiful presentation. A touch point like that is incredibly important; it can change the relationship."

Capricia talks about how food was also elevated and leveraged as a tool of diplomacy. "We had been missing out on many wonderful opportunities to engage more fully with our counterparts. Coffees, breakfasts, lunches, teas—so many important discussions were happening at the table," she explains. "So, we thought about every element of that dining experience. What are we serving? What are the courses of this meal and what are the culinary ingredients? Who is serving it? Who is creating it? What is the design of the table setting, from seating to centerpieces? What could be a bridge to our guest? Where is the connection with that person that we can try to create to draw them in closer to us, for them to feel an affinity with us? "We created the State Chef Corps and invited chefs from all over the country who we believed represented, first of all, the United States and our ideals," she continues. "We selected chefs who would understand that our focus was about more than simply a great meal—we wanted food to be purposeful. One of the first events of this kind that we had was a state luncheon that was jointly hosted by then Vice President Biden and Secretary Clinton to welcome the Chinese vice president, who was on track to become their president. We reached out to chef Ming Tsai in Boston and invited him to create a very special meal. We certainly don't ever want to make a completely Chinese meal for a Chinese leader, as we wouldn't want to go a foreign destination and be served steak and potatoes. Our goal was to lift this occasion using the tool of food to create the best bilateral experience. We wanted to take the opportunity to say, 'We are the great quilt of the world, and your culture is a part of our culture.' Ming Tsai did just that. The fish was a wonderful bass that was caught in the United States, so it was all American. Everything was sourced in the United States, but the seasonings and the herbs created this great fusion of flavor.

"When I escorted our guest upstairs to the Monroe room, chef Ming Tsai was there, standing with Vice President Biden and Secretary Clinton. Many leaders from around the world are guarded in moments like these, but our guest just relaxed, beaming with this sense of 'You respect me. You are welcoming me so beautifully into this very important place with this extraordinary chef.' It was an important diplomatic moment."

The decor at the meals was intentional and important. "You want to have some sort of warming element on the table, but not elaborate floral arrangements that could be a barrier," Capricia explains. "With flowers, you have to be very careful of allergies and careful of certain color selections. You don't want to offend someone with a color choice that reflected mourning, such as all white in many countries. The table can set a tone, like a bare, sterile table conveys a sense of this is all business, no frivolity. We would likely only have flags in the room, but the table would be prepared with notes and pens only."

Capricia and her team were deliberate and strategic in their choice of the room where an interaction would happen, as well. "One room could provide a warm and inviting environment while another would be a little cooler in nature," she says. "Sometimes, we wanted someone to feel uncomfortable and a little on edge. Maybe it might be the size of the room. It could be the ceiling height. It could even be the temperature of the room. A lower ceiling height will force people into becoming more decisive, making more concrete decisions."

She provides a practical illustration. "People like Russian President Putin don't want to feel attached to any alliance with the United States," she notes. "So, they want to float and be vague. They love big rooms with huge areas of space between you and themselves. That amount of space can create an uncertain atmosphere. When we control the circumstances, we are likely to want to, literally, pull them into closer collaboration. It's the same dynamic with table size, making the width closer depending upon the agenda.

"If, however, it is a relationship that we feel comfortable with, and the occasion is purely social, then you will see us really relax all of those elements. You will see a bigger, maybe grand, table. You will see a different space. In the White House, the selection may be the state dining room as opposed to a cozier space, like the family dining room."

Preparing the host of an event is as important to Capricia as engineering the environment. She likes to make sure hosts are incredibly well-briefed beforehand and supported with a little "cheat sheet" at a table covering everyone and everything from the actual seating arrangement (including pictures of guests) to the why's behind how that arrangement was made.

Various high-level leaders Capricia has worked with each had their own hosting style, she says. "Bill Clinton wants to know everything about you. He's incredibly curious. He's constantly asking questions and drawing information. 'Where are you from? What do you do... etc.' Once he gets someone talking, he finds the thing that you have in common with him. Whatever it might be, he finds that intersection point and makes you feel like you're the only person in the room with him."

She adds, "Barack Obama has his million-watt smile. It's innate in him. He walks in and everybody feels, 'Oh, I want to know you. You're just wonderful.' He enjoys greeting people individually, framing the discussion, and then he likes to get down to business.

"Hillary Clinton likes to set the mood. She likes to have food on the table. She wants to make sure everyone's cared for. 'Do you feel comfortable? Do you need something to drink?' She's very much a caretaker."

Preparing the host—even a very famous host—isn't always enough to guarantee success though. You need to provide supportive back-up as well. "It is incumbent upon the host to begin the exchange, but there are those who lack the hosting gene, and they need to be prompted," Capricia explains. "I will brief another designated attendee on the flow of the engagement, and to be prepared to prompt discussion to assist the host with elements such as introductions at the table and presenting the issues to be discussed. The host will absolutely chime in, picking up on the cues. It's understandable. Our hosts are incredibly busy people who lead incredibly busy lives, and they can't remember everything all the time. Our job was recognizing when and how to utilize our well-tailored soft power tools to prepare and assist our leaders to achieve diplomatic success."

WHAT WE HEARD AND LEARNED

- Use soft power to bring people in and encourage collaboration
- Always look to create additional connections
- Prepare and support your host
- Create bridges of understanding between those who differ

LESLIE MCGUIRK
STAR USES ASTROLOGY TO
BRING PEOPLE TOGETHER ... AND
IT ACTUALLY WORKS

"We are all part of this giant dance of the planets and the stars—and to me, astrology is one of the greatest, most creative things on this earth."

LESLIE MCGUIRK, COLLABORATION ARTIST

LESLIE MCGUIRK HAS WRITTEN several beloved children's books, but she is better known as an astrology expert. And she has some ideas about how people can make collaborations more effective.

Leslie knows that many people will be skeptical about her advice, so she's quick to say, "Don't believe anything I tell you. Just entertain the possibility that I might be onto something. When you have a direct experience of what I'm talking about, then you will understand that there is something to this astrology thing that's been around for thousands of years."

Leslie has no use for the popular astrology that's in newspapers and magazines. "Writing horoscopes and fortune-telling is the lowest level of thinking. It's a really horrible disservice to the actual science of astrology." She adds, "Everyone knows their sun sign. I don't really care about that because it's not that interesting to me."

She has a different sense of what astrology is all about. "It is human design," she explains. "Everything in nature has a pattern, including us. Plants grow from seeds. Imprinted inside of seeds is the system of what that plant will become. Astrology is the vibrational map of what was above your head when you were born. A good astrologer can read the energy of the sacred geometry between the planets and how we are set up. It's like the owner's manual in your car's glove compartment. It does not tell you the future; it just tells you the best way to operate your particular vehicle because you have free will, you're in charge of what happens.

"I think one day we will have complete proof that there is a lot of science behind astrology," she adds. "Just take the moon, which regulates every body of water on the earth—and we are 90 percent water. There's a correlation. The moon does not make you crazy during the times when it's full, but definitely things are more heightened. So, there's an influence. That's all astrology is. It's just a navigational tool. The sky has always been a navigational tool for people who are in ships. How did they get around? They followed the stars. So why do we, as modern people, think that we're still not affected by the whole universe? We are all part of this giant dance of the planets and the stars —and to me, astrology is one of the greatest, most creative things on this earth.

"When you plan an event," Leslie advises, "astrology is one way to make sure you have the best outcome. Think of an astrologer as similar to a meteorologist. Astrology is akin to the weather for a day. There are some days that are more gnarly than others. Get an expert to consult the cosmos and then pick a day that could be more uplifting, where things you want to do are going to flow, where things will be easy. Choosing a bad day makes no more sense than planning your wedding during a time when you're going to have heavy rainfall."

Leslie takes on the negative associations people have with full moons and inverts them. "Full moon times are great for having things be more memorable and more heightened. Everyone's going to be revved up and excited. You want people to leave your event feeling as if their life was changed. So why not use the full moon energy?"

Leslie also thinks that event content should be crafted with an eye to appealing to four archetypical groups of people she identifies with fire, earth, air, and water properties. "You need to feed all those qualities. If you have an event where you are metaphorically weak in one area, it's not going to be as strong. For the fire and air people, you would need that event to be fast-paced and very dynamic. That's what they love. The earth and air people don't need all the pyrotechnic stuff, although they could enjoy it. But their energy is softer and gentler."

Leslie suggests that because of the nature of our times, you should pay special attention to the earth element. "Groundedness matters because of what's happening with cell phones and computers. We are very disconnected from the rhythms of nature and from being connected to the earth."

She also proposes literally catering to the element groups. "To please the fire people, serve spicy foods or anything to do with heat. Think chilis and peppers and anything that's the color red," she says. "Someone in the earth group is like a rock; they don't want to move. Serve them anything that keeps you grounded and makes you feel safe. Think comfort food like potatoes. The air people are always about the intellect and the mind. They like trying variety in many different things. For the water people, anything with liquids. Think soups and things that are gentle in a liquidy way. At a good event, you should have a little bit of everything, just like in cooking. You don't want all spicy because then the people who don't care for that are not going to be happy."

Leslie explains what it means when Mercury is in retrograde, and the potential effect of that state on gatherings. "It happens at random times throughout the year for a couple of weeks. It's a ridiculous thing to over-stress because people don't know what the heck it is," she points out. "Simply put, there are times when Mercury, the planet of communication, appears to be going backwards in the sky. During these periods, for most human beings, things don't go as planned. Planning an event during Mercury retrograde is probably not for the best. But be aware, while 80 percent of the population is not in sync with those time frames, those born during Mercury retrograde like these times."

Leslie envisions events where you gather information about the participants' time and place of birth prior to gathering. "I would look at the Mercury sign of every single person who's at the event." That sign, she explains, highlights how a person communicates. "Is it in the style of fire, which is aggressive and passionate and direct, or do they communicate more with water style, which is gentle, soft? Air represents mental activity. Earth is about practicality. These are the people who want everything to make sense and to be verified. Once you understand someone's communication style, it just makes it so much easier to get the whole system of how the entire group works."

Leslie likes the idea of astrology-based group activities as well. "What I would do is explain astrology using metaphors," she says. "Then divide people into different categories of fire, earth, air, and water. It's a fun way to get deeper into the individual people and connect the group as a whole. Everybody's interested in it, even if they act like they aren't, because who doesn't want to know about themselves? I tell my clients I'm 95 percent accurate with figuring out your wiring system. I don't entirely understand why it is accurate as it is, but I know it is. It's fascinating."

WHAT WE HEARD AND LEARNED

- Think of astrology as a navigational tool
- Consider astrology-based group activities
- Find out the major astrological chart elements of those with whom you're gathering
- Craft content with awareness of fire, earth, air, and water properties

HOLLY PETERSON

PACE-SETTING HOSTESS SHORTCUTS PATH TO SUCCESSFUL COLLABORATIVE GATHERINGS

"Keep it short, keep it simple, keep it elegant."

HOLLY PETERSON, COLLABORATION ARTIST

BEST-SELLING author and journalist Holly Peterson is often described as a consummate hostess because of the gatherings she has at her homes. She's developed a set of rules to keep things moving and to keep guests happy. Holly also attends a lot of charitable and business events, and she is adamant that they should adhere to the principles behind her rules.

When you arrive at one of Holly's gatherings, she stands at the door to welcome you and to introduce you to others. You can break into a circle or approach someone with a lot more confidence and comfort if you've already been introduced. She is dismayed that some hosts at events don't introduce a guest to at least three other people right off. "I get a huge amount of satisfaction from connecting people. I feel great accomplishment when two people I introduced become friends or do business together without me. I don't get upset that they're hanging out without me afterwards. I like it."

Holly also likes name tags. "If it's any kind of professional anything, they're wearing name tags in my house," she says. "That's the point. You're trying to network, and you're trying to meet the guy who's running this and the woman who's doing that. It's a waste of people's time not to know who's-who. I don't require them in a social situation unless it's a parents' night. Then, of course, I make them wear their name tags because who can remember every name from school drop-off."

Another rule: The cocktail hour at a Holly party isn't a full hour. "People arrive at your house a little grumpy and low on blood sugar and thinking about homework and their 6 a.m. flight to Cleveland the next morning. You've got to be really sensitive to that," she says. "Nobody wants a long cocktail hour. If I could, I would make this an edict across America. They want one drink, maybe two. They want a few filling, yummy hors d'oeuvres. Then they want to sit."

The meal itself is also different. "I never, ever serve a first course," Holly says. "Whether it's a seated dinner or a buffet, it elongates the evening into just too many sections that make it unpleasant for people. I think that when people sit, especially at a dinner with place-cards, when you go straight to the entree it's fabulous for everyone. It's liter-ally the meat of the evening right away, no waiting. That part of the evening is done in 45 minutes at the most. It makes the seated part much shorter. You don't need to talk to the person on your left or right for more than 20 minutes.

"Move the party along as fast as you can," she continues. "I think that the people who want to stay for the after-party and have long desserts and coffee and drink a little too much are staying on their own terms and of their own volition. They're not forced like kindergarten to sit at a table and eat. So, I do really short drinks and really fast, one-course meals because it gives people the freedom to leave for an early flight or homework hell with a kid."

Holly applies the same thinking to other events. "If you have 1,200 people at the Plaza for a benefit for some cause, it's the same thing. Move along as fast as you can. When they're seated, you have a lot of food and a lot of wine ready. I see nothing wrong with a bottle of red and a bottle of white wine on the table. I like to have family-style, extra food on the table like fried artichokes, breadsticks, olives, and all kinds of yummy things like that for noshing. Then when the waiters come with the food, you get your meat right away."

Holly has a request of event planners: "Please don't come up with 20 things we need to do after dessert." She suggests, "Front load presentation as much as you can. If you have nothing to do by dessert and dessert is just dessert, people are smiling. Nobody wants to have had two or three drinks, a glass of wine, an entree, a dessert—and *then* be confronted by the first of four award presenters."

Holly connects brevity with modesty. Her advice to people who use her home who want to do longer presentations: Get over yourself; whatever you're doing is not that interesting. "A speaker should be modest and to the point," she says. "Keep it short, keep it simple, keep it elegant. Keep it brief. If the audience wants some more information, they can email you afterwards. When you're presenting, it's easy to get a little too excited about what you have to present. It must be bullet points. It must be short. It must be well-produced. You can put it all out in a pamphlet if you want to give them more information. But don't do long presentations. Then you just hear fidgeting and coughing."

WHAT WE HEARD AND LEARNED

- Get into people's heads to entertain properly
- Provide name tags
- Skip the first course and go right to the entree
- Front load presentations as much as you can

ANDREA SULLIVAN

ORGANIZATIONAL PSYCHOLOGIST ON UNDERSTANDING BRAINS AND BODIES IN COLLABORATION

> *"When everybody's a stranger, it can be very scary. It's really important that people have an early connection with other people in the room. It creates a sense of safety."*

> *ANDREA SULLIVAN, COLLABORATION ARTIST*

ANDREA SULLIVAN IS FOCUSED on not just what to do when facilitating a meeting, but also on why any particular activity might, or might not, work. She is acutely aware of, and fascinated by, emerging neuroscience, and has a strong sense that physiology plays a large part in what people do. "This is not just brain neuroscience," she explains. "This is neurophysiology. We're talking about the whole body and the complex systems of individuals and groups."

Andrea's lens starts with the insight that "Our nervous systems talk to each other without us being conscious of what's happening. We're made partially of electromagnetic energy. Our cells communicate via electricity and magnetic centers. Our electromagnetic field radiates out from three to 15 feet beyond the body. Whatever energetic state we're in begins to affect other people's energetic states. When our electromagnetic fields connect, something called emotional contagion happens. Our physiology tends to synchronize, and we experience similar mental and emotional states."

To Andrea, this interpersonal connection is only logical. "It's how evolution works: We used to be single cells, which combined to form multi-cellular organisms such as ourselves. Now that's happening on a larger scale, with human collaboration becoming an evolutionary imperative."

Knowing about this dynamic helps her define what she, as a facilitator, should do to encourage and sustain serendipity in collaboration. Facilitators need to have a much greater ability than usual to stay present and aware in the moment—because, of course, their emotional state will influence participants, she explains. "A facilitator manages their own emotional state because it's going to spread via emotional contagion. You want it to spread. You deliberately leverage co-regulation. Co-regulation is where one nervous system impacts another nervous system. Maintaining control of themselves and, to the extent possible, of the interactions between participants, is essential to creating the right emotional space that will allow certain key shifts to happen.

"The first shift has to do with the autonomic nervous system, which is composed of the sympathetic nervous system and the parasympathetic," she continues. "The sympathetic is the 'fight or flight' one. It's the one that mobilizes us when we're under threat. When we have the sense that we are in danger, a survival program kicks in and we can't be social.

"The parasympathetic nervous system calms things down. It is the 'rest and digest' one. When we're in the parasympathetic nervous system, then we can collaborate. There are multiple benefits to parasympathetic arousal. It's basically healthier. It lowers heart rate, it helps your immune system, and it allows for much greater creativity."

Applying these research findings to collaborative moments, Andrea mentions *neuroception*, a process whereby we are always scanning the environment for danger. "What happens with meetings is that when people come, they're in a state of uncertainty," she says. "They don't really know what's going to happen. Who's going to be there? What's the agenda going to be like? Is the venue going to be comfortable? That uncertainty arouses our sympathetic nervous system. There's a little bit of a threat there.

"Thinking of a workshop, thinking of an event, thinking of a team-building meeting—the very first thing that has to be handled is psychological safety. Psychological safety really begins prior to the event. You have to prime people prior to the event. Give people the information they need in an easy-to-read format. How, when, what, who, where—all that stuff is context that they need. They also need a way to ask their questions before they come. Send out the messages beforehand with the tone that you want to create. It's all part of getting people ready to shift to parasympathetic mode."

When it comes time for the gathering to convene, Andrea advocates for slowing down, bringing awareness to what is happening, and getting intentional in our thoughts. "Once people gather, a great, effective practice is starting workshops with meditation, leading people through slow and deep breathing," she says. "If you breathe out twice as long as you breathe in, it automatically brings you into a parasympathetic state. Breathing in raises your heart rate; breathing out lowers your heart rate automatically and calms you. It's such a simple thing. It's amazing."

Andrea also points to connecting people as a way of shifting participants into a less-threatened frame of mind and body. "When everybody's a stranger, it can be scary. It's really important that people have an early connection with other people in the room. It creates a sense of safety, a sense of 'OK, I know who's in the room. I can deal with these people," she says. "I love what I call a 'mingle process,' where everybody in the room says a little bit to someone else and then they just switch to speak to a different person. Even in a large event, you don't have to meet everybody. If you feel a little bit of intimacy with a few people, you feel OK about the group and the room."

Andrea is always aware of the physical transformations that happen as people meet and interact. "This isn't just a matter of the states of the various individuals involved. New research in the field of interpersonal autonomic physiology sheds light on a phenomenon called physiological synchrony," she explains. "Using new tools, researchers can measure almost everything: heart rate, respiratory rate, even brainwaves on a larger scale. They've found that everything comes into coherence between people under certain situations. If you look at musicians playing a piece, even if they're playing different parts of the piece, their physiology comes into total synchrony. Their hearts will start beating at the same rate. They'll start blinking at the same rate, breathing at the same rate.

"There are obvious practical implications to understanding the science as well," she adds. "When people are synchronized, they are better at collaborating—and more willing to collaborate. If you can get a group of people into a state of where their physiology synchronizes, they are more willing to work with each other."

While the benefits of having participants in a parasympathetic state are many, it wouldn't be effective to have them there all the time. Andrea points out that the sympathetic nervous system and the parasympathetic nervous system each should be harnessed— cautioning people to avoid seeing the sympathetic state as a fully "negative" place. "We can't be in positive emotion all the time," she says. "We need to do our tasks. The sympathetic state is best for that. Our vision literally narrows. We focus on the task. We're not looking for possibilities. When we harness the sympathetic system, we're not going for negative emotions. We're activating the task-positive network, the part of the brain that helps people move from our wonderful visions and desires and our hearts into the concrete performance."

Andrea cautions that the emotions associated with the two states aren't equal. "Negative emotions, such as those aroused by the sympathetic system, are much stronger than positive ones," she notes, and suggests sandwiching concrete task elements between more positive, creative elements. A common mistake, according to Andrea, is introducing the concrete task focus too early. A beneficial social/emotional space must be established first for people to work and collaborate at their best.

"Another, somewhat parallel way that physiology researchers characterize the brain involves identifying a default mode network and a task mode network," she says. "The default mode network is our social brain. When we're not focused on a task, our brain automatically defaults into thinking about, 'Who's here? What's the power structure?' It just happens automatically."

This theory identifies specific emotional 'attractors' that a facilitator can learn and use to nudge participants into one state or another. "The default mode is activated by positive attractors and brings about a host of positive physiological changes," she explains. "Blood pressure goes down. There's neurogenesis—more neurons are being born. Working memory is enhanced. There's perceptual openness. We can look at the big picture. We can see possibilities. There's a learning orientation. We are more resonant with others."

Andrea's understanding of social interactions informs how she guides certain group activities, and points to a common misstep. "One of the things that really interferes with collective intelligence is social importance. People are going to follow the leader who has the most perceived power in a group. Smart leaders will express their opinion last."

Even better, Andrea suggests, "When you're brainstorming, have it be synchronous instead of sequential. My preference is that people write down their thoughts on sticky notes and then the facilitator puts them on the wall. You don't follow because as soon as the people higher up in the hierarchy or with more power express an opinion, then you get other people agreeing with that. And that totally interferes with collective intelligence."

When faced with almost *any* question relating to a collaborative event, Andrea will apply research-informed thinking. Her sense of the implications of new and emerging neurophysiology research extends from details of a productive environment to the very future of the human race. She believes we are caught in a transition right now where we need to expand our vision of survival beyond the individual or communal level.

"In terms of evolution, we're at one of those points where it could go either way," she says. "We're all going to survive or none of us are going to survive. The good news is people learn ways to survive."

WHAT WE HEARD AND LEARNED

- Work to make a room feel safe for all those in it
- Design the social and emotional space as carefully as you do the physical environment
- Use the sympathetic and the parasympathetic nervous systems deliberately
- Don't let social status hinder brainstorming

FOSTER COMMUNITY...

BELONGING

BERNIE BANKS

FORMER GENERAL, NOW PROFESSOR, ON DIVERSE TEAMS FOR ULTIMATE EFFECTIVENESS

"We have an 'all boats rise' kind of approach, as opposed to 'let's see which boats are most promising and let's spend a lot of energy on that select group of boats and kind of leave the other boats to do the work' ... The aggregate of betting on everyone leads to much better outcomes than just betting on a select few."

BERNIE BANKS, COLLABORATION ARTIST

BERNARD (BERNIE) BANKS has superb academic credentials. He is the associate dean for leadership development and inclusion as well as a clinical professor of management and organizations at Northwestern University's Kellogg School of Management.

But his observations seem far more practical and real-world than academic. He draws on a long career in the United States Army. In 1995, he was selected from over 40,000 officers to receive the Army's prestigious General Douglas MacArthur Leadership Award. In 2006, the Apache Helicopter unit he was leading in South Korea was designated as the top Apache Helicopter unit globally in the U.S. Army's annual best aviation unit competition. During his time in service, he led multiple military units ranging in size from 10 to 3,000-plus people. He is analytical about the ways in which the military can be different from other sectors, as well as aware of where it sets examples that non-military organizations should consider when approaching collaboration.

"One of the things we understand in the military," he explains, "is that we attract people from every corner of American society. These people have a variety of perspectives regarding a variety of things—but regardless of those perspectives, they have to figure out a way to work well together in order to meet our charter on behalf of the American people. I think that unifying function of mission and service to the nation, and ensuring that our actions pass scrutiny, is something that's a little different than you see in the private sector or in various communities, where things can become very polarized. That's not to say that the military is any better than anyone else, but the military has some unique external forces that it has to take into account when thinking about how it goes about doing what it does day-in and day-out."

One factor is that U.S. military team members join on a voluntary basis, he points out. "We're opt-in, as opposed to trying to find a way to opt out. I think attracting those who want to be there strengthens us. There might be times, based on national needs, where we might have to go to mandatory conscription, a draft. But in our current operating environment, given our talent needs and given the benefits we see associated with being a volunteer force, I believe a voluntary force is the right model for us today."

An aspect where the military again differs from other sectors is in how it prioritizes the investments it makes in its people. "What makes the military special is that—unlike many organizations that figure out who they see as having the most potential, and then make a lot of bets on that group—the military bets on every single one," Bernie says. "We have an 'all boats rise' kind of approach, as opposed to 'let's see which boats are most promising and let's spend a lot of energy on that select group of boats and kind of leave the other boats to do the work.' We make differentiated bets, putting more money on the group that we think has the potential to make a greater difference—but we invest in everyone. It's in our best interest to ensure that they all become more competent. The aggregate of betting on everyone leads to much better outcomes than just betting on a select few."

Bernie thinks that outdated perceptions of the military persist. "Many people believe that the military is a highly directive type of enterprise. In fact, the military has evolved because our operating environment changed. Today, in a dynamic environment we have dynamic teams. Today's U.S. military is one that's fostered around small teams being empowered to take prudent risk. The current construct in the military is about the extension of trust, the demonstration of professional confidence, allowing teams to figure out the 'how.' Of course, we give them a clear what, why, and what success consists of. To have great accountability, certain things have to be present: You have to have clear expectations, you have to have the clear capability to meet the expectations, you have to have clear measurement, you have to have clear feedback, and you have to have clear consequences.

"In the military, we have a saying, 'The enemy always gets a vote,'" he continues. "In order to be able to compete effectively, you have to be able to pivot rapidly. You'll come up with plans, and then those plans will frequently be rendered invalid by an adversary who is also thinking very intently about how they could throw you off your game. Both parties are doing what they can to bring about their desired outcome. The speed at which change is enacted today is reflective of the demands of the environment in which we operate."

Bernie differentiates between collaboration and teamwork, both of which he sees as essential. "The difference is subtle," he explains. "Collaboration is all about harnessing different perspectives; teamwork is about learning how to coordinate your activities effectively in order to achieve an outcome. Great teams believe in harnessing the power of collaboration because it allows them to think differently about how they might go about their activities. That's collaboration. In teamwork, we have a series of tasks that we must learn how to do well in concert with one another, and amplify our ability to do that effectively ... that's the core of teamwork. Collaboration can help you think differently about how you operate as a team, but it is not the exact same thing as great teamwork.

"When I think about a team that I was a part of that collaborated well in service of addressing a significant challenge, I think back to a time when I was serving in Korea," he adds. "I was part of an organization where we were being asked to develop a new capability that would allow us to have better visibility on where all our assets were at a given moment in time. The plan to field this system, what it took for us to become competent at utilizing it, and to do it all in the midst of what was already a very high operational tempo environment … all that put significant pressures on the organization. But because of the talents that existed within the organization, and a willingness to think creatively about how we could leverage those talents and challenge the status quo and experiment, we fielded that system in record time. Our organization went from being in the bottom third globally in overall organizational performance to being evaluated as number one globally. That was a direct result of collaboration, teamwork, risk tolerance, a learning orientation, a dedication to becoming masters of our craft, and being resilient and working through adversity."

He offers some advice to people looking to recruit for their teams. "Consider character as well as competence. The unfortunate reality is that many organizations focus on competence, while they leave character to chance. But it's the combination of the competencies your team members possess, and what character informs their actions, that plays an outsized role in determining how your organization behaves. If you can, open the aperture to ask how are we going to focus on both competence and character, and highlight the importance of character? I think that's a better way to go about team development."

WHAT WE HEARD AND LEARNED

- Unite on a mission
- Invest in everyone
- Let teams figure out the "how'
- Consider character as well as competency

STEVEN CLEMONS

NEWSPERSON USES REAL-TIME COLLABORATION TO SOLVE REAL PROBLEMS

"I was a bag boy in a commissary on a U.S. airbase in Japan where we only got paid through tips. If you're a boring bag boy and you never engage your customers, you're not going to get much of a tip. I became extroverted because it was good for bag boy tips."

STEVEN CLEMONS, COLLABORATION ARTIST

STEVEN CLEMONS JOINED forces with Ben and Justin Smith to lead the live event arm of their venture Semafor, a modern news brand with an emphasis on global news. Prior to this new post, he was editor-at-large of The Hill. He's also been Washington editor-at-large of *The Atlantic* and the editor-in-chief of AtlanticLIVE, the magazine's live events series. He authored the blog The Washington Note, which *Time* selected as one of their "Best Blogs of the Year" in 2010. Further back in his past, he was a technical advisor for the film *Rising Sun*, which starred Sean Connery and Wesley Snipes. He also had a role in the film *State of Play*, starring Ben Affleck.

The story of how he developed the powerful personality needed to be such a powerful public performer is simple. "I was a bag boy in a commissary on a U.S. airbase in Japan where we only got paid through tips," he remembers. "If you're a boring bag boy and you never engage

your customers, you're not going to get much of a tip. I became extroverted because it was good for bag boy tips."

Steve discovered his power as a connector early in his career. He
recounts his time with the Japan America Society in Los Angeles. "It
had a kind of pecking-order crowd. You had a lot of seniority and
stratification among senior Japanese executives and senior Americans
who dealt with them. All of us young people had to get the scraps.
We'd show up, but nobody would talk to us. The system was archaic,
and people were connecting over status and whatever they did yester-
day. There was nothing new or dynamic or nimble. I had an incredible
opportunity as an executive director of this non-profit membership
organization."

Through this, Steve says he realized something about human
behavior: "If you have a room and a podium and chairs, people will
walk into that room and pay attention to whatever the rules are set by
the person who's hosting. All of a sudden, I had the power to introduce the person who didn't know anyone to the people who did. I had
the power to take young Black and Hispanic students from college and
introduce them to CEOs of big companies and help them have a
dynamic interaction."

Steve leveraged his position and his realizations to create new
social environments where people could connect across age and status
barriers. "I created something called the 5:01 Club. At that time, many
people got off work promptly at 5 o'clock, so 5:01 was the first moment
of non-work time. I would go to a restaurant, maybe get nachos, have
the Japanese consul general or the president of Toyota Motors come
over. I'd also bring in people from the community: students, teachers,
professionals—every mix of people in the Little Tokyo area of Los
Angeles. It basically broke through all these barriers of not
connecting."

His 5:01 Club idea subsequently spread around the globe and
gained extensive media coverage.

Steve brought everything he learned in Los Angeles with him when
he moved to the East Coast. "When I moved to Washington, I knew I
wanted to create zones where people knew they would be able to be
connected," he says. He discovered that gatherings in his new location

could also benefit from his personal touch. "Often, when you went to a party in Washington, D.C., people expected you to figure out your own way. I proactively help people meet each other."

Steve has thoughts about the science and art of introducing oneself. "There's a certain penetration of space that you do when you say hello. In that moment, you need to be a little modest, because it's really not about you. It's about that other person. You ask the other person questions. People resonate with that. It's a key part of creating the right climate."

The focus of a gathering is as crucial to him as the greetings. "The biggest mistake that most think tanks, businesses, and media groups make is that they over-celebrate whoever's speaking, and they under-attend to the audience," he says. "Your focus should always be the audience, the people there. Make sure they have a good time. Make sure they feel connected to whatever content you're putting together. That gets them to want to come back."

Steve's approach to hosting events involves both careful preparation and ample spontaneity. He feels you need sufficient humanity and surprise to make things interesting. "I get so bored when people do a book event, or a policy event, and they just recite their work or deliver something that was prepared for them. Even the questions are canned and asked in a sterile way. They bring nothing of their lives to it. They bring none of their suspicions or concerns or their jealousies or their envy—whatever it may be. They miss out on the fascination, the magic.

"You've got to invest a little bit in knowing your audience, and that requires work," he adds. "It requires looking at business cards. It requires remembering something of the stories of other people. A key to success is using other people's stories to connect with them in such a solid way that they feel like they have been given permission to be their full selves in your space."

When an event concerns medical issues, he says, "I try hard to get my people to bring in a real patient—someone who, for example, has a lived experience with Alzheimer's or the rare disease we're talking about."

So, how does Steve manage to know enough for all of the diverse events he hosts? "You need to know the topic and have a facility with it. Which is significant. You don't have to be the world's leading expert on it. You need to know what makes it compelling and interesting."

Steve also focuses his pre-event preparation on edges. "Every single issue out there has an edge. I want to know that edge better than anyone. I don't want to know what everybody else knows about the whole industry. I don't have time for that. I want to know the controversies—I want to know the opportunities. I want to know what's gone badly, and what's gone well. If I can become a specialist in that edge, it gives me an edge in the conversation."

Steve has developed techniques for making hybrid events work for all. "I think the challenge in my role on stage is how to make the person online feel as special, if not more, as a person in the room. We're not wired to do that. We're wired to look in the eyeballs and pay attention to the people in the room. I get questions from remote participants all around the world. When I can, I get video clips from their iPhones. I put their questions to, say, senators, and have them respond in real time. I do this so our audience out there feels that they are equal. You've got to get that right."

As for the challenge of "reading the room" with a virtual audience, Steve has a few hints. "You can see them by attendance level. You can see them by Twitter traffic. I make available my Twitter and other social media so people can reach me during an event and send me things."

During longer events with multiple presenters, some of whom are being brought in remotely, Steve has another way to read the virtual room. "I can get the feel from the speakers who've been watching the rest of the program. They've been an audience for a while. Are they bored or are they turned on? If they're turned on, then I know the audience is, too."

Steve believes that the best events satisfy a genuine human desire to interact with people who are different and that the interactions he hosts and moderates could even help bridge the massive rifts that hinder things in Washington, D.C. "We ought not to buy into the notion that we'll only talk to one side of the aisle, or one perspective. I believe in conversations in a safe space among people who don't agree with one another. It's not just divides between Republicans and Democrats; you have divides within parties. I can't get people to do what I want them to do, but I can create experiences that open their apertures, where they have a bit of a different experience."

WHAT WE HEARD AND LEARNED

- Greet everyone
- Balance hybrid participation
- Read the virtual room
- Have difficult conversations

ARTHUR PEARSON

VETERAN OUTWARD BOUND ICON ON COLLABORATION IN LEARNING

"That is frequently the trickiest part of the journey, because why should you bond with a bunch of complete strangers who you don't know?"

ARTHUR PEARSON, COLLABORATION ARTIST

ARTHUR PEARSON SPENT MORE than 13 years, from the mid 1970s to the late 1980s, as the program director at the Hurricane Island Outward Bound School. He was as invested as anyone in the practices and traditions of the legendary outdoor programs that challenge young people to explore their personal potential. Today, he has the knowledge to question and examine the elements of the traditional Outward Bound experience, and the drive to guide the organization's expansion into other formats—such as programs in local schools and neighborhoods that cultivate a passion for learning, for collaboration, and for discovering greater success in school, work, and life.

"The traditional Outward Bound experience," he explains, "is social learning in a really simple, primitive setting. It's as simple as it gets. It's like dialing back all of the complexities of modern life and filtering them out. You end up in a sort of Stone Age situation: a bunch of humans sitting around a fire in the wilderness, trying to keep warm and feed each other. I think there is something about the simplicity of it and the fact that it is done in what is, approximately, a family unit. The ground floor of beginning to build a team of young people who will actually work together and collaborate is that they first need to feel some sense of belonging with that core unit. Perhaps that is as simple as, 'We're all in this together. These other individuals that I'm together with now will take care of me. They'll treat me as one of the pack.' That is frequently the trickiest part of the journey, because why should you bond with a bunch of complete strangers who you don't know?"

Outward Bound gets past that hurdle by immersing people immediately in problem solving together in a playful way. Most team building is best done using playful activities, Arthur notes. Research shows that people learn to trust each other when they smile and laugh together, which are signs of trust, he adds. Early in an Outward Bound course, there are activities that get people to joke around together and be goofy together. That breaks down that initial hesitancy.

Arthur points out a classic example of the practice. "We ask everyone to stand in a circle, raise their right hand, reach across the circle, and connect with somebody else's right hand—then raise your left hand, reach across the circle, and connect with a different person than you have with your right hand. Everybody's reaching across the circle, holding hands with two different people. It's a big tangle. The task is to untangle that into either a circle or a figure of eight, which it always does, by the way. The process of untangling is inherently silly. You have to touch other people. You have to make eye contact. That's conducive to developing trust and a sense of affinity with another human being. It stimulates hormones in the brain that move you to feel that this other person is not the enemy."

From a fun, team-building starting point, Arthur says the next place you go with the group is towards harder collaborative tasks. "It might be something like, 'Here's a set of materials including small pieces of bamboo and some rope. I want you to make a bridge that spans six feet of boiling lava,'" he explains. "Something like that. Something hard and, hopefully, at some point frustrating. It's no longer just playing and laughter. Now you need to communicate and listen to each other."

This is a point in the process where new capabilities can emerge.

"Often someone—most likely a tall, white male who's always been called on by the teacher—speaks up and says, 'I know what to do. Try this and that.' And it doesn't work. Now he's got to shut up and listen while, say, a quiet little girl in the back explains a different way of seeing the problem that makes it much more practical to solve the problem.

"This, incidentally, illustrates why people say that diverse teams are more productive," he continues. "When you're on an Outward Bound course and are encountering a really difficult problem, the fact that different people view the problem radically differently is your only hope with a complicated-enough problem. The more diverse the team, the more different ways to approach the situation, the greater the likelihood that you'll find a way to solve the problem.

"From there, we keep raising the difficulty of the tasks, frequently raising the ambiguity and timeframes. The final expedition of a course is a four-day task such that you are continually exercising this cycle of needing to communicate," he adds.

The progressions experienced in an Outward Bound course correlate closely with learning theory. "Jean Piaget, a Swiss psychologist who spent thousands of hours observing children, says that learning is an iterative process of thinking how something works, finding out that your understanding is inadequate, and having to readjust your understanding to accommodate new data," says Arthur. "He describes the dynamics within that progression. There's an uncomfortable moment of disequilibrium when something does not fit your understanding of things. The only way to resolve that discomfort is to integrate this new data into your understanding of the universe. That is the learning cycle."

The Outward Bound approach is also consistent with the work of another foundational learning theorist: Lev Semyonovich Vygotsky, a Russian psychologist, who, like Piaget, focused much of his work on children. "Every graduate student can tell you that Vygotsky explained the Zone of Proximal Development (ZPD)—the space between what a learner can do without assistance and what a learner can do with adult guidance or in collaboration with more capable peers. The ZPD basically is the demonstration that learning is a social process. There are huge swaths of life that are impossible to learn sitting alone with whatever set of books you might have. There are skills and abilities that you can master only in the presence of supportive peers, more competent learners, and/or more advanced learners. That's why it matters that we do Outward Bound courses in groups. It's why, some people say, we grow up in families. We've looked at great instructors at Outward Bound courses and put that together with learning science. We were struck by the 'craft wisdom' of our people who haven't read Piaget or Vygotsky. They still get things right. They've found their own ways to great results with kids. Craft wisdom and the science of learning and development seem to, basically, converge."

Arthur has also given extensive thought to how organizations can work together. "Organizationally, the most productive collaborations that I've been part of are where, basically, all of the individual organizations, to some degree, subordinate themselves to a set of common goals. For instance, in the summer learning community in Boston where there are probably 60-plus separate non-profits that provide summer learning services to Boston public schools, all of our students are evaluated using the same metrics. The same evaluation tools across the board. Many of them are, perhaps, not the evaluation tools that we would have selected acting on our own. But we subordinate that because we want to be part of the coalition. We all want to serve kids outside in the summer. We all agree that academics is important, and we're all willing to be evaluated using the same evaluation tools."

That's collaboration, he adds. "With this common ground, we can meet together and see how we can learn from each other. 'What are you doing better than I am? I'm going to think about doing it differently, because you're getting a better result than I am.' Those, for me, are the most thrilling collaborations between organizations."

WHAT WE HEARD AND LEARNED

- Build teams trust with laughter, eye contact, and touch
- Ratchet up the challenges in a learning cycle

- Apply learning theory to program development
- Notice the strengths of those you collaborate with, and draw inspiration and knowledge from them

NICK SAKELLARIADIS

MINOR LEAGUE TEAM OWNER IN CONTINUING MAJOR SUCCESS WITH COMMUNITIES

"When I would run into friends, they'd ask, 'What are you doing?' I'd reply, 'I'm trying to buy a baseball team.' And all of a sudden, they'd ask, 'Can we participate too?'"

NICK SAKELLARIADIS, COLLABORATION ARTIST

NICK SAKELLARIADIS DIDN'T ACHIEVE his childhood dream of playing center field for the New York Yankees. Nor did he succeed at his Plan B, getting rich enough to buy that team. But he hit a home run with his Plan C: becoming part owner of a thriving Minor League Baseball team that has amazing bonds with players, fans, sponsors, and the local community.

When he evaluated the Dayton Dragons, the High-A affiliate of the Cincinnati Reds, he knew it was the team he wanted. "For various reasons," he says, "it was not available immediately for purchase at the right type of number. It took a year for the transaction to take place. In the meantime, I retired from my day job in the financial services industry. When I would run into friends, they'd ask, 'What are you doing?' I'd reply, 'I'm trying to buy a baseball team.' And all of a sudden, they'd ask 'Can we participate too?' There are two of us who own and control the team, but we ended up selling little tiny pieces to dozens of friends who wanted to have the fun and the thrill of also being base-ball team owners.

"That's turned out to be fantastic," he continues. "I've been able to bring my friends with me for weekend outings to watch the games. We have conference calls and annual meetings in New York to catch up. That's been a terrific part of the whole experience—not to mention, they often provide good feedback on business matters that pertain to the team."

Nick is quick to point out that the Dayton Dragons were already a success before he became involved. "The formula was already work-ing. This team had the longest, and still has the longest, consecutive sellout streak in the history of American professional sports. The secret sauce really comes from our great management team, led by a guy named Bob Murphy, who was there when the team was organized in 1999. We bought the great team, the great franchise, and the wonderful management that helped build it."

Nick adds, "Our management is monomaniacally focused on making the fan and their family have a positive experience at the game. Family experience is the key to the success of this organization. Once you get the fans, you get the advertisers and you get the spon-sors, and you get this virtuous circle of 'everybody wants to go to the games but tickets aren't going to be available, so we better buy season tickets before the season starts to make sure we can go to the game.' As a result, every year when the season starts, we've pretty much sold all the advertising and sold all the tickets. The only thing that remains is executing—making sure everybody loves the experience—so that they want to do exactly the same thing the next year."

The Dayton Dragons organization engages in extensive training to ensure that fans have the right experiences. "The training emphasizes, 'Take care of the fan.' It involves things like going through case studies of 'What to do if these 16 things happen.' For example, if a fan complains that he or she has the wrong seat, rather than fighting with the fan, what we train everybody to do is put yourself in the shoes of the fan and try to accommodate them. Maybe the fan has been mistaken, but rather than fighting them, let them have the seat. The worst thing that happens is we're out a few dollars because the seat has to be exchanged."

Nick and his team make the fan experience about much more than just a baseball game, instead prioritizing building a family-friendly entertainment experience. "We have 200-plus goofy, family-friendly, funny little things that take place before the game, in between the innings, and after the game," he says. "There might be a toddler race from home plate to first base. Another would be bringing senior citizens from the retirement home to sing Beatles songs. Of course, we have goofy mascots running around and doing stunts on the field."

His metric for entertainment success is simple: "If I go to a major league game, I see people leaving their seats and going to the restrooms or getting food between the innings. In our stadium, they're doing that while the game is taking place because they don't want to miss any of the skits."

Things are kept to family-friendly standards. The atmosphere has a spirit like a good high school game, where everybody's rooting for the kids. Players aren't booed, but supported as if they're family. Nick explains that this helps build the connection between the players on the field and the fans in the audience. This engaging support for the fans creates the feeling that the team is a collaborative community between fans and players.

The fan/player connection is also fostered by off-field interaction. "Many of our players are in the 18 to 22 age range. Probably a third of them are away from home for the first time. We have a 'Booster Club' whose vetted members help the players adjust, often hosting them for free in their homes. The players are literally embedded in the community."

The team members, in turn, reach out to engage with the local community. "We are very involved in the public school system. We have a program where we give tickets, hats, jerseys, and merchandise to the schools. The teachers use the gifts to promote whatever behavior is important to them in the classroom. We have players who go out to these schools and talk about what it's like to be a baseball player and that sort of thing. Every game, we have a certain number of the players who will stay for an hour and a half after the game to sign autographs and meet the kids."

Nick is acutely aware of the good that his team can do. "There's cooperation between the team and the community that builds civic pride. As the biggest gathering place in the area, up to 10,000 people, we can provide a lot of visibility for good causes. We honor veterans, we honor churches and synagogues, we honor charities. This builds collaboration with whole swaths of the community."

He illustrates this with an example from 2019: "In the middle of the eighth inning, 15 people lined up on the third baseline. All of a sudden, a fellow dressed in black goes up to a microphone. He announces that these 15 people have passed the requirements for United States citizenship and, as a federal district judge, he proceeds to swear them in.

"The 15 are ecstatic to be joining the country. You can see their joy. They're jumping up and down. It is incredibly moving. In an intimate stadium, 10,000 people are on their feet, screaming their lungs out, celebrating the creation of new American citizens," he remembers. "That kind of thing creates bonds not just between the Dragons and its fans, but also between new American citizens and their new host city in the United States."

WHAT WE HEARD AND LEARNED

- Make people smile with unexpected surprises
- Create an experience that goes beyond the field and brings whole families in
- Make community involvement contagious
- Invite and engage with the larger community around you

ANGELA SCALPELLO

COMMUNICATIONS CONSULTANT ON CATALYZING SERENDIPITOUS CONVERSATIONS

"I really believe that the best conversations have questions where we aren't looking for specific answers ... Pushing instead of pulling, and telling more than asking, dooms innovation and creativity."

ANGELA SCALPELLO, COLLABORATION ARTIST

"MY EXCITEMENT always came from aligning groups of people behind a strategy to deliver business results," says Angela Scalpello. She has a passion for helping organizations unlock the power of people to drive change and transformation. After a long career during which she played an amazing range of roles—HR, information systems implementation, risk management, payroll, staffing, employee communications, employee relations, learning and development, and more—she opened a consulting practice, The Scalpello Group.

In truth, the roots of her practice go back all the way to her childhood.

"I was always somebody who gathered people together," she remembers. "I started a little day camp in my neighborhood. I started a little summer school in my neighborhood. I ran the milk delivery program in third grade. I was the fourth-grade class president. I was the student council president in high school. I was always somebody who was fascinated by human behavior. In college, I said to somebody, 'I feel so bad. I don't have hobbies.' He said, 'Don't be ridiculous. Observing how people behave together and gathering people is your hobby.'"

Even in childhood, Angela's style involved: "Always asking more than I told, and pulling more than I pushed." She describes herself as innately curious to hear other people's stories, always asking, "How has this been for you? What would you like?" "In fourth grade, I remember saying to somebody, 'What platform should I run on? What's important to you?' Even today in my consulting practice, I never do anything without doing check-ins and saying, 'How is this going?'"

Angela is thoughtful about the kinds of questions she asks. "I really believe that the best conversations have questions where we aren't looking for specific answers. 'What if we could? What would that look like? What are your aspirations? What's the common ground?' This matters. Pushing instead of pulling, and telling more than asking, dooms innovation and creativity

She is even a fan of asking a problem question, an approach she learned while working at the Ogilvy & Mather advertising agency. "You start a brainstorming session with the basic ground rules that all ideas are welcome and there will be no premature evaluations of them. You get all the ideas out there, and then you start asking questions about them. But if the group gets stuck, you put out the worst idea possible—deliberately, to be provocative. Often those terrible ideas are the spark that gets you to the idea that really works."

While asking a "problem question" could expose you to criticism and judgment, Angela thinks that's helpful. "People often think that you create trust and then you can show vulnerability. But the research shows the exact opposite: You show vulnerability, then you can create trust."

The services Angela provides to clients often leverage, no surprise here, questions and conversations. "I'm certified in something called 'conversational IQ.' The idea being that healthy conversations create trust and in turn, create the space for people to co-create and innovate. I also am certified in The Four Rooms of Change, which helps individuals, teams, and entire organizations understand where they are in the change process. It involves answering questions like 'Where are we?' 'How do we feel about it?' 'What do we want to do about it?' It's an extremely powerful tool for getting organizations to be more about 'we' than they are about 'I.'"

Angela likes to send a particular TED talk to all her clients. In it, Margaret Heffernan explains why it's time to forget the pecking order at work. She starts out with a story about somebody who tried to create a super flock of chickens by breeding the best egg layers. Over time, the result wasn't a super flock. The chickens were so competitive, they pecked each other to death.

"The takeaway from that story is a line I use all the time: Relationship Before Task," she says. "Collaboration is even more important today because the innovations are coming out of teams. I'm always amazed when people try to put together teams to do some hairy, audacious goal, but the people don't really know who they're working with. We need to know each other.

"'What's the thing you want people to say about you when you're not in the room?' is a terrific question," Angela continues. "Your answer can tell me more than just what you want your friends to say about you. It can reveal your value system. People rarely say, 'I want them to say, 'Wow, he has a lot of money.' People often say, 'I want people to say I'm helpful. I want them to say I'm kind. I want them to say, 'I've never let them down.' Now I know so much about you."

Angela builds on the chicken story with a strategic observation. "The more you compete internally, the more you take your eye off the ball of competing *externally*. We all have only so much energy. If I'm spending all my time competing with you, what's happening in terms of what we should be doing externally?"

Angela has a recommendation for diffusing competitive culture as well: "Add more women. When women are inserted into a group, there are much more balanced speaking times. When there is only one woman in a room and the rest men, it can still be a little hard. When there's at least another woman in the room, it's easier for a woman, and everyone else, to speak up. More people speaking up and sharing." (Angela is, appropriately, a member of the advisory board of the Institute for Women's Leadership at Rutgers.)

She has observed not just how women have different collaboration skills than men, and how women can advocate for each other. "Women often amplify what other women say. It happened in the Obama administration when the women realized that the men in his inner circle were getting more airspace. The women got together and said, 'We have to amplify our voices.' So if I was part of that and I said something that was overlooked, a woman teammate might say, 'Hey, I want to stay on what Angela just said.' They also got men, as partners, to do the same."

Angela plays an active role in getting more people to join the conversation when others aren't playing that role. "I'll be the person who asks, 'Hey, David, what do you think about what John just said?' I give you that pathway to be able to comment on what somebody else said. I do that not to make you come up with a creative idea, but to help you hear your own voice and to be comfortable with it."

According to Angela, the right conversations are crucial to organizational success. "When you read about a company that's lost its creative mojo and you see a line that says they had developed a risk-averse culture … that happened in conversations. No one jumped on a table and said, 'We're going to be risk averse.' People started to respond to ideas saying, 'You know what? We tried that once before and it didn't work.' Or, 'That's a bit too risky.' And no one stopped them and said, 'But what if we could do it?'

"As we move into the future, companies that understand that collaboration requires relationships and takes a little more time will be the ones that succeed," she adds. "Companies need to play the long game. Social scientists tell us that the need to belong is greater than the need for security. Being embraced as part of a team, getting the feeling that I matter, that what I say matters, that what I do matters to this team—all that has a powerful impact. It's how you create stickiness among team members."

WHAT WE HEARD AND LEARNED

- Show vulnerability first to build trust
- "Relationship before task"
- Women team members can diminish destructive competitiveness
- Understand the power of the need to belong

ADRIAN SEGAR

ADVOCATOR-IN-CHIEF OF THE UNCONFERENCE ON COLLABORATIVE ENVIRONMENTS THAT PEOPLE LOVE

"In a fishbowl, anyone in the room can speak—but to speak, you have to be sitting in one of four chairs that are in front of the room. Anyone, at any time, can go up to one of those chairs, if there's a chair empty, and take it."

ADRIAN SEGAR, COLLABORATION ARTIST

ADRIAN SEGAR, the founder of Conferences That Work based in Marlboro, Vermont, is known for having co-invented, run, and documented the "unconference"—a different kind of participation-rich and participant-driven event. These gatherings do away with tony outside speakers and big media productions in order to shift the control to the participants.

In 1992, Adrian developed this new kind of conference because his interests weren't being addressed by the conferences he attended. "The problem was I would go to traditional physics conferences, where the focus was on relatively few speakers," he explains. "I felt very frustrated going to those. I think a lot of people do, because I wasn't interacting with the people sitting next to me who also had a lot of interesting information. I had no opportunity to connect with them while the lectures were going on. I became interested in creating conferences that were much more participatory, in which we would discover what people actually wanted to talk about right at the event."

People began to contact Adrian about his new version of conferences, and he quickly found his new calling and passion. Adrian designed and facilitated a number of unconferences, and he was always eager to share his discoveries. In fact, he has authored three books that detail his approach: *Conferences That Work: Creating Events That People Love; The Power of Participation: Creating Conferences That Deliver Learning, Connection, Engagement, and Action;* and *Event Crowdsourcing: Creating Meetings People Actually Want and Need.* It's not surprising that Adrian has been named one of the 100 most influential people in the event industry in several global polls of over 20,000 event professionals.

Adrian has mapped out all the necessary elements for his type of conference. While these events are not agenda-driven, their phases are highly structured and targeted. "First off," Adrian explains, "you learn individually and collectively what people are interested in. During this initial process, you also discover the other people in the room who are resources for you, or who you are resources for. All that information shapes the outline of what happens. The result is an on-the-fly program that actually optimizes the event for everybody there."

In the middle of the conference, you run the program you have just created. "It's very different," Adrian explains. "Most of the people who are presenting or leading those sessions didn't know until maybe the day before that they were going to be doing that. So no one is expecting something polished or a lecture. These conferences are full of sessions that people chose. They're about topics that people really care about. The sessions themselves are popular.

"These sessions are much more interactive than old-style presentations," Adrian continues, "You discover the 10 other people who are really fascinated, or want to learn more, or know a lot about something that you're really interested in.

"The last part of these kinds of conferences is a set of closing sessions that increase the likelihood that each person individually will actually do stuff. There's a session that sets aside time and has a structured process for people to think about what they want to change. It allows them to figure out what they are going to do specifically in terms of measurable outcomes that they create for themselves. And there's a piece of a session that also includes small group work, which also increases the likelihood that change will actually happen. We all know that if we make a resolution about something and then we talk to a group of people who are supportive about it, we're much more likely to follow through."

Adrian says that the techniques he pioneered are particularly effective with smaller groups of, say, 100 or fewer people. He points out that while huge galas get a lot of media attention, data from venues shows that most meetings in the U.S. have no more than 100 participants. But that doesn't mean his approach doesn't work for larger gatherings. He suggests that you simply and naturally subdivide the larger group into communities of interest.

Adrian provides an example: "I did a medical conference with 500 people who were running very large medical offices in the United States a few years ago. It turned out that there were differences between how, let's say, oncology medical offices worked from obstetrics. So, it made sense to divide those 500 people into 10 groups of 50 by the medical specialty of the organization that they were working in."

In his events, in his books, and in discussions, Adrian provides details about specific techniques used in each step of each phase of various types of unconferences. For example, he has proven the value of something called "a fishbowl," and even has names for modular variants of the technique such as "a fishbowl sandwich."

The fishbowl addresses the challenge of preventing a few people from dominating a discussion. "In a fishbowl, anyone in the room can speak—but to speak, you have to be sitting in one of four chairs that are in front of the room. Anyone, at any time, can go up to one of those chairs, if there's a chair empty, and take it. There's a moderator in one of those chairs, who basically moderates what happens in the other three chairs. If all the chairs are full and someone walks up, then the person who's been speaking the longest has to step down."

The fishbowl is typical of Adrian's techniques: thought out, proven, simple, and surprisingly easy to accomplish. And thanks to his work, meetings can be both more spontaneous and more purposeful.

WHAT WE HEARD AND LEARNED

- Flip the script with a participation-rich and participant-driven "unconference"
- Drive your unconference via structure and participation-driven process, not agenda
- Use techniques like "fishbowl," which prevents a few people from dominating a discussion
- Provide structured time at the end of conference for attendees to make specific resolutions for future change

AMANDA SLAVIN
COLLABORATION WIZARD ON THE PROGRESSION OF LEVELS OF ENGAGEMENT

"I think it's always been ingrained in me to create this feeling of belonging, of inclusion, of connection, of community."

AMANDA SLAVIN, COLLABORATION ARTIST

AMANDA SLAVIN IS the co-founder and CEO of CatalystCreativ, the experiential marketing agency that was funded by the late Zappos CEO Tony Hsieh. The company is deeply focused on engagement, and it has developed expertise in targeting millennial and Generation Z audiences. Its clients range from NPR to Dell, from Coca-Cola to the New York City Ballet, and from Starwood Hotels to an NFL franchise. She's the author of *The Seventh Level: Transform Your Business Through Meaningful Engagement with Your Customers and Employees.*

Amanda is a natural-born convener. "I've been creating experiences since I was three years old," she remembers. "I would pile my stuffed animals on the stairs every single day and sing and play piano for them. In first grade, I created a snack exchange between my fellow students—bringing them all to the table and making sure that I was facilitating conversation and that everyone was included. I think it's always been ingrained in me to create this feeling of belonging, of inclusion, of connection, of community. While I was getting my

Master's in curriculum and instruction, I wrote my thesis on something called 'the seven levels of engagement.' I developed a methodology for measuring engagement, which I thought would help in my understanding of education and the challenge of inspiring children. At the same time, I was throwing events on the side and interning at events companies. I was really living these two lives."

Amanda graduated with a Master's in Education in 2009, right in the middle of a deep recession. She ended up getting work in the hospitality and marketing and events industry. But she held on to the thinking about stages of engagement, and she applied it to business. At this point, it's part of her DNA, and the DNA of her company. "Our secret is to use the levels of engagement thinking that I had studied relative to education. We look at where a person is, and deliver experiences designed to move them up a progression through various stages of ever-deeper engagement."

To her, the progression of engagement is just common sense. "You wouldn't ask someone to marry you if you'd never gone on a first date with them. To me, following the natural progression is treating human beings like humans."

In her system, the first level of engagement is "disengagement." Amanda explains that "most people think that disengagement is the enemy of engagement—when, in reality, disengagement is the first level of engagement." The next level up is unsystematic engagement: when a person is confused by messaging.

The third level is frustrated engagement. "That's when," Amanda explains, "you're trying to connect with a brand or connect with a message, but you end up getting distracted in the process. This is pretty much most of the social media experience. Getting people through the bottom three levels is important, because if you're not ensuring that they are being done properly, you really can't increase engagement."

Level four is "structure dependent engagement," which is instruction-based. "Here you ask for behaviors like 'Comment below;' 'Like this post;' 'Email me back;' 'Respond to this message.'"

The fifth level is "self-regulated interest." This is where influencer marketing and partnership marketing might come in. Your target's interest is piqued, but they're still not likely to be emotionally connected to the brand.

Level six is "critical engagement." A brand or a message is inspiring the target person to set goals and transform their own life. And the seventh level is "literate thinking," where people engage based on personal values and beliefs.

"You can actually identify an action per level," Amanda says. "You can ask, 'If I have 60 percent of my customers in disengagement, how am I going to elevate them? The format indicates what you need to do. I'm going to be on the right platforms. I'm going to ensure that I'm speaking to them properly. I'm going to be ensuring that I am actually talking to the right people."

After years of using this model for her own work, Amanda has come full circle and is a teacher again, sharing how to use it with others. "We've been building out a full curriculum to educate agencies, brands, and cities about these seven levels. We work with them to identify actions associated with each level. And we're actually developing worksheets and a series of workshops." She now has a platform that teaches the framework called CatalystU.

Thinking about engagement naturally led Amanda to think about millennials and Gen Zers, who have different engagement styles and needs. "Millennials," Amanda explains, "have been on digital tools since a very young age. In general, they need a way to share. Putting this phenomenon into a 'Seventh Level' context, they need to feel that their personal values and beliefs align with a message. I'm older, so when I go to an event, I don't actually use my phone. But the way that millennials are actually experiencing the event is by using their phones. That's a part of the event. That's a part of the experience. If you don't have creative opportunities for these creators to create, it's not really going to work.

"People in Generation Z," Amanda observes, "also tend to have different dynamics around engagement. They need to see that whatever they're doing is of value and can make a significant change. They want to create movements. They want to create their own reality. You want to give them opportunities to develop content, to share their voice. Generation Z is really making sure that they feel heard and valued.

"A good approach is to ask generation Zers, 'What do you want to see?'—and then really ensure that you're going to be able to deliver, because I think they've seen so many brands say all these different things and then not necessarily follow through with them," she adds. "Because if they don't support a company's message, they will go on social media and try to actually take that company out of business. They will emotionally bully brands into doing what they feel is right. For them, a brand needs to stand for something, and it should be authentic in the sense that it needs to make sense throughout."

Amanda, always a close observer of communications and behaviors, has advice for how agencies should speak. "There are all sorts of words, abbreviations, acronyms, and phrases that make sense within our common vernacular within a professional specialty—but that doesn't mean that they make sense to anyone else. Create a list of these words and banish them. We've now gotten to the point where we define what we mean in our scope of work."

WHAT WE HEARD AND LEARNED

- Be a natural convener of people
- In a gathering, move participants up a progression of engagement
- Give millennials a way to share
- Enable Generation Zers to create movements

JONATHAN STEFFERT

NEW ZEALAND'S CULTURAL ATTACHÉ IN D.C. CAN'T AFFORD TO TELL A TYPICAL STORY OR HAVE A SO-SO PARTY

"The future is in storytelling. That's where people are getting news from now. It's about scaling the story to start with 'Who am I? What is my place in the world? Where have I come from and what values do I stand for?'"

JONATHAN STEFFERT, COLLABORATION ARTIST

JONATHAN STEFFERT IS the Cultural Attaché for Public Diplomacy and Public Affairs at New Zealand's Ministry of Foreign Affairs & Trade based at the New Zealand Embassy in Washington, DC. His job is, in a nutshell, to make Americans fall in love with New Zealand. He knows he can't compete with some of the big players in the diplomatic arena in terms of budget. "Somebody once said to me, 'Small embassies can't afford to throw bad parties.' That's something that I've always held onto." So, he finds ways to make the stories he tells, in all sorts of ways, more compelling. "I have to put this hyper-thoughtful lens over every opportunity and ask who the story is about, who is benefiting from it and who is missing from it."

Storytelling is a New Zealand trait. Steffert grew up, like many New Zealanders, immersed in Maori cultural practices like '*Waiata*' or songs that are used to teach, record the past, or even settle historical debates. "The future is in storytelling. That's where people are getting news from now. It's about scaling the story to start with 'Who am I? What is my place in the world? Where have I come from, and what values do I stand for?'" Everything Steffert does or arranges as part of his job stays true to New Zealand's unique culture and to his upbringing, so it's fundamentally and fascinatingly authentic.

"I want our guests to know the receptions and events we host are worthwhile to attend and are filled with people of value to them and New Zealand as the convener of conversation. It's about knowing how to build an experience and what I can do to be thoughtful, including the guest list I create and the kinds of community I convene. I take advantage of things like art, culture and friendships, even at a reduced scale. It creates better impact and more substantial outcomes."

While Steffert can create big events when that's called for, he focuses on smaller gatherings. "Traditionally, public diplomacy involved a lot of receptions of, say, 350 people. Those are intimidating environments. You get more value from doing a concentrated event around a dinner table with a few high-level people where we can share a bit about our shared values. The scale allows a more personal and in-depth conversation about the theme, like environmental values and why we care. We revere the natural world and are sustainable by nature, and have success sharing our message with broad audiences, but there's impact when you have the opportunity to invite people on a journey, and that is most effective through thoughtful nano hosting.

"I argue it's far better to curate a sensory experience at a smaller scale because I see success as a guest telling one of their friends, or contacts that they had a good time at the New Zealand Embassy or the New Zealand Ambassador's Residence. Our guests telling that story is far more powerful than me telling it."

Often, the stories he tells or arranges to have told are delivered experientially in a way consistent with New Zealand culture. "A lot of what we do is based on the sensory element of what it means to be transported somewhere." Transport and voyages are important themes in the country's cultural narrative. "The ceiling of our Grand Hall depicts a giant boat, what we call *Waka* or canoe. The supporting beams form a structure over this ballroom space that alludes to the Polynesian voyaging journey and story."

"That's just the space. What are you hearing, and what are you smelling? When you walk into the New Zealand Embassy you hear songs and sounds of native birds and wildlife playing on the sound system and are enticed by the smell of lamb cooking on the barbecue that we purposefully put in front of sliding doors, knowing that the wind is going to pull the aroma through one door and push it out another door. We get the lawns mowed the day of an event because there's nothing better than the smell of clipped grass and a barbecue. So, we passively transport you even before you've had a glass of our wine or are welcomed by a New Zealand accent."

Steffert doesn't rely on environmental cues to do the whole job. He also trains his team and equips them with the right stories to tell. "I brief our staff. We do a small stand-up to discuss who we're hosting, complete with a look-book of those that we're focused on saying hello to and stewarding. I use this opportunity to introduce what we're serving and the story behind the experience. When guests arrive, they move through registration, where they collect a glass of wine and are introduced to the vineyard and tasting notes."

Steffert's event hospitality team is a little different, too. "We invite all our staff to our events because we like to focus on the equity aspect of it. The team working at the immigration office processing visas are also part of our New Zealand story. The person working reception is the first New Zealander our guests often interact with. Including a variety of people at various levels is an intentional advantage. Because if you are the Chairman of the Joint Chiefs of Staff at the Pentagon and you meet the receptionist at a New Zealand embassy event, that says something about who we are and our values."

Steffert equips his executives and diplomats as carefully as he does his hospitality team, so they can tell compelling stories wherever they are. "I issue them with a variety of tools that they can deploy for meetings. For example, any New Zealand diplomat you meet will likely have a pocket full of friendship pins and various other items that tell our New Zealand story. So if one of our diplomats walks into a busy reception, makes contact with you, but thinks, 'I really want to chat, but I'm working the room and don't have a lot of time,' they can remove their friendship badge and use it as a tool, 'Can we make time to have a cup of coffee? I'd love to get together.' The act of giving creates a lasting impression; it sparks a connection. Particularly when you take it off your shirt and give it, instead of pulling something from your pocket."

Giving is, of course, a typical diplomatic tactic. But as Steffert and his team practice it, it comes from a more profound, sincere place packed with storytelling significance. "In New Zealand, the word *manaaki* is an expression that shows care. Care for your contact, and care for the connection. But more than anything, we are generous in our friendship, generous enough to say, this is mine, and I'm wearing it, but our connection is important to me, and I want to give you this."

"How do you tell people we're from New Zealand? We do that through the generosity of spirit and acts of kindness. We give natural gifts, sometimes trees. And we love to give honey. We give wine (that's an easy one). And we support different ways to tell the story that leaves the receiver thinking, 'That was an unusual gift to get. I liked it. I'm going to tell someone about it—or better still, I will use it myself.'

"This was best illustrated when former Prime Minister, Jacinda Arden, gave late-night talk show host Stephen Colbert a chilly bin on his show packed with beef. (You call that a cooler in the United States.) It was full of meat from a New Zealand company that operates in the US. It was leaning into New Zealand 'humour', New Zealand kind of sensibilities, and barbecue culture. But it was also elevating a New Zealand story. Our food and beverage story is brilliant. It's a primary industry story that highlights a range of values, including why grass-fed is good for the world. Sure, there's a bit of lunacy in giving someone a box of meat … but that creates an endearing element."

The gift made Colbert an even bigger fan of New Zealand. He had already liked the country and liked to talk about its role as the site of most of the production of the fantastically popular Lord of the Rings movies. So, this is a story about a gift that told a story about a country that has a knack for telling stories.

WHAT WE HEARD AND LEARNED

- Smaller can be better when you're storytelling
- Transport your audience
- Root your stories in authentic values
- Train and equip all team members

DEBORAH SZEKELY

LIFE LESSONS ON COLLABORATION FROM RANCHO LA PUERTA RETREAT

"People, by themselves, are nice by nature. It's just like a tree grows; it just grows. Niceness is a normal state of affairs. Anger comes when you've been frustrated, mistreated. You're not born angry."

DEBORAH SZEKELY, COLLABORATION ARTIST

DEBORAH SZEKELY HAS BEEN many things over her long life, including an activist, diplomat, philanthropist, and writer. She has been influential and instrumental in Washington, D.C. She has founded a museum. Her personal odyssey includes stops in places like Tahiti. She is currently the proprietor, heart, and soul of Rancho la Puerta in Mexico. And she is regularly called the 100-year-old godmother of whole-body wellness.

Today, Rancho la Puerta's incarnation as a sought-after retreat destination is the result of a long evolution. Throughout all of the changes, Rancho la Puerta, nestled at the base of a mountain traditionally thought to have magical properties, has always been known for its magnificent natural surroundings.

Equally important to the experience it provides, but less noted and celebrated, is the way Rancho la Puerta promotes the exchange of ideas and development of friendships. First, Deborah wants the Rancho to be full of happy people. "You're not going to want to connect with sourpusses." To achieve that, the ranch has few fences and few rules. It's meant to be a transformative experience where you are more relaxed and open.

"At the ranch," Deborah says, "You're yourself. People, by themselves, are nice by nature. It's just like a tree grows; it just grows. Niceness is a normal state of affairs. Anger comes when you've been frustrated, mistreated. You're not born angry."

The ranch helps its guests shed the protective armor they wear in the outside world with exercises like mountain climbing in the morning. As a result, Deborah says, "You open up. You're breathing hard. You're more flexible. Your mind is impressionable."

While the ranch gives its guests great latitude and freedom to design their own experiences there, the exception is dinner. "You have no choice where you sit," she explains, "I want them all to meet each other, not stay in cliques. That's intentional."

The resulting connections are what keep its guests returning year after year. "The big thing that brings people back is the friends they made. When I write letters about coming to the ranch, I say, 'You will make friends forever.' Everybody goes home with one or two friends."

The story of the ranch's growth is a saga in and of itself. World events drove Deborah and her husband to Mexico. "My husband had a good job, and we were going to England. I was going to go to college there. Everything was planned, but the World War got in the way. So we came to Mexico. We had no choice. We had to go someplace, and it was cheaper in Mexico than Canada. We both spoke Spanish, and my husband didn't speak English. He spoke French and Spanish, but not English."

In its early days of the ranch, guests stayed in tents. "They were movable," she remembers. "Four young people could move them. I put them in all kinds of places. I once painted them as rainbow cottages. I tried to do interesting things with them because they didn't have sewage. They didn't even have electricity—we used kerosene lamps and every room had three flashlights."

Deborah's inspiration for the schedules of activities came from an interesting source. She tells the story: "Initially, the retreat's main attraction was daily lectures by my husband, Edmund Szekely [a Hungarian philosopher and psychologist]. He lectured every day at four o'clock. Everyone went there. But after a while, he got bored and became repetitive. So, I led exercise classes to keep the energy up. Remember, I had just graduated from high school, where I had learned calisthenics. The early classes were basically high school calisthenics. Then we hired a yoga teacher. As we hired more staff, we developed the present fitness style of teaching. But essentially, the day's schedule was based on my high school schedule."

High school is a theme for Deborah. She likes to stimulate conversations by asking guests about their younger selves. "I ask them 'When you were 14 or 15 or 16, what did you think your life would be like?' Everyone opens up. They talk about how they were beginning to think at that age, and they reflect on how it's different from what they are doing. Many people pick someone they admire at that time. It's interesting how many of them hold on to that inspiration in one way or another."

Some of the signature rituals of the ranch were started to satisfy Deborah's curiosity. There are weekly "speaker dinners," where the diners are people who are presenting at the ranch. "The origin was pure self-interest," she says. "I wanted to know what the guests were hearing." But Deborah soon recognized that these intimate dinners were yielding other benefits. "I found that the real benefit is that the speakers got to know each other, and shared knowledge and information." Deborah has a tip for making these gatherings of seven or eight people work: "There's always wine so that the speakers relax and chat."

Deborah improves the lives of hundreds of people every year, and she created an equally strong legacy back when she was working in Washington, D.C. She recalls that, "I fundraised for Republicans and Democrats. I had connections on both sides." One artifact from her time there is still important. Deborah heard a number of people in Congress complain that nothing was being done to help incoming legislators get up to speed. "So I had a dozen retired chiefs of staff create a comprehensive management guide to setting up and managing a congressional office." The 17th edition of the resulting book, *Setting Course*, came out in time to help the new members of the 117th Congress.

Deborah is proud that it is still relevant. "AOC talks about the book. When people are going on about things, she says, you haven't read *Setting Course*. You should do it at once."

WHAT WE HEARD AND LEARNED

- Put up few fences and few rules
- Add physical activity, and wine
- Foster forever friendships
- Use talk of the past, and nostalgia, to spark conversation in the present

IAN ZISKIN
GURU ON COLLABORATIONS OF ALL SIZES

"My way of thinking about it is you have to go slow to go fast. You start off with a process of involving a bunch of people who were affected by a change. It takes time."

IAN ZISKIN, COLLABORATION ARTIST

WHAT DO you do after nearly three decades of being a top HR executive at Fortune 100 corporations, including Northrop Grumman, Qwest Communications, and TRW?

If you're Ian Ziskin, you keep working to transform the field as president of EXec EXcel Group LLC, while also being part of important collaborative coalitions. While you're at it, share your expertise by writing and co-editing four books, including *The Secret Sauce for Leading Transformational Change*, and serving on a host of boards.

Ian has spent a lifetime gathering insights while working for large companies. "The fundamental basis of building a culture of connection was engaging people in changes that affect them," he says. "Whether it was from a diversity and inclusion standpoint, creating employee resource groups that enable people to influence the work environment, or whether it was major change efforts in terms of how we were running the business and the kind of work environment we were trying to create … It turned out to be the most powerful formula for doing collaborative culture change."

However, Ian is realistic about the challenges involved in this approach. "Creating a more diverse and inclusive environment is a double-edged sword. The good news is you get multiple lenses through which people see a problem or a challenge, and the great creativity and innovative ideas that come from all of that debate and discussion is great rocket fuel for driving a more collaborative kind of culture. On the other hand, there are divergent perspectives. People disagree, and therefore it takes longer to get alignment, agreement, consensus, and therefore action.

"My way of thinking about it is you have to go slow to go fast," he continues. "One of the universal principles that I've encountered in all these different environments is that the people who are leading the change feel like it's not moving fast enough. And the people who are affected by the change, or in some cases victimized by it, generally feel that it's moving *too* fast, and they like to slow it down. So, everybody's looking at the same problem, but from two very different angles. You start off with a process of involving a bunch of people who were affected by a change. It takes time. It feels slower for somebody who's impatient, as I am. It feels like you're going through a lot of extra steps. But on the back end, what I generally have found is the level of alignment and support and agreement is stronger and therefore execution is better. It's longer lasting, and it actually moves faster at the end because people have been included in the change."

Ian points out both the value and challenges of celebrating success. "People like to stop and pause just long enough to recognize and celebrate what's been accomplished," he notes. "But in order to do that effectively, a couple of other conditions have to exist. First of all, the most important one is knowing what success looks like—not only the end result, but interim steps along the way. If you don't have agreement about what progress looks and feels like, it's really difficult to stop and celebrate it.

"The second thing about celebrating and recognizing people for their contributions is it's easy to say thank-you to the people who have been most actively involved and maybe most helpful," he adds. "It's a little bit harder sometimes to thank people who are more resistant, who are skeptical and push back or ask tough questions. While it seems like they're resisting things, quite often they actually push the organization to be better in terms of asking the hard questions that nobody else wants to ask. And that makes the outcome better."

One of the ways in which Ian fostered collaboration in the past was by being an affiliate research scientist with the Center for Effective Organizations (CEO), a research center in the USC Marshall School of Business. "The premise of an organization like CEO was basically building a collaborative partnership between academicians and practitioners," he explains. "The goal was having actionable research that was done in an academic environment, but that had highly practical and pragmatic application to real work environments. This is sometimes a bridge that's hard to build. The way we did it was by having practitioners and their companies as sponsors of the center. They were very actively involved in shaping and influencing the kind of research that got done so that it was in fact applied and very practical. Having a strong collaboration between both proved to be a very effective model."

While Ian works in a range of areas, including leadership development and HR transformation, he has devoted special attention to enhancing the role and effectiveness of coaching. He co-founded both the Business inSITE Group (BiG) strategic partnership and the Consortium for Change (C4C), a community of over 70 (a still-growing number) independent coaches and consultants.

C4C, created just a few years ago, responds to a few premises. "One being," Ian explains, "that as an independent coach or consultant, it can be difficult to compete for business with larger boutique firms, and particularly the much larger big consulting firms. So, C4C represents an opportunity to have these independent coaches and consultants collaborate with one another in competing for and going after business. We basically gave people a larger infrastructure and platform to compete from.

"A second premise is the idea of referring business to one another," Ian continues. "Just using myself as an example, if a coaching engagement came on the radar screen for me, but it wasn't really in my wheelhouse, or I didn't have time to do it, or the price point wasn't right for me ... I now could refer it to somebody else in C4C who I trust to do a good job.

"The third premise, which probably is the one that's grown the most, is simply building an environment of sharing best practices, and teaching one another good practices for running our respective independent businesses. Helping one another, sharing tools, and sharing frameworks is a way of continuing to invest in yourself and your own development and build trusted relationships with people. As those relationships continue to get built, people are increasingly collaborating with one another."

Ian makes it clear that the quality of the C4C members is key to its effectiveness. "The best kinds of people to be part of C4C are those who have what I call a spirit of abundance. They believe in sharing what they know. They teach others what they know, and they have a willingness to learn from them. They *collaborate*."

WHAT WE HEARD AND LEARNED

- Engage people in changes that affect them
- Go slow to go fast
- Learn from active engagers and the people who push back
- Invoke a spirit of abundance, freely sharing what you know

DREAM THE OUTRAGEOUS...

CREATIVITY

CHERYL CECCHETTO

HOLLYWOOD EVENTS PRODUCER CASTS HER COLLABORATIONS

"Whatever your path in life, be it event producer or teacher, etc.—any front person needs to consider how they address their audience. It's very important that they speak eloquently, concisely, in a positive, confident tone while imparting valuable, detailed information."

CHERYL CECCHETTO, COLLABORATION ARTIST

CHERYL CECCHETTO, the owner and president of Sequoia Productions, is the collaboration artist that the entertainment industry calls on to make sure their events are spectacular.

Sequoia Productions has produced the Academy Awards Governors Ball for 33 consecutive years, along with the Primetime Emmys Governors Ball and Emmy Creative Arts Ball for 25 consecutive years. These events are huge. Emmy events were at one time North America's largest annual seated dinners, and are now non-conventional galas totaling a stunning 7,500 guests.

Cheryl is able to sell to Hollywood because she can talk Hollywood. She started from a background in set design and theater, and began her career as an actress (See her *Golden Girls* rerun!) Her vocabulary and thinking reflect Hollywood. For example, she calls events "films with one take." She pitches event ideas the same way movie people pitch films in their world.

Cheryl is all about presentation, and that shows in what she'd like to share with aspiring collaboration artists. Typically, she is direct, no nonsense, and even a bit dramatic in how she expresses herself, including her obligatory measure of Canadian eloquence and respect.

"Whatever your path in life, be it event producer or teacher, etc.— any front person needs to consider how they address their audience. It's very important that they speak eloquently, concisely, in a positive, confident tone while imparting valuable, detailed information," she says.

Cheryl trains her staff to high presentation standards. She not only selects people who already have great communication skills; she continues to train them. "I think it's very important for staff to make group presentations, and to take turns running recorded, internal meetings," she explains. "I ask them to watch our Zoom recordings and notice how they present themselves, and how many times they say the words 'um' or 'like,' and whether they 'cut off' other participants. Some may feel put on the spot, however I believe that feeling uncomfortable is a necessary ingredient for growth."

She continues, "I believe it's important because our projects are high profile and high stakes, with so many transactions required to bring them to fruition. It's very important that each member of the team presents as their best self."

Cheryl gives detailed feedback. "I will ask them to count their 'ums' and 'ahs,' and to notice any superfluous hand movements and whether their bodies are engaged. I encourage them to look around the room to include everyone.

"To be in the event business," she continues, "you need to have presence and presence of mind. You need to be able to read the room, the whole room, make eye contact, and ensure the client, via excellent communication, that their event is of the highest importance and that you fully understand and support their vision. To do that, you need to know how to speak."

WHAT WE HEARD AND LEARNED

- Think of gatherings as "films with one take"
- Give honest, productive feedback
- Learn how to express yourself eloquently, concisely, and confidently

MICHAEL CIRINO

NOVEL EXPERIENCE CREATOR PUSHES BOUNDARIES AND RAISES THE BARS

"It's just a great excuse to collaborate with people."

MICHAEL CIRINO, COLLABORATION ARTIST

MICHAEL CIRINO IS the founder and creative director of A Razor, A Shiny Knife, a creative agency whose work includes experiential marketing, culinary events, interactive installations, and tech-fueled experiences like laser-branded sandwiches and drone photo booths. The company works with world-renowned clients like Pepsi, Hearst, Google, UNICEF, and Sotheby's.

Michael has always focused wide-ranging thinking—and has never been shy. For example, he made the case and convinced the restaurant critic for *The New York Times* that underground dining experiences should be covered in that paper. But perhaps Michael's greatest claims to fame are the logistical miracles he modestly calls "stunts." One of his earlier stunts was a fabulous dinner served in a New York City subway car.

"It was a six-course meal of gourmet food accompanied by very fancy service on an L-line train as it traveled from Manhattan to Brooklyn," he says. "A lot of the details for the whole thing were designed so we would actually fit in with that unique environment. We live in a society that has food-safety handling rules and rules about fiery desserts. Doing any kind of dinner party on the subway is not an easy thing. But we set out to provide all of the things you'd want at a nice restaurant: a multi-course tasting menu, elegant tables (that hung from the ceiling), fine China, crystal glassware, sparkling water and chilled still water—everything. There were 12 people dining on the subway, and it took 84 staff to serve them. The complexity of the challenge added value to the project itself.

"Planning took us about a month," he adds. "A lot of the problems that we incurred came from the MTA code of conduct. It says, for example, that you can't put anything on the ground. We couldn't use a tray jack. So we needed four more people to hold all the things."

Michael continues, "People were getting on and off. They were walking through our car. We came prepared to be a part of the community, so we could, for example, give kids in a family that showed up snacks. The guests didn't know what was happening. They were told they were going to have a picnic and to meet on the corner of Eighth and 14th. When they came down to the subway car, our maître d' seated them. Roughly every three subway stops, one whole team would get off and another team would get on with all new china. We tried to provide the pomp and circumstance of a fancy restaurant."

Nine guests had bought tickets and reserved their seats ahead of time, he explains. "I solicited three more people on Sixth Avenue. We had the nine diners buy tickets, because people who *didn't* have to buy tickets often didn't show up. But we refunded their money the second they got on the subway. This wasn't about money; it was a proof of concept.

"*The New York Times* wrote about it; 1,500 other publications wrote about it. So, the things that I dream up to connect people can also turn into real things, right? There was actually a party on the subway that was really difficult to do."

Another "stunt" that A Razor, A Shiny Knife executed to perfection was a 100-course meal. "It was started off as a joke," Michael recounts. "I was sitting with the chef of a three-Michelin-star restaurant that served 12 courses over five and a half hours. I said, 'I could probably do 100 courses in the same time, or less.' We built a 150-foot-long table.

And we put 10 seats at one end, and then we laid a thousand plates out on the rest of the table. Chefs plated the food on those dishes. There'd be 10 waiters walking down the 150-foot table with plates in each hand. Each would stop behind two of the 10 guests, lean in, and put the plates down. Realistically, there's no way anyone could eat 100 courses. We told the ten people with seats that they should bring three or four friends, and we ran it like a relay race. If you sat down five times, you'd eat 25 courses. When you were seated at the table, your job was to eat. You were getting a course of food that was roughly three or four bites every two minutes and 15 seconds. By the time you had them, you saw people walking down the table with the next course. (It takes 30 seconds to get 150 feet.)"

Having the guests eat in tag-teams left time for diners to talk about the dishes when they weren't at the table. "They were explaining their personal experience in real time. Recounting codified those memories and made them a little bit stronger," Michael says, adding that the four chef teams were carefully scheduled so that they would have time to interact with the diners. The team that plated course one also served course five, and so on.

"My job," Michael reports, "was to make sure people knew that stuff was going to happen, get them excited about participating, and let them know they didn't have to take out their phones because we had photographers taking pictures of every dish."

A highlight of the meal was the huge cake celebrating the birthday of one of the diners. "Why not have a birthday cake at every meal?" Michael asks. "We brought the guests that weren't at the table into that experience, getting them ready to sing. Everybody knew their place. It was a flash mob for a second. The birthday woman didn't know that they were going to sing, and then she had all these random guests singing to her in the middle of this crazy culinary experience.

"I see this kind of meal as a fun way of collaborating with the culinary and the experiential space in a city," Michael says of the greater significance of his stunts. "If I bring a 100-course meal to Chicago, think of the chefs that I could work with, the baristas, the bartenders, the bakers, the butchers, and also the musicians, the crafts people, the artisans responsible for China, the floral design, and the artwork on the walls. It's just a great excuse to collaborate with people."

WHAT WE HEARD AND LEARNED

- Use stunts as proofs of concept and to get media attention
- Charge for the stunt: People who don't buy tickets often don't show up
- Provide photographers so participants don't have to take photos and can concentrate on the experience
- Go fast, but make time for interactions

CHRIS AND JILL DRURY
DUO LEADS A COMPANY THAT'S PIONEERING NEW MODELS OF EVENT INTERACTION

"We look for ways to learn from each other."

CHRIS AND JILL DRURY, COLLABORATION
ARTISTS

JILL TAUB DRURY and Chris Drury of New York-based Drury Design have changed events for clients including IBM, Google, and Goldman Sachs by pushing for innovations that meet new audiences where they are.

Chris makes it clear that while they are known to be early adopters of technology, content comes *before* any tech. "You have to figure out who the audience is. Then the messages. Then the value proposition. Then you establish what the content is. Then you decide who's speaking," he says.

One of their signal accomplishments was to activate the hallways at events. "Back in the day, you came into a space with a stage, you saw the show, you were done," Chris remembers. "You left the big space and hung out in hallways, waiting for workshops." Jill adds to his thought, "It's completely different now."

While the idea of using the hallways creatively seemed obvious to Chris and Jill, the path wasn't easy. "Even IBM was hesitant," Chris says. "You would have thought that as a tech company, they would get it, but they didn't. Jill and I went into our own pocket, and we created the first social space out there. It started out with highboys and couches."

"We had charging stations which were, at that point, basically power strips," Jill adds. "We branded everything. The highboys were branded on the tops. It was all very clean. The furniture was white. Essentially, we took the branding from the event, and we applied it to the social space." Chis observes, "Now everybody does hallways, and everybody does social. It's moved past the hallways and into the streets, which is phenomenal."

The Drurys are aware that shifting the focus and control at events from the stage to social centers sometimes made clients nervous. "One day, an alarmed client came to me and said, 'They're moving the furniture,'" Chris recalls. "I told them this was a great sign. That means that they own the space, and they feel comfortable here, and then they'll do what they want to do. You want people to be comfortable here, to grab chairs, to get together, to get to a whiteboard."

Creating the right spaces wasn't always enough; sometimes they had to be evangelists for new social media, Chris explains. "We brought in people to teach clients and attendees what Twitter was and how it worked, because we wanted to use it for the event to be able to get people to engage."

Jill describes how things have changed: "Back then, we had to explain to clients that if they had 10 percent of their participants using social media, that was good." Chris adds, "Now, if we got under 90 percent participation at some events, we would ask, 'What's wrong?'"

It's not surprising that the Drurys cite metrics and statistics when talking about success in creating innovative gatherings where serendipitous collaboration can occur. Their clients have included top accounting firms who like to see numbers. Chris describes how one such client came to see the light. "Deloitte wasn't initially interested in the things we were talking about and demonstrating. But when they saw the ROI and other metrics—then, all of a sudden, they took it seriously. They became experts."

Jill and Chris were also among the first to help clients understand that they should embrace new media habits that could compete with an event's main stage for attention. "Years ago, when I brought up programming for a 'second screen' experience, people thought I was out of my mind," Chris says. "They said, 'What do you mean? They're going to look at their *phones*? I want them to look at me on the stage.' And I answered, 'They're looking at their phone already.'"

"We had video from the back of the arena that we'd show to the clients," Jill adds. "We'd say, 'See all those lights? Those are people on their devices. We need to capture their minds when they're on their devices; let's do content that works for them.'"

The Drurys are also in the vanguard of cognitive events. "A cognitive event," Chris explains, "is one that learns who you are. It reasons. It looks at what you do, and it makes recommendations on things that might be right for you.

"Exploring this area presented challenges," Jill adds, "We're mostly right-brain people in terms of what we do, but for one of our events we had to learn how to program IBM's new Watson system. The client wanted for the cognitive event to showcase its cognitive computing approach."

The Drurys now see event breakout sessions as deserving more attention, much like hallways once did. "The breakouts are, oftentimes, the last thing on the list," Chris says. "Planners focus on everything from the keynotes to the parties before saying, 'Somebody has to do the breakouts.' Unfortunately for that kind of thinking, breakouts are where most of the hands-on learning happens." Jill adds, "They have to be more engaging."

Chris has strong opinions about how venues should change as well. "I think hotels are not right for what we want to do and what people want to do now. That's why we started going into hallways. Hotels need to understand the way people actually want to experience content or meetings on their premises. Get rid of the walls, create spaces, let people mix, let them go to where they want to be able to get content."

Jill sums up, "Audiences are evolving. They're changing, and their expectations are different. And you have to meet those expectations."

Chris adds, "Luckily, technology is constantly evolving, too. You have to see where it is now, and where it could be used to enhance events."

The Drurys are acutely aware of generational preferences and behaviors, both in their team and at events. Chris says, "We want to keep our employees engaged and passionate and excited and wanting to step up and bring whatever they're interested in up to the plate … how is that any different than what we want at our events?" Jill says, "We have employees who have been with the organization for 30 years or more. And then we also have people who are 20 years old. We look at how they think and how they learn. We look for ways to learn from each other."

"A baby boomer," Chris starts, "wants to know exactly what's going to happen. It needs to be set out in front. They need a set course. They need to analyze it. They need to think about it."

Jill provides the contrast. "A millennial will come into a situation and say, 'OK, what's going on? What's fun to do here? What do I like? Where do I go towards? Where can I have impact?'"

Jill points out that even an audience that has similar roles and training will have different generational needs. "When you look at an event and your audience is all technical or they're all pharmaceutical, whatever it might be, they have a common interest. But the ages are really different. It can be extremely difficult, particularly on the training side. People learn differently."

WHAT WE HEARD AND LEARNED

- Activate the hallways at events and create unexpected social spaces
- Be aware of generational differences
- Teach clients and attendees when helpful
- Look to learn from each other

TAHIRA ENDEAN
PEOPLE-CENTRIC, PURPOSE-DRIVEN, INTENTIONAL DESIGN INSPIRES INVOLVEMENT

"We can't take care of people until we've taken care of ourselves."

TAHIRA ENDEAN, COLLABORATION ARTIST

VANCOUVER, British Columbia-based Tahira Endean is an event producer who's passionate about intentional event design and the integration of technology to enhance the human experience at events. She has, literally, written the book about events: *Intentional Event Design: Our Professional Opportunity*. "This book is not about logistics," Tahira explains. "It's about the bigger-picture thinking behind the logistics, and about understanding why we need to have strategies in place. What I want is for us to be able to reframe what the event industry is and to have tools to do that."

The book reflects two linked, people-centric principles. The first is that "businesses invest in events because they provide a catalyst for behavior change, leading to business growth," she says, adding the second is that participants attend events "because we crave face-to-face opportunities for learning and intelligent conversation with like-minded individuals." The upshot of these is that "We're not going to have events if we don't create spaces that people feel are valuable," she explains.

Tahira puts people-centric, purpose-driven design first because, she says, "There are still many events where we're doing the same thing in the same way that we've always done it. We are not thinking about how people have evolved very rapidly in this digital age. We have the same needs that humans have always had around our basic care. We still have this deep need for human connection. But we also have new needs related to arriving with a super-computer. We need to think more deeply when we're spending tens of thousands or millions of dollars on events. It's not about what the decor is. It's about the entire environment, and how that is going to drive conversations between people. Success at an event is not the number of leads you've generated. It's the number of quality conversations that have been had. It's our responsibility to provide the catalyst for that when we're doing any event, social or otherwise."

She talks about a sequence of intentions that is pertinent to events. "Intention one really is people-centric, purpose-driven design. Two is looking at how we integrate and embrace technology. Intention three is designing for the optimal brain experience. Four is optimizing learning and performance. Intention five is space flow and seating design. Intention six is five-senses design. The final intention, intention seven, is wellness. Not just wellness for our participants, but for us—because we can't take care of people until we've taken care of ourselves."

One of the frameworks Tahira refers back to is the CED, the Certified Event Designer process that began in Europe nearly a decade ago. "It's a framework, a design process specific to events that gives us a fundamental basis for looking at our stakeholder needs. Not just the meeting owner, but also groups that are participating. For larger organizations where you're doing multiple events over the course of a year or longer, having consistency shouldn't mean that your events are the same. It's about having a consistent framework, so you understand what you need to do in designing your events to meet the needs that you have taken the time to drill down to."

She explains the value of this process. "We have an industry that's based on hierarchical layers. You will quite often have a meeting owner who's at an organization and then an agency, and other agencies hired to do specific tasks. There's quite often a missing link to what the owner really wants. Going through a process that owner has signed off on allows you to better articulate what's important to all of those collaborators."

When designing events, Tahira pays attention to Dunbar's Number, first proposed in the 1990s by British anthropologist Robin Dunbar. "It suggests that your largest community can be 150 people," she explains. "When you plan an event of 10,000 people, you need to think about how to break it down into these smaller communities."

"At any point in time," she explains, "You'll have five people who are very close to you. You'll have 15 people who are part of your core. Those people will shift over time as you change jobs or move roles or move to a new community or go to an event. When you're at an event, you're going to have your core people who you're going to spend time with. You're also going to have some new people, which may be why you came to the event. The upper limit for building our social villages is about 150—and for event design, finding ways to bring small communities together creates the most memorable experiences."

"Session planning," Tahira adds, "is about creating sessions that are going to attract people who have a similar interest. And, of course, avoiding 'sage from the stage talking' and using learning and performance design. You want to create opportunities for people to talk to each other. Smaller, deeper conversations in a trusted environment is how we build communities."

"When we build a trade show," Tahira continues, "we want to move beyond having people walk down aisle after aisle looking at the middle level and averting their eyes from the logos they're not interested in. We design a much more open, inviting experience where people make eye contact with people on the same level and have conversations. Those conversations drive business."

WHAT WE HEARD AND LEARNED

- Use people-centric, purpose-driven design to create spaces that people feel are valuable
- Pay attention to Dunbar's number. Group attendees into small communities

- Measure event success by the number of quality conversations
- Remember wellness for participants, your team, and yourself

STEVE GOTTLIEB
PLATFORM CREATOR INCREASES PARTICIPATION BY USING TECH TO ALLOW COLLABORATORS TO CHOOSE THEIR OWN JOURNEYS

"I was at a TED conference, and I heard an anthropologist talk about workplace rules and why factory workers should have access to their cell phones on the factory floor. He said, 'Autonomy over where you direct your attention is now a fundamental right.' And the light bulb went off."

STEVE GOTTLIEB, COLLABORATION ARTIST

STEVE GOTTLIEB IS the founder and CEO of Shindig, a virtual platform architected and engineered for hybrid and virtual applications in events as well as other sectors. Steve comes from the music business. He was the founder of TVT records, one of the largest and most successful independent record labels in the history of the United States. He discovered and spearheaded the careers of artists such as Nine Inch Nails, Ja Rule, and Pitbull.

Steve's 25-year career in the music business paved the way for Shindig. "It was all about things that didn't depend on top 40," Steve explains, "but that depended on super-serving super fans and creating evangelists and tremendous word of mouth. Really nurturing deep senses of community. That was really what Shindig was intended to enable. I first thought about it for artists' fan engagement. It was a platform for artists to do Q&As with fans, but also allow the fans to share their passions with one another."

Steve remembers an "aha moment" that pointed out what the platform needed to be able to do to have dramatic relevance for the event industry. "I was at a TED conference, and I heard an anthropologist talk about workplace rules and why factory workers should have access to their cell phones on the factory floor. He said, 'Autonomy over where you direct your attention is now a fundamental right.' And the light bulb went off. I realized that the lack of personal autonomy was a downside to most webinars and the like. You're just supposed to sit there and listen and be good attendees. This seemed all wrong. The whole idea of permission marketing was based on meeting your audience halfway and meeting them where they were. But what had happened was, we got them into webinars and then we just jammed them with messages. No real interactivity, no ability to bring them up on stage and take their questions and really hear them out in a meaningful way."

Steve spotted an unrealized technical opportunity. "The infrastructure was no longer just fixed telephone wires. But no one had leveraged the fact that we now had a computer in the middle, so we could rearrange all of the connections on-the-fly. That meant that with the right development, we could have 1,000 people in an event, and they could suddenly be in 500 different conversations, and then all listening to the stage again. And we got 27 patents around that concept."

Shindig was developed over a long time. Steve explains, "It wasn't built as a response to COVID. There are a lot of enterprises that came in and just glued together solutions by adding, say, speed dating to Zoom. Shindig was conceived a decade before COVID, with the thought process of, 'What if it were possible to convene people online and give all the interactivity, the rich nuanced experience, of an in-person event virtually?'"

You can create many of the dynamics of an in-person event on Shindig. But the goal of the technology has never been to replace in-person events or event planners and facilitators. Steve explains, "In devising the tech, we worked with the understanding that tech could not *recreate* events. That you couldn't use AI to pair people. You couldn't force people into conversations. You couldn't ignore the social hierarchy and just assume, 'Oh, the CEOs are going to sign up to meet with the non-CEOs five minutes at a time.'"

Steve declares, "Virtual events require more planning genius—more of someone creative to really make the experience unique and inventive and dynamic, and something that is worthy of people's time."

Shindig's business arrangements are aimed at empowering event practitioners. "On a lot of other platforms," Steve details, "every feature is a new add-on. They get you in cheap and have lots of add-ons. Our go-to-market philosophy is completely different. We have a very straightforward price per user, per hour, which is cut in half for social impact non-profits and educational institutions. That's what makes sense for events. We think events require complete freedom and imagination to conceive, and so we don't charge for features. We want to give you all the features so you can imagine something great."

While Shindig is designed to enable self-service, the company also does a lot of training and hand-holding. "We learned long ago," Steve says, "that no one reads instructions. We have regular client trainings. We offer white-glove services where we'll help you produce an event."

Steve offers an example of the versatility and innovation possible when leveraging shindig. "We're talking with one of the very big, prestigious event institutions right now about their upcoming event. They're thinking about a super-exclusive event effectively just for all the speakers, where the speakers will assemble in one place and get to rub elbows. The audience will all be virtual and online. They'll have this combination of a very high-level exclusive in-person event and a global virtual event."

For the most part, Steve sees technology as creating the potential for even more compelling events. "This is really just the beginning. There'll be more ongoing transformation unleashing greater creativity and efficiency. Hybrid and virtual events will set new standards in terms of the savings of time and money and connecting people. We're going to love these events."

Along with all of his optimism, Steve is clear-eyed about some of the challenges that will be facing the events industry. The first is competition for attention. "A world with a plethora of events, 365 days a year, is going to up the ante for what it's going to take to get everyone together for an in-person event."

Steve sees a dynamic that will drive change in events. "Offering a live stream is going to have profound implications. The first people who are going to want to take advantage of being remote are going to be the high-value speakers who are not going to want to deal with travel to make an appearance. And once you lose some of those high-value speakers, you diminish the incentive for the sponsor and the audience to come. You no longer offer the chance to rub elbows with a high-value player."

Unlike some entrepreneurs who position technology as an instant cure-all, Steve describes a slower and bumpier path forward. "Tech changes slowly. Adoption is often very slow. In fact, to be honest, we're likely to see some retrenchment post-pandemic as everyone begins to focus on getting to a new normal. People are going to have to learn again."

While Shindig is purpose-built for events, its inherent flexibility makes it interesting in other areas, such as education and training. Steve illuminates, "It allows a teacher to go from addressing the entire class to giving individualized attention to individual students, and then going back to the head of the class."

WHAT WE HEARD AND LEARNED

- Give audiences autonomy as to what they pay attention to
- Deploy feature-rich platform and business arrangements to encourage creativity
- Plan extensively for virtual events
- Train and hand hold to ensure tech adoption

FRANCISCO J. NÚÑEZ
CHOIRMASTER LEVERAGES DIVERSITY AND MENTORSHIP TO CREATE HARMONY

"Teach children and they flourish. Their brains will get bigger, and they'll want more. Once you change children's brains, their lives will change forever."

FRANCISCO J. NÚÑEZ, COLLABORATION
ARTIST

"YOUNG PEOPLE'S CHORUS OF NEW YORK CITY, or YPC, as we often call it, is a hybrid of many ideas I put together—informed, originally, by my childhood experiences," says Francisco J. Núñez. "I am Latino. My father is Black. My mother is Latina. And the idea of coming from a blended family was unusual, especially back in the '60s. Our way of life was good. Lots of love, and lots of education. But what had made my life even more interesting was meeting children from across the financial spectrum. They had different ways of thinking and living. I learned about a greater range of options. That's what YPC is about: creating options through community for many children."

Francisco has clearly met that objective. Over more than 35 years, the program has grown and morphed so that it now serves many participants and is internationally recognized. It has the agility and depth to take on many artistic challenges. "We used to be only 200 children. We're now 2,000: 600 active children, plus 1,400 more in schools. At a YPC performance, you might actually see a bunch of nine- and twelve-year-olds, or you might see a group of teenagers, or you might see a combination. We're about to record a new opera for Gordon Getty that will include men and boys ages eight to 18, and some girls. We are unique in that way."

According to Francisco, YPC is about surrounding children with the finest teachers, the most excellent music, the most beautiful spaces, and audiences that appreciate what they achieve.

"Music is very hard," he says. "Not everybody is born a prodigy. But if you work very hard at something, you will become very good at it. If you work at singing really well, you'll become a very fine singer. Teach children and they flourish. Their brains will get bigger, and they'll want more. Once you change children's brains, their lives will change forever."

The path to this impressive success was not always easy. Francisco had to push back against prejudices and create opportunities. "Early on, I was told 'New York City is not a choral city. New York City is an instrument city.' In most of the programs that had singing, it was part of an instrumental program. A settlement house, like Third Street or Bloomingdale or Henry Street, might have violin or piano classes. If they had the choir, it was there for socialization or to teach soft skills. Boys' and girls' clubs were also doing the same thing. The focus of their music programs was not artistic excellence. It was bringing young people together, creating community."

Francisco had sensed that this didn't have to be the case. He was aware of choirs that were based on artistic excellence in Europe and in a few places in the United States. "I brought together children from different parts of the city, different places on the financial-resources spectrum, different religions, different ethnic backgrounds, different skin colors—all to make music at the highest level. Today, New York City is a choral city. Singing is everywhere."

Francisco has been able to leverage the professional talent pool around New York City. "You can read about and imagine what you want to be when you grow up," he says, "but it's a far richer experience to work directly with someone who does it. You feel the energy. You feel the impulse. You see every nuance, every facial expression, the sweat pouring down. Then you hear the singing or the playing of the instrument or the way they speak. That affects a child in a profound way. We surround our young children with experts who are enthusiastic, who give back and don't take. It makes a difference for everybody: the children, the adult professionals, and the audience.

"It's funny how people know when it's real, when the connection is really happening," he continues. "Very few of us understand the creative mind, much less, 'How do I become great?' But if the right person is put in front of you, you can see, 'Here's one way of doing that.' It transfers into everything else. When we have mentors like that in front of us, we feel inspired. 'You looked at me and validated my singing. Now I want to be like you.'"

One of the challenges Francisco faced was the lack of music for choruses like YPC. "Collaboration means stepping out of your own comfort zone and entering another genre and learning from it and evolving. I had to step outside of the choral world. It's a limited genre, based on an old tradition. The repertoire, especially for children's choirs, is limited. Handel's *Hallelujah* chorus is not really for children. It's for adults. A Mozart requiem was not written for children. I stepped out of my genre, went into the concert world, and asked, 'Are there any composers who respect children enough to write great music for them? Will you write for a children's choir?' The answer from everybody was: 'No. If I write for you, I will be stigmatized as an education composer, and no one will respect me anymore.'"

In 2001, to persuade composers to take that leap, he created a program called Transient Glory. Transient Glory was the concept of singing music during that transient time of life before we become adults. "We don't have the same experiences as adults. We haven't had a job. We don't have children. We might not be in relationships —but music can be written for us. I was able to convince four major composers—Michael Torke, John Taverner, Elena Kats-Chernin, and Norah Kroll-Rosenbaum—to write four amazingly difficult, beautiful works. All those pieces got published."

YPC has not only expanded the ages involved, the range of musical genres, and the audiences—it has also added movement. "When I was a child, we sang and we danced all the time. I was called jumpy because I was always a person that needed to move," Francisco observes, "In European culture, the concept of movement while singing is seen as lesser in the art world. That's not necessarily the case in the rest of the world. Dance is one of the most important communicators that we have. It's innate in who we are as animals. It turns us on to each other. To me, dancing and singing at a high level just makes us better people."

WHAT WE HEARD AND LEARNED

- Aspire to artistic excellence
- Embrace diversity
- Step out of your comfort zone
- Create spaces where people can communicate

BRYAN RAFANELLI

EVENT MAESTRO CREATES
OPPORTUNITY FOR SERENDIPITY
BY PLANNING EVERY MOMENT

"I always want my creative team to imagine the outrageous … I want them all asking, 'How can we make an amazing, dream thing happen?'"

BRYAN RAFANELLI, COLLABORATION ARTIST

BRYAN RAFANELLI, founder and chief creative officer of Rafanelli Events, is a legend. In addition to his work for corporate functions and non-profit events, Bryan and his team have designed more than a dozen events for the White House during the Obama administration, including state dinners and the holiday decorations in 2015 and 2016. They've worked on weddings for clients like Chelsea Clinton and Matt Damon. They designed and executed the November 19, 2022, wedding of President Biden's granddaughter, Naomi Biden, to Peter Neal—the 19th wedding ever hosted at the White House.

Rafanelli-designed events are tremendously creative, but they are never random. "I plan every second," Bryan explains. "If I learned anything from working at the White House, it is 'plan every second.' I do this with my team all the time. We walk through plans for an event, and we walk through it again. No matter whether it's something as small as a wedding or some giant, corporate thing, we do the same thing: go over it and over it, so we can watch for what could happen.

We know what's going to happen every second while the guests are there. And, by the way, they don't know that. It's really thinking through what people are going to see and how they're going to feel."

It's telling that Bryan speaks of what he does with his team. One of the biggest challenges he faced in scaling up his business was how to "replicate" himself so the company could grow. This wasn't an easy task—because Bryan has very demanding standards. "I always want my creative team to imagine the outrageous," he says. "I don't want them to think about timing, moving, costs. I want my production team to be smart, but also think about how far we can push things. I want them all asking, 'How can we make an amazing, dream thing happen?' It's critical to start there, because if you start in the middle, you end up with mediocre."

The importance of teams is something that was reinforced while Bryan worked in Washington, D.C. "I was part of a team. The White House is packed with people who have done extraordinary things— the butlers, the ushers, the floral department. They've been there for a long time. This is their career. We complemented what they do, and tried to expand it a bit."

While he compliments the White House team, Bryan feels that Washington events, in general, could use a bit more pizzazz. "I think with political events—and I say this with love—the expectation is so low that a little bit of organization and theater goes a really long way."

Planning every second of an event includes, naturally, thinking long and hard about sensory experiences like music. "We are always really careful that we don't have an overwhelming IMAX theater kind of experience," he explains. "We don't want to blow them away with sound. We want them to feel comfortable all the time, unless there's some big, giant thing that's about to happen. There should be recorded digital music that is at the right level so that everyone can have a conversation—but they can hear Aretha Franklin, or whomever, in the background. And it should be fairly familiar, by the way, because people like things that are familiar. If there's a little toe-tapping happening in a cocktail party, we have scored."

Bryan also has ideas about how to use technology to create a visual rhythm in a performance or event. Plan every second means *program* every second, he explains. "A screen that had been providing a pleasant background, for instance, will light up with activity between speakers, performers, etc. Such movements tap into the cadence of surprise.

"As a baseline," he continues, "we have to have three to five 'wow moments' at our events. Keeping somebody's mind moving through a 120-minute experience requires that something happens every 20 minutes or so to make the guests feel like something's happening, but it's not the same thing."

Bryan demands that these wow-moment "reveals" be relevant to the story the event is telling. "I'm a real stickler for saying, 'This just can't be some fabulous thing made out of 2,000 light bulbs strung across the sky.' It has to have some kind of connection back to the client's brand, product, service, or cause."

WHAT WE HEARD AND LEARNED

- Draw on structured creativity by planning every second of an event or collaboration
- "Imagine the outrageous"
- Deliver "wow moments" regularly to keep people enchanted
- Aim for the dream. If you start in the middle, you end up with mediocre

SANDY SAFI

CONNECTING THE WORLD BY
CREATING FOMO PHENOMENON

"There's a lot of ways to feel compensated for operating an event. There are financial upsides, and then there's just simply the love of doing it."

SANDY SAFI, COLLABORATION ARTIST

EVEN AFTER EXPANDING a charming ritual that started in France into a massive business in cities around the globe, Sandy Safi, who co-founded Dîner en Blanc International, is awed time and time again by the energy, creativity, and cooperation of people eager to participate in a rare, fun, exclusive event in a surprising place.

A Dîner en Blanc is an elegant pop-up picnic in which participants dress in all white. They bring their own food and tables and tabletop gear to an undisclosed location, guided by hundreds of volunteers. Sandy learned of the traditions of Dîner en Blanc from her partner, whose father had started the event in Paris in 1988. She was excited to discover different ways to replicate and scale up the event in other countries and for different cultures.

Sandy was unprepared for the tidal wave of interest that followed an article about Dîner en Blanc in New York City. "We announced that we would be doing it in New York, and the press picked up on it. And suddenly, we had thousands of people saying they wanted to attend, signing up on our waiting list. And it grew from there." That's an understatement. Sandy estimates "maybe 170,000 people attend across the various events, and we have a waiting list of over 1,000,000 people."

Dîner en Blanc International took on the challenge of figuring out how to make it possible for there to be Dîner en Blanc experiences around the globe that had local flavor and flair, while still preserving the unique qualities of the event. There was no precisely matched growth model to follow, so Dîner en Blanc International evolved its business model as it grew.

"We started receiving requests after the New York event from all over the world," Sandy explains. "We were not set up to run around the planet and reproduce this event in so many cities. So, we asked, 'How can we give people a turnkey solution to create this event, to respect the tradition and where this event came from while still making it financially feasible?'"

The result was a licensing model. "We license only teams that are qualified," Sandy notes. "We vet them. We will license out to people in a particular city. There needs to be two to three people who are leads on the project—people who actually know the city, have good relationships, have experience of how to set up stuff in their city."

Dîner en Blanc International gives the licensees a lot of leeway as to what they want to do with the event. Sandy says, "Some of them work on a for-profit basis. A lot of them also look for just the networking opportunities that they get through the event; they look for the connections that they can build. It's a window of visibility. There's a lot of different ways to feel compensated for operating an event. There are financial upsides, and then there's just simply the love of doing it."

At first glance, it may seem like running these events would be relatively simple because so many of the logistics are handled by the attendees. But as Sandy details how things happen, it becomes clear that these beautiful meals, which seem to be so full of spontaneity and serendipity, actually require—and this will not surprise people who have run events—lots of planning and support. "The infrastructure that's around these events that you might not see is actually quite impressive and important to make sure that people are safe and well taken care of. We also abide by regulations like permits and insurance requirements. There's a lot of red tape to gathering so many people in public spaces."

Each Dîner en Blanc is a perfect platform for partnerships, and Dîner en Blanc International puts clear parameters around what can happen. "Partner activities," Sandy states, "need to align. Things on site have to add value to the attendees' experiences. We don't do billboards. We don't do anything that is distributed. There's no paper onsite. There is nothing like that. You have to bring an experience on its own, into the event."

Sandy makes it clear that there is still a lot of room for creativity. "A Champagne company could bring a step-and-repeat onsite and provide extra bottles, or they could provide bottles to a press area or a media area. They could bring influencers on site. I think travel and tourism is a great bracket for partnerships. We've had a partnership with a cruise line where they just wanted to show the different components of their cruise, so they rebuilt some components or experiences on site."

Speaking with Sandy, it becomes clear that her mantra might well be "believe in your event." When she describes her Dîner en Blanc experiences (and she gets to attend a lot of these events), her eyes light up. They are still almost magical for her.

There's wonder in her voice as she says, "I take the time to walk through every single city and to see how the participants react and what they bring to the event. And you do feel a very big difference if you attend, let's say an event in New York City [versus] an event in Melbourne or Singapore. Maybe in some places the emphasis is put more on the food, and in others on the fashion. In still other places they're just chilling, laid back, and want to have a nice evening out. In some cities, people are a bit more competitive about what they're wearing. People really go all out. Short of bringing a chandelier and a generator to an event and setting it up, they deck those tables. It's unbelievable."

Sandy is quick to point out an aspect that might be easy to miss: "It's also a green event, right? People are bringing their real plates, real forks, real knives. They're not supposed to leave any garbage behind. They're bringing tables and chairs, and then taking them home."

WHAT WE HEARD AND LEARNED

- Create contexts for magical, surprising moments
- Integrate local flavor and flair
- Demand extensive attendee participation
- Plan and support extensively to preserve the sense of serendipity

SARAH SHEWEY

MAKING TRAINED TALENT ON DEMAND A REALITY

"My best advice to anyone at any stage of their career is to figure out what makes you different and just do a lot more of that—and keep going."

SARAH SHEWEY, COLLABORATION ARTIST

SARAH SHEWEY IS a self-confessed tech and data geek, and a deep thinker about the nature of events—as well as an entrepreneur who is changing the very structure of how events are executed. She's the founder and CEO of Los Angeles-based Happily, a nationwide network of freelance event specialists in the United States. She's also a co-founder of TEDActive, and the driving force behind EXP, an event where the people behind the world's best experiences come together to share war stories and best practices.

"Happily began as a nationwide network of freelance event planners and event teams that are available on-demand for production agencies, community managers, leaders, organizers, and individuals who are planning events," she explains.

Sarah reveals the spark behind Happily. "I saw a trend of freelancers and people wanting to work for themselves, but they didn't necessarily have the structure to support them in doing that. Happily was designed to attract these entrepreneurs. While at TED, I noticed that a lot of people have ideas, but not the best ways to execute them. So, there was an unfilled market niche."

Demand for the services that Happily provides is driven by brands' aspirations. "Brands come up with huge campaigns. They've got all of the data analytics. They understand their customers. They know that they need to put on a tour or hold a summit. They turn that over to agencies, saying, 'Make this cool. Bring this to life.' The agencies work really hard, but they are smacked by short lead times. The execution stage has gotten really short, while these campaigns keep getting bigger. Two months away from an event, people start to freak out about all the details. That's where Happily comes in. We fill all of the gaps in the logistics. Our mission is to make sure events are executed better than the way that they were planned.

"Happily puts out fires all the time" Sarah continues. "We test prospective associates for their flexibility, ingenuity, and equanimity when confronted by the unexpected. We present scenarios written by senior producers inside of Happily and myself and ask, 'How do you respond to this?' We've had over 50,000 people apply to work with us. Everybody loves taking the exams. They're tough, because there's a layer of subjectivity to them."

Sarah describes Happily as "sort of like an execution layer in the stack of experiential. (We've evolved to also offer creative agency services as a layer on top of the execution.) We're the onsite team, so we feel all of the mistakes. We troubleshoot them, live and in real time. Sometimes companies will get so overwhelmed when they have like thousands of people coming through the door, they miss important interactions. They can, for example, forget to greet people.

"We'll break it down to an executional instruction. 'You have 10 seconds. Here are the five words that you can say in those 10 seconds: Thank you for being here,'" she explains. "'Thank you for being here' helps people realize that they are now stepping out of their homes, their cars, whatever. The phrase makes people feel present, and also graciously makes them feel a part of the conversation. It invites people to participate and engage."

While Sarah has lots of practical secrets like this one to share, she also always looks to see what changes may be on the horizon. "You've got artificial intelligence. You have blockchain that's coming out, and that's the future. There's all this tech stuff that will redefine the future of work and life. As AI automates things, and blockchain starts to actually help distribute work across the planet, then the layer that actually needs the highest quality of work is going to be the creative layer.

"In this future, we will have free time because the robots will be doing tasks for us," she adds. "What are we going to do with that time? How are we going to stay relevant? That's where that creative economy comes in.

"The whole thing about artificial intelligence is that it becomes, essentially, smarter than us. We're becoming more and more dependent upon our devices, and we're feeding them our personal data. AI looks at individual data multiplied hundreds of thousands of times and anonymized. AI will be able to predict behaviors in our lives. It'll break our behaviors down to a science. But the future won't be one where we, as humans, have become repetitive and predictable, because that creative layer will help us reimagine and re-contextualize ourselves. This is going to be the most important piece of continuing evolution and innovation.

"Anyone in the events business," she continues, "knows that experiences and events and face-to-face interactions with somebody are where the real, unpredictable magic happens. AI will be trying to basically capture and bottle that magic. And every time they bottle it, we are going to use creativity to shift again and keep innovating."

Sarah created an event, EXP, to bring experience economy pioneers together to share best practices in an experiential learning environment. As you would expect, every step was thought out. "We intentionally kept the guest count super low. We started out with one-on-ones, putting two people together and saying, 'Figure out why we put you together.' Next, we moved into workshops of five to eight people. Tiny workshops, 90 minutes long, intended to be super deep dives on a subject matter. Getting into things that people usually don't talk about. Small workshops so that you become best friends with the people that are in there with you. People have enough time to share what their struggles are or ask questions and get into it. Then, we double it and have groups of 20, 25 people engage in local activities that have a social impact component. We'll be documenting information from work-shops and putting it in a book that people can buy, so that there will be lessons learned that are democratized and shared with everyone.

"Thinking about that creative economy future," she says, "my best advice to anyone at any stage of their career is to figure out what makes you different and just do a lot more of that—and keep going."

WHAT WE HEARD AND LEARNED

- Network with freelance talent
- Embrace changes on the horizon
- Look to make a social impact locally
- Find your talent and keep going

JOHN WOO

CONNECTING PHYSICAL AND VIRTUAL AUDIENCES BY BREAKING THE "FIFTH WALL" IN HYBRID GATHERINGS

"Ultimately, events are about converting hearts and minds to your message, your platform."

JOHN WOO, COLLABORATION ARTIST

JOHN WOO IS the senior vice president of creative and strategy at Spiro, a global brand experience agency and part of the GES Collective, one of the world's most experienced face-to-face event organizations. As 2020 halted face to face events, John and his colleagues met the challenge of hybrid and virtual events with a combination of calmness and innovative thinking.

The calmness came from their sense that many things are fundamentally unchanged. John says, "The attendee journey really hasn't changed at all. Whether it's a hybrid or IRL or fully remote…they're all live experiences with and for someone." Today, as the lines between IRL and URL have become even more blurred, the team still approaches the challenge of how to reach audiences where they are vs. a more traditional methodology. "You can really be smart with your technology," he notes, "but you shouldn't let your technology drive what the experience is. You really need to get back to the core of why you're doing an event, who it's for, and then build from that point."

For John, it all starts with a deep understanding of the audience. "The more that we know about them, the better. When you really start thinking about it, you have a target demographic, and you have subgroups within that demographic. It's actually easier for us now to really sub-identify these subgroups and these sub-cultures. We can deliver better and more tailored messages to them in order to try to create stronger connections with the content, the messaging platform, and what we're trying to communicate about the brand."

But it's about more than just the content, John cautions. "You need to know how your audience is consuming it. We get inside the social media feeds. We see what they're talking about online. You start to see behavior patterns. Some people will be really big outliers who want to adopt everything. Other people will be stealth-lurking in the middle of your chat room, listening to everything and only putting their own point of view out every once in a while. You have to start digging a little deeper between those layers to identify who those people are and what the right experience is for them. How does it translate for them online (URL) or in person (IRL) or both?"

John describes a few of the typical personalities they are encountering. "There are 'browsers,' people who walk quickly by the experience and see if they like it or not before they engage—people who love to multitask, especially online. You get that a lot when you're doing breakout sessions or even a live session, because people want to try to catch a little bit of everything," she says. "Then there are the ones who are super-focused. They're very organized, very planned. They're very intentional about what they do, and who they connect with in-person or online. Then there are people who are real big brand advocates and loyalists. They're your ambassadors, your amplifiers."

John emphasizes that getting those types identified early on really helps in experience design. "Audience intelligence facilitates customization of experiences. Ultimately, brand experiences and events are about converting hearts and minds to your message, your platform. Is it really enough to convert one person and let them be an amplifier for your message? Do you try to find the outliers in your chat rooms and the ones that kind of dive in and check out your website every once in a while, and target them specifically with experiences?"

The Spiro team gets innovative when they think about the implications of new channel and medium agnostic ways audiences attend events and brand experiences. "We have been talking about the idea of 'the fifth wall,'" John explains. "They say 'the fourth wall' is between the audience and the story, or between the story reader and the story itself. In the theater, it is the imaginary separation between the stage and the audience. The fifth wall happens in the spaces and experiences in-between – connecting the IRL and URL attendees. The fifth wall is between the online audience and the in-person audience. An event is really about networking around common ideas and thoughts and like-minded people. To be able to connect the people that are online and in-person we need to bridge that fifth wall."

John illustrates the concept further with an example. "You know how when you went to any event in the past, there was typically a big photo op area at the start of the experience? What if you had a large wall there that was actually made up of iPad screens, and on all the iPads were the faces of the online attendees who were welcoming the in-person audience? The online people would get a chance to be the ones who welcome people into the physical exhibit space. If you take it further, an in-person attendee could take an iPad off the wall and walk around with it."

John also issues some very practical cautions about panel discussions. "If you stick to a script too much, then there's no spontaneous interaction—and what's the point of the panel? Also, when you think about a panel meant to facilitate participation across multichannel attendees, you have to be careful about the technology you choose. Some multiple screen technologies don't handle interruptions well. You can literally have five people talking at the same time, and no one will hear anything."

John also has suggestions to make about program length. "People don't tend to retain a lot. Especially when it's too long of a format. We try to go for bite-sized nuggets, meeting the audience where they're at. We're taking large, 45-minute sessions and turning them into 15- to 20-minute sessions. It's like crafting a good headline, and it changes the format a lot. Your headline is not meant to be three sentences long. Your headline is meant to be big, punchy, impactful, and memorable.

You just need to make sure you hit your salient points, and then people can walk away with something that they can share. The editing process has become much more important now, because you can't just give someone an hour of platform—people will just tune out."

Paradoxically, John points out that while programs are getting shorter, events are getting longer. "The event has a different definition than it did a short while ago. 'During the event or brand moment' is now a much longer period of time because it lives so long online. Even those who participate in person can still access and experience the content online."

"Humans crave connection to each other," he says. "And it is our job as experience designers and creators in this post-covid era to facilitate the fifth wall connection, to meet the audiences where they are, and to push the boundaries of blending our digital and physical realities."

WHAT WE HEARD AND LEARNED

- Clarify your goals when gathering
- Look for subgroups within your group
- Don't just focus on the content; know how your audience is consuming it
- Go for bite-sized nuggets of content

LET WONDER LEAD...

CURIOSITY

LISA BELZBERG

CONSCIOUS CONNECTOR
BREAKS DOWN BARRIERS TO
CREATE LARGER CARING
COMMUNITIES

"People are craving intimacy and friendship and genuine, authentic relation-
ships. Once I know what they want, it feels right to put them together."

LISA BELZBERG, COLLABORATION ARTIST

LISA BELZBERG IS A CONSCIOUS, almost compulsive, continuous connector. Her social calendar is crowded with events like dinner parties, where she brings together people who she feels would benefit from knowing each other. She thinks deeply about how to make each guest comfortable and how to engage them. At times, over the years, she has used her prodigious, natural social skills to create sustainable collaborations. A good example is the organization PENCIL and its Principal for a Day program, which she started and ran before turning it over to new management talent.

Lisa explains the inspiration for the initiative. "I had walked by schools and thought, 'I'd really like to know what's going on in there.' I asked myself, 'How can we gain entry into the schools?' As I began to do a little bit of homework, I realized the schools are very isolated, which means that the principals are very isolated, which means, in terms of public education, Black, brown, and low SES children are further isolated. There's 1,000 reasons in every urban and rural area why that ought not be the case. There is every social, emotional, societal, and economic issue why public school students, the customers and workforce of tomorrow, should be more integrated into their cities. At the same time, there are principals who haven't had an opportunity to learn what's going on outside of their building because they're always putting out fires. I thought, 'Let's see if we can just completely, organically, bridge these gaps by getting business and community leaders into schools, and actually into the principal's office.' The initial commitment was easy: a day."

Lisa makes it clear the initiative was not about asking for money. It was about developing a relationship between two communities that share geographic areas but are often worlds apart. The idea was to bring an interested CEO into a school principal's office for a day to experience the day-to-day rewards and challenges. "It was about the greater civic community understanding what's going on in its classrooms," she says. "The key to it was them gathering together. Then they develop relationships because a CEO and a principal have the same issues. There were plenty of principals who said, 'That CEO was great, but what I really need is someone who's four or five years out of college. I can use the CEO for my own professional development, but my kids can't relate to him. My kids need someone closer to them, so they can say, "I can do that. I see your path now."' We continually evolved it based on the feedback. The key to all of it was just really listening."

Deep, authentic interest and curiosity was a key in the program's success. If an outsider CEO came into a school thinking, "I'm coming to help out these poor public schools," there could be a problem, Lisa explains. "But if they start the process thinking, 'I'm coming in because I really want to learn what's going on. I need to learn about it for my business. I need to understand it for the tax base of the city.' Then you can have mutually beneficial relationships."

Lisa watched as each year the program grew and grew. While there was never an expectation of money, many acts of collaborative generosity ensued. "There was a classroom of kids in grade 11 who needed SAT tutoring," Lisa remembers. "A company paid for a bus that would bring them to their office twice a week to learn and practice

SAT strategies. Employees of the company got to do some rewarding SAT tutoring, and the students got the experience of seeing what an office looks like. Those kids had more of a chance of college. The larger focus was always about connections and making connections. It was about creating community in New York City, as opposed to having public schools in silos."

At regular monthly meetings, it became clear how much everyone was learning—and as the program grew, its impact expanded. "Bodega owners who participated thought, 'The kids who walk by are part of my community, I have a responsibility to them. If I see them skipping school, I can report it to the principal.'"

When new programs were piloted and spun off, there was no empire building. "We, as an organization, wanted no naming control or power over anything," Lisa explains. "We were involved in the first years to make sure that the program got off the ground, and then you never heard our name again—because you don't need to. The program was established in school after school, city after city, country after country, bringing together communities that have mutuality of interest but didn't know how to enter each other's worlds."

Lisa is currently focusing on smaller, more intimate collaborations. "I'm going to continue making sure there's genuine intimacy amongst people that fosters goals and concrete accomplishments. People are craving intimacy and friendship and genuine, authentic relationships. Once I know what they want, it feels right to put them together."

Lisa is a big proponent of social gatherings to foster those moments. "People are craving intimacy and friendship and genuine, authentic relationships. Once I know what they want, it feels right to put them together."

WHAT WE HEARD AND LEARNED

- Bridge gaps by putting people in places unfamiliar to them
- Start with a small commitment, like a day together
- Go into new environments genuinely curious about what happens there
- Let programs expand organically

SARAH BROWN

QUIET ACTIVIST, SPOUSE OF FORMER BRITISH PRIME MINISTER, TAKES DELIBERATE STEPS TO CREATE CHANGE

"All the time you're getting closer to the truth. New knowledge brings you new vantage points, and new information."

SARAH BROWN, COLLABORATION ARTIST

SARAH BROWN HAS BEEN INVOLVED with activism and movements for change since she was a teenager. She is the chair of the UK charity, Theirworld, and she's the executive chair of the Global Business Coalition for Education.

Furthermore, she has friends in high places. She's married to Gordon Brown, who served as prime minister of the United Kingdom from 2007 to 2010, and has had a unique vantage point to see how change is made at the top. Her campaigns have seen her team up with activist supermodel Naomi Campbell, former U.S. First Lady Michelle Obama, and global legends from Graça Machel and Melinda Gates to Bono and Annie Lennox.

Sarah, who actively works to make the world better, has very clear ideas about how to make things happen—and she makes active use of her significant profile and platform. "It never occurred to me," Sarah says, "that there wasn't something you could do or an action you could take. Everybody can play their part, and everyone can do something. You've got to work out what you want to change. Who's the person that can change it? If you can't make the change, someone else has to do it. And when's a good time to do it? Just because you've decided something should change doesn't mean that the person who can make the change agrees with you, or that they could do it that day, or that they've even got all the information to make that decision."

Sarah sees engineering change as a process like the scientific method. She advocates for trying something out and, if it doesn't work, then trying a different route. "All the time, you're getting closer to the truth," she explains. "New knowledge brings you new vantage points and new information. So you then change the way you're going about it."

In her mind, there is a clear process as well for getting those you need to work with you to willingly collaborate. "Once you know the thing you want to change and who can do it," she explains, "then think about what the journey is for that person. You have to think about what it is that's going to facilitate them making a decision, unlocking the political world for something, deciding to put a budget towards something, deciding to change a piece of legislation, all of those things. How are you going to persuade them, and how are you going to give them the opportunity to do it? It's crucial to find a good moment for them. Not your moment; *their* moment."

"Once you've got their moment in your mind," Sarah continues, "You have got to put the pieces together for them. Make it easy for them to do what you want them to do. Then you have to mobilize as many people and voices as you can to persuade that person to take that moment. If you can mobilize the different groups in communities, all asking for the same thing, you're a lot closer to getting the person who can make a difference doing so."

Suffice it to say, when it comes to creating change, Sarah believes in planning. "What I have learned, particularly from my time being in government—but it was even obvious before—is you have to do the preparatory work. Once you're in the room, it's too late."

Sarah is realistic about the teams that form to create specific changes. "You're not going to have everyone pulling together all the time. You've got to galvanize and create good moments where everyone can come together. And in the meantime, people are going to go and do their own thing and build their own things that they're doing. Also, other things come up along the way."

To get to the point of being a collaboration artist creating real change with Theirworld—which uses all of its connections and expertise around advocacy to really look at what's coming up next at United Nations meetings—Sarah had to go through some learning experiences. "I've had to learn how to use my own voice. For a long time, I thought you could do it quietly. You could write the letters and hold the placards and organize events and let someone else speak," she says. "But I found that if you do that, then you lose the chance to deliver the precise message that you want to be heard."

Sarah's early lack of comfort and experience speaking in public ultimately led to an important lesson: "There's a brilliant opportunity when you don't think anyone's looking to learn to hone your voice. I made the terrible mistake of waiting until I had a big platform and then deciding I needed to speak on it," she says. "I had to make some of the world's worst speeches of all time in front of people who were actually listening. I'm not joking when I say this: I boldly invited some of my friends to the very first public speech I gave to a big audience. I was speaking for a group called One Parent Families about the issues that were facing single-parent families. I got to the end of the speech, and I passed out cold. I'd spoken very well, but I'd forgotten to breathe. I fainted in front of everybody. One of my top tips is that breathing is really important!"

Sarah also had to gain some perspective. "I've had to learn over the years that not everyone's going to like what you're asking for or think it's convenient or think it's helpful. They may think that you're a bit annoying."

Sarah believes that finding and using your own voice can be transformative. "You've always got a slightly bigger sphere than you think you have. Learn to use your voice, write a good letter, get out there," she advises. "People are always looking for somebody who can speak up for an issue. You'll get invited to the next thing, then you'll get invited back. You become the good person that can talk up for something."

WHAT WE HEARD AND LEARNED

- Know the change you want
- Identify the person that can make it happen
- Mobilize voices to persuade that person
- Create the right moment for that change agent to act

COLIN COWIE
CELEBRITY EVENT PROFESSIONAL INTERSECTS HOSPITALITY AND ENTERTAINMENT TO MOTIVATE ACTION

"It's all about how I make you feel. We are continually manipulating and enhancing all the senses to tell a story with a carefully thought-out beginning, middle, and end."

COLIN COWIE, COLLABORATION ARTIST

COLIN COWIE, founder of New York-based Colin Cowie Lifestyle, is one of the great celebrity event professionals. His approach to designing truly special events is so different that he had to coin a phrase to describe it: Colin Cowie Hospitainment. He defines this as "the crossroad where traditional hospitality meets programmed entertainment in a way that we get to tell a meaningful story."

Colin is all about stories. "I think it's our responsibility to listen deeply and to tell stories—and to be a good storyteller, you have to be a good listener," he says. Colin sees opportunities to tell stories everywhere, and he tells them with sound, with light, with props, with colors—with anything that will appeal to the senses. He tells stories with words too, in a deep, rich voice and a slight accent that reveals that he's originally from Zambia.

To give you an idea of how he thinks about stories, here's what he thought about one of the more prosaic environments in our world today: an elevator. "We do a lot of work with real estate developers," Colin explains. "In most places, an elevator is a single, harsh experience with bright, white light. For me, an elevator is an opportunity to tell the story. Here's how the experience can change throughout the day. In my world, there's classical music in the morning at eight o'clock. It's bright and it's light. At six o'clock in the evening, it's a different rhythm. The light is dimmed down, and the volume comes up a bit. And by midnight, it's sexy. The lighting has come way down, and the music has changed. That tells a story. We are continually changing and enhancing all the senses to tell a story with a carefully thought-out beginning, middle, and end."

Colin thinks of his events, and even of his presentations to clients, as opportunities for seduction. He's always looking for a chance to further enchant an audience. But his seductions are never about himself. "Every person, every couple, every car, every hotel, every product has its own DNA. We start with that DNA, and we tell a story that's further enhanced morning, noon, and night. Add to that spring, summer, winter, and fall, and we're looking at different colors, different textures, different temperatures. This allows us to tell a unique story every single time. And that way, no two things will ever look the same."

Colin and his team find the DNA by asking a lot of questions. A few of them might be: "Where do you vacation? Do you have a favorite color? Can you identify a favorite flower? What are your favorite restaurants? Do you follow a particular designer? How do you entertain in your home? How do you prefer to be entertained? Where do you go when you travel?

"People open up because they love talking about themselves," Colin explains. "And then of course, you study their Pinterest board, Facebook page, and Instagram account. This information allows us to proactively create a guest experience we know will resonate with them and create an emotional connection. That is the goal with every client."

In an oversaturated world, Colin is a ruthless editor. "It's about knowing which 90 percent to say no to so I can figure out the 10 percent I can use to tell a compelling story. That way we're telling their story with their ingredients. It's not about us. It's all about them."

Colin's story is inspiring in itself. After a stretch in the military, he decided that he didn't want to spend his hardest-working years in places like South Africa during Apartheid. "So, I came to the United States" he reveals, "with $400, a big dream, one suit, and an ever-present sun tan."

Colin started in Africa and is now based in New York and Miami, but the big breaks that launched his career happened in California. He started at the bottom of the ladder. "I got a job at a catering company, and I watched what they did. I figured out what the rental company did. And six weeks later, I resigned and started my own business. I called it Colin Cowie Lifestyle—and this was before everybody started using the term lifestyle.

"It was a small catering company," he continues. "I ended up doing a luncheon for the producer of the movie *The Graduate*, whom I'd met the year before in the south of France. I was at their house for lunch and his wife told me she was having a party in two weeks' time for LACMA, one of the museums. I offered to help with the party."

Colin says his big break started when he was teaching cooking classes at the Beverly Hills High School adult program. "One day, a lady asked, 'Can you freeze pasta?' I replied, 'Why would you want to do that when it takes only eight minutes to cook?' One of the students in the class was the wife of the president of *Playboy*, Hugh Hefner. She asked me to be a food consultant for an upcoming event. She asked me what I would do for an event they had been planning. I jumped in and told and retold the story eight or nine times. Each time, it got bigger and better. Then, I looked up and saw, standing in front of me, Hugh Hefner in his pajamas. He asked, 'Can you do this?' I had two months, and absolutely no clue how I was going to do it. And I think it was probably one of the best-produced events I've ever done."

WHAT WE HEARD AND LEARNED

- Find the "story DNA" of those who gather
- Be a good listener
- Tell stories with sound, light, props, colors, as well as words
- Seduce your participants

LAUREN KOTKIN
PHILANTHROPIC SPECIALIST HELPS UNLOCK THE RICHES AND ENERGY OF THE WORLD THROUGH CONFERENCES

"We can have four generations in conference sessions. Someone who is a Millennial could be sitting at a table and sharing different ideas with a Greatest Generation person."

LAUREN KOTKIN, COLLABORATION ARTIST

LAUREN KOTKIN IS the senior director of education for Exponent Philanthropy, a Washington, D.C.-based association for small staffed foundations. The association has been gathering for conferences for more than 20 years—and recently has made a major change in how the content for its conference sessions is developed.

"Exponent Philanthropy," Lauren explains, "is a membership association of what we like to call 'lean funders.' In a lean organization, you just have a couple of people and everyone wears multiple hats and really knows what's going on. Since many of the participants work in relative isolation, the social and networking aspects of the every-other-year conferences are highly valued."

The two-and-a-half day conferences differ in many ways from typical conferences. They are built over an unusually long timeline because Exponent Philanthropy likes to post descriptions of all of the sessions when it opens up registration six months before the conference, so that its members can decide if they want to attend and start considering which sessions they want to participate in. For years, they built the program via a small group of staffers. "For 20 years," Lauren explains, "we curated all the content in-house. Seven or eight staff members would each plan seven or eight sessions, including finding speakers and crafting the content.

"Recently, we heard from members that they wanted to be more active in conference design, so we opened up the process, inviting session proposals," Lauren continues. "We were hoping to bring new voices, but there were also certain stories in this community that are worth retelling over and over. We have some very inspiring members who we will bring back on multiple occasions because we want more people to hear that message. The selection of which sessions to accept was done in a name-blind mode. The reviewers do not see who was behind the proposals. Once they made their recommendations, we looked at the list. Sure enough, there were new names."

The challenge for Lauren and her team was how to get member voices to be more active in conference design while still maintaining content quality. "When we issued a call for sessions for the next conference, we built in a process where those who wanted to design sessions were coached by me and a colleague," she notes. "The very first step in our coaching process was to have them get on calls with us to talk about their content. We had two or three required phone calls with each content session designer around content, as well as optional ones after that to really get at the crux of what they are trying to do in the session. The biggest problem was lack of focus. When you think about a conference session, you want to help participants focus in on the one thing you want people to remember when they walk away."

A big part of those calls, Lauren adds, was making sure that it was not too much for the timeframe. "Sometimes we'd tell them, 'You have 75 minutes,' and they'd send us a plan for two and a half hours of content. I always felt, 'You have 75 minutes. It's not that I didn't give you enough time. It's that you haven't yet created the best program to get what you need to get across.'"

A key part of enabling the new session content developers was giving them a guidebook that reflected years of experience. Another aspect of the coaching process was starting with a required webinar to learn about the conference and the audience. "This audience is very particular," Lauren says, "and content should reflect who they are. We're very confident we understand our audience, but not every session designer or speaker is necessarily as familiar with the community. This is an opportunity to explain who is in your audience so we know the speaker will be speaking to the audience. Conference sessions are more likely to be successful when the speaker really knows who is out there."

Lauren illustrates the value of this component. "It's a small nuance, but how you talk about grant size matters. A speaker might use a $2 million grant as an example, when the average grant size among our members is closer to $30,000 to $40,000. It's hard to relate to that example when you think, 'We don't have $2 million.'"

An important step in the coaching process is refining the session title, she adds. "I have a great admiration for newspaper headline writers. They summarize exactly what's in the article and the feeling of it, whether it's going to be a movie review, whether it's going to be a positive or negative review, if there's a slight twist on the content. We try to emulate that with our titles and our descriptions to get at the crux of the matter—in an entertaining way, if possible.

"After the title, there's a short 50-to-60-word description, with perhaps two or three bullet points on learning objectives," Lauren continues. "We also include session formats, so if you are really not in the mood for small-group discussions, you can pick a different session that may have a different format, such as speakers.

"You can read about what people say will happen to philanthropy because millennials are here. What we're seeing is, it's the same energy. It's very inspirational to do philanthropy, and it also can be crushingly hard because you're trying to solve something."

Lauren expects the Exponent Philanthropy conferences to keep evolving and keep welcoming new voices. "We can have four generations in conference sessions. Someone who is a millennial could be sitting at a table and sharing different ideas with a Greatest Generation person."

WHAT WE HEARD AND LEARNED

- Engage your community in content development
- Clarify content focus and tailor to your audience
- Support new content developers with tools and scaffolding
- Bring multiple generations together to build on each other's perspectives

ANITA MCBRIDE

D.C. INSIDER SHINES SPOTLIGHT ON THE POWER OF FIRST LADIES

"Through history, first ladies feel a sense of responsibility as a figure that many people look up to. They are caretakers, almost mothers of the nation in a certain way."

ANITA MCBRIDE, COLLABORATION ARTIST

ANITA MCBRIDE PLAYED essential roles in several U.S. presidential administrations. She has, for example, tackled the daunting operational issues involved in transitions between presidents. She also played a key role in the staggering number of changes that were made in the wake of September 11, 2001, to make the White House safer. Her practical competence and command of how things get done in Washington is impressive. She's the embodiment of the spirit that has kept our government going.

Anita also has a unique perspective on a set of women who have played a tremendous, but often under-appreciated, role—and she feels that we could all benefit from knowing a bit more about how they operated and contributed.

One of the many high points of her career was serving as chief of staff to First Lady Laura Bush from 2005 to 2009. She directed the staff's work on the wide variety of domestic and global initiatives in which Mrs. Bush was involved. She had primary responsibility for the first lady's efforts to support U.S. foreign policy objectives in human rights, women's empowerment, global health, and human freedom. She also directed Mrs. Bush's travels to 67 countries in four years, including historic visits to Afghanistan, the Middle East, and the Thai-Burma border.

Her current work as executive-in-residence at the Center for Congressional and Presidential Studies in the School of Public Affairs at American University in Washington, D.C., is greatly informed by her experiences with various first ladies. She directs programming and national conferences on the legacies of America's first ladies (the First Ladies Initiative) and their historical influence on politics, policy, and global diplomacy. She has been collaborating with co-authors on a book that tells the stories of the frequently under-appreciated contributions of first ladies.

Shining a spotlight on the first ladies is consistent with Anita's sense of how Washington actually works. "Political wives have unsung power. Any organization that needs support would be wise to call on the spouses of elected members of Congress. For that matter, a spouse of any head of any organization—corporate, philanthropic, whatever—can be an important resource.

"I study first ladies and think about future first spouses," she adds. "It's a different role than that of president. The president has a raft of defined statutory obligations. The First Spouse doesn't have a position description at all. Some of what they choose to do is based on their expertise and interests. Other things are thrust upon them. That said, the two positions are collaborative and complementary. Through history, first ladies have felt a sense of responsibility as a figure that many people look up to. They are caretakers, almost mothers of the nation in a certain way. Every single American, whether they supported their husband or not, should feel that their first lady cares about them."

Anita cites two first ladies as being particularly important in the evolution of the role. "Eleanor Roosevelt pioneered the role of activist first lady. No one before or after has come close to her in that. She ushered in a different view of the role of first lady, even though the structure around her was minimal. She pretty much redefined the position on her own with a few female journalists that she had befriended, some White House staff, and resident staff.

"The first lady that put the structure in place for a bonafide Office of the First Lady with resources and personnel was Rosalyn Carter," Anita continues. "She had chaired the Mental Health Commission for the state of Georgia for her husband when he was Governor of Georgia. When they came to Washington, he wanted to put her in charge of a National Mental Health Commission—but the rules governing personnel at the time did not allow a family member to have an official role. (This is the post-Bobby Kennedy days.) Rosalyn did not want just an honorary chairmanship title, because she thought that implied someone who showed up for photo ops and cut ribbons. She really knew her material on this, and she wanted to dive into it. It caused a ruckus amongst the Office of Legal Counsel, Department of Justice, and the White House Counsel's office. There was nothing in place governing whether an actual first lady could take on an official role if appointed by the president. The upshot was a complete review of the authorities vested in the White House to assign personnel and staff to the first lady. That led to the White House Personnel Authorization Act of 1978, which formally created Office of First Lady positions. It changed everything."

Anita recounts how First Lady Barbara Bush made an instinctive gesture that had a profound impact. "In 1989, there was tremendous stigma around AIDS. People didn't know how you got it. Could you get it by touching someone? By being in the same room? Barbara Bush went into an orphanage in D.C. where a baby was dying of AIDS, and she picked up and hugged that child. It was a bold thing to do, but Barbara Bush didn't think of it in that way. She was a mother and a grandmother, and a child was sick and needed a hug. When Barbara Bush died, the woman who had run that center was interviewed and she said that the first lady hugging that child when people were so fearful of being around anybody with AIDS changed everything."

Anita continues, "In contrast, one figure in history who did not get the credit for what she overcame, what she contributed, and what she could have contributed is First Lady Pat Nixon. The history books need to be reopened on her, and really examine what a leader she really was. There are so many aspects to her and her life that people just don't know, from her being the caretaker of her family at an early age, to putting herself through University of Southern California, to her effort that 'people are my project,' encouraging a spirit of volunteerism in our country. She was one of the most traveled first ladies in history and the only first lady to be designated as 'official representative of the United States' on her diplomatic travels. More historic preservation and acquisitions for the White House collection happened under her, more than any other first lady, including Jackie Kennedy. But she was maltreated by the president's inner circle, who did not want Mrs. Nixon to have a high-profile role. Yet she persevered as best as she could. She helped to lead an effort within the Nixon administration to get more women hired in senior positions in the federal government. These stories of Pat Nixon are not widely known. Because of her husband's unpopularity and the Watergate scandal, her significant contributions are overlooked."

First Lady Laura Bush got a bit more credit for her good works— but Anita, who worked closely with her, still feels that she is underappreciated. Anita had met Laura Bush at various times, and she was aware of what the first lady was capable of before she got the call about the chief of staff position.

When she was working in White House management and administration, a colleague told her what Mrs. Bush had done with her staff the day after the 9/11 attacks. "We had all been told the night before, via a communications tree, to come back to work. It was important for the world to see the White House back at work. Mrs. Bush gathered all her staff together. She wanted to hear from each of them. What happened to them? Where did they go? How were they doing? She brought in a Methodist minister to pray with her staff and to give them strength."

Laura Bush's actions in the wake of 9/11 are emblematic of a shift that Anita noticed. "There was more empathy from that point on. The country was experiencing so much grief and shock. We lost 3,000 people. We realized that there were people out there determined to kill us. There was empathy for the families, for the friends, for the country. Empathy for each other."

While Anita works actively to center and elevate the first ladies, she seems to underplay her own collaboration prowess. "I think people trusted me to have an answer—or if I didn't have an answer that I would get one. I wanted to solve people's challenges. I really loved the work."

WHAT WE HEARD AND LEARNED

- First ladies have their own agendas
- First ladies can have more flexibility than the president
- First ladies gestures have huge cultural impact
- First ladies rise to the occasion during crises

ROGER NIERENBERG

TEACHING BUSINESSPEOPLE COLLABORATION THROUGH IMMERSION IN THE ORCHESTRA EXPERIENCE

"I wanted to create a circumstance where people who were not initiated, who did not perform when they were children, would actually feel the music."

ROGER NIERENBERG, COLLABORATION ARTIST

ROGER NIERENBERG IS a veteran classical music conductor and the creator of the Music Paradigm, a learning experience that helps organizations become more effective by giving participants a chance to sit inside a professional symphony orchestra as the musicians and conductor solve problems together.

Roger's original goal and passion was for a broad cultural change. "The kind of music that I love, that I believe in, was year by year becoming less important," he explains. "Fewer and fewer people felt it was relevant to them. There were large parts of the population that were untouched by this music. I wanted to see if I could do something about that. I wanted to create a circumstance where people who were not initiated, who did not perform when they were children, would actually feel the music. I asked myself, 'Where did I fall in love with music? How did it happen to me?' For me, unquestionably, it was sitting in the orchestra, playing. I felt this electricity and this energy and the vibrations on my body. I thought,

'That's where I want people to be. I want them to have that experience.'"

In the course of figuring out how to bring classical music to life for more people, Roger discovered a powerful way to help organizations of all kinds become more collaborative. Part of the challenge of getting people to appreciate classical music is, he says, that "many people are quite blocked, quite inhibited, about classical music." He explains that the moment people understand the experience is about classical music, they are not sure that they're really going to appreciate it. "They don't like that feeling. They're intimidated."

Roger wanted to create an environment that was definitely not intimidating. So he focused the subject not on music, but on things that people feel competent and strong about—their own careers. The discussions became about collaborating, about leadership, about diversity—about whatever was most relevant to a particular group's values. While their minds were occupied thinking about those issues, Roger found participants became curious and open to the music. "Once they're in that state," he says, "the music can reach them. It can really affect them."

Conversely, Roger found that focusing on how an orchestra performed was a great way to get people to think about the critical collaborative issues they and their organizations faced. "We start off with very simple observations," he explains. "I ask the participants to choose a musician and just observe their amazing coordination, strength, speed, whatever. Then, I look around and pick somebody who seems to be engrossed in what's going on. I hand the microphone to them and say, 'So, what did you see?' And they make some kind of observation.

"My job is to contextualize that observation and show that there's real wisdom in what they've said," he continues. "From those observations, it becomes observations about teams, and then it becomes observations about the whole. I start to draw inferences from those observations about the way people work, because fundamentally the way musicians work is the way other people work—except it happens really fast in amazing feats of collaboration."

Part of why this approach works is that orchestras are highly collaborative to begin with, so they can provide concentrated examples of how things work and how they can go wrong. "Orchestras are by their nature collaborative," Roger points out. "There are people who are skilled as soloists, but they know that what the orchestra is about is the *collective* of how they play."

Roger, like any great conductor, brings a distinct vision and passion to his work—but he is acutely aware that a major part of his job is to listen and understand where his participants are, and then meet them there. "No orchestra is going to play it exactly the way that I've imagined it. So, I listen to the orchestra and, at the same time, listen to my idealized version. I subtract one from the other, and I arrive at a gap analysis that shows me what needs to be done in order to bring them closer to each other."

Roger applies a similar analytical process to figuring out what needs to happen to integrate a new member or temporary replacement into his orchestra. Then he provides the new member with *experience*, not instruction. "I'll create some kind of collaborative exercise for them," he explains. "I'll try to figure out what element of collaboration will come most easily. Will it be tuning together? Will it be the ensemble? Will it be creating the sound? I want to find some way that they can succeed at collaborating. That opens the process. It also gives you a success model that you can refer to. 'Remember how well we did that? Can we do that with this passage?'"

WHAT WE HEARD AND LEARNED

- Get people curious by asking them to make observations
- Identify gaps in where you are versus where you want to be, and look for remedies
- Do a small thing together, like tuning your instruments
- Determine where participants can successfully collaborate— and build on that

CHARLIE PALMER

CHEF AND HOST COOKS UP
COLLABORATIVE EXPERIENCES

"The dining experience brings people together. It inspires conversation. It makes people think and talk about things—not just food and wine, but about their lives. I think that's a really important thing for us in the world that we live in today."

CHARLIE PALMER, COLLABORATION ARTIST

CHARLIE PALMER GRADUATED from the Culinary Institute of America and then went on to build the Charlie Palmer Collective, which includes restaurants, hotels, and event spaces across the country. He has taken his expertise in food and wine and applied it in creating environments where people collaborate and in helping young people learn to be better citizens in their communities. Along the way, he has supported many charities, especially those in the communities where he operates. He has even orchestrated collaboration by great chefs in an annual fundraising event he created.

"The dining experience brings people together," he says. "It inspires conversation. It makes people think and talk about things— not just food and wine, but about their lives. I think that's a really important thing for us in the world that we live in today."

Charlie has responded to market demand by providing more corporate and group experiences. "People are so much more knowledgeable, in general, about food and wine and dining, no matter what walk of life they're from," Charlie explains. "They're bolder and interested in digging deeper. There's this massive interest in food and where it comes from, how it's grown, and the magic of the kitchen." Charlie, who spends a lot of time in California's wine country, is particularly aware of how people are thinking about wine. "There's great interest in so many people about, say, a specific varietal, how it's made, what happens in the vineyard, what makes it different.

"Our approach," he continues, "has been to add something special to everything we do. We add things to move the experience from being a simple dinner to being a special dinner for 25 or 40. For example, we could start with an informal panel discussion during the cocktail hour. And then part of each course could be a little demonstration of one ingredient or technique that's going in this dish, or one thing. A lot goes on in the kitchen that people really don't know about. It makes sense to create a simple, quick demonstration—that 'aha' moment of 'Hey, this is how that's done.'"

Charlie also makes these events different from a typical fine-dining experience by adding media. "We'll add a 12-by-14-foot visual screen to a sit-down dinner not as the center of attention, but as a complementary background. Imagine seeing an entire field of artichokes when we are demonstrating an artichoke course."

To deliver amazing experiences across his hospitality empire, Charlie has to rely on teams. He keeps those teams aligned with his sensibilities with a simple guideline: Be nice. "Everything we do in hospitality boils down to just being nice to people. Once people realize that you're nice, everything is so much more enjoyable. Everything's so much more relaxed. Everything tastes better. We've had tough customers, people who are not naturally relaxed or easy-going. But when they react to niceness, they're different people. They realize that you really care about them, that you really want to take care of them. You really want them to have a great time. It just changes the playing field."

Charlie sees his long involvement with City Meals on Wheels, a charity that delivers meals to the home-bound elderly that might not eat otherwise, as logical. "For someone who cooks for a living, who nurtures people, it's just a natural thing because we're feeding people —whether we're getting paid for it or donating our time."

At one point, Charlie was even able to create a high school cooking program that fed into City Meals on Wheels. "We took kids who were interested in food. They prepared meals in one of the kitchens and delivered them. They were learning how to cook and learning kitchens, but they also learned how to be a good person. All my children have helped make deliveries. There's nothing more inspiring."

Charlie's own event, Pigs and Pinot, has been growing for over a dozen years. "It started as a simple dinner where some winemaker friends of mine and I raised money to build a library for the local school." In recent years, the event has benefitted several causes, including scholarships to learn culinary arts and the wine business. "Somehow, I've become the orchestrator of events where four, five, or six chefs are going to each do a dish. I know the chefs I invite. I ask, 'Could you do me a favor? Could you do a dish?' And when they say yes, which they do, I get more specific. 'Could you do squash? Could you do a bird?'"

The desire for quality and different experiences goes across the spectrum for Charlie—extending, much like the food does, beyond his professional world and into every area of life. He points to his family to illustrate a way to pursue meaningful experiences together. "For the last 10 years, we haven't given our four sons junk," he says. "They get experiences—like when our twins turned 21, we took them to Barcelona and Madrid. We didn't buy them the newest, greatest computer or whatever. We gave them experiences, because that's going to make a difference in their lives. It meant a lot to them, and it'll mean even more to them five or 10 years from now when they say, 'Remember when we were in Madrid and Barcelona? Remember that Picasso we saw?'"

WHAT WE HEARD AND LEARNED

- Believe in the magic of the kitchen to connect and nurture
- Be nice to people
- Welcome all ages to your table
- Trade the pursuit of "things" for "experiences"

BEN PARR
ENTREPRENEUR, INFLUENCER, AND WRITER PAYS ATTENTION TO ATTENTION

"Attention doesn't have an on/off switch. It comes in stages. You have to build short-term attention by disrupting expectations, and build long-term attention, too. That's how you get anything done over the long term."

BEN PARR, COLLABORATION ARTIST

BEN PARR—THE author of *Captivology, The Science of Capturing People's Attention*—has spent his life looking at how people connect. A goldmine of information on collaboration, Ben focuses on attention because, he believes, "Attention is the fundamental currency of the modern economy. It doesn't matter what industry you're in—whether you're in events, you're in startups, you're in media, you're a musician —attention is the lifeblood of your business.

"It's hard to capture attention these days," he adds. "There are more and more distractions than ever before. The increase in information that an individual is exposed to has been exponential. Yet most people don't have any clue how the psychology of attention works. No one had ever done a book that gathered the research of the last 50 years on attention. There's so much knowledge that should be shared."

Ben stresses the importance of establishing expertise in order to gain credibility. He feels business executives need help in this area.

"People automatically listen to experts," he says. "Edelman, the PR firm, does a survey every year of what kind of people are trusted most. And two-thirds of respondents always say they trust experts in academia, and at the very bottom of the list are CEOs. We don't trust CEOs. If you're an expert, you need to talk a little bit about that expertise."

One of the things he talks about in the book "is the disruption trigger," Ben explains. "We pay attention to the people and things that violate our expectations of how the world is supposed to work. If you do a typical monotone presentation with 10 bullet points, you're going to fail as a speaker. The less predictable your speech, the better. I had a confetti cannon that I would light off in the middle of the crowd. I would always find that right after I did that, people would start paying much more attention to my talk and my speech."

Attention doesn't have an on/off switch, Ben notes. Instead, "it comes in stages. You have to build short-term attention by disrupting expectations, and build long-term attention, too. That's how you build a top tier conference. That's how you get anything done over the long term. The big thing I would say for delivering long-term attention is to really focus on the power of participation."

The goal, after all, isn't just to give a killer speech, but to create a two-way relationship between speaker and participant, Ben cautions. "Certain speakers give their speech and leave without interacting with the event participants. That doesn't really build a relationship; it actually demonstrates coldness. It demonstrates you don't care. Do the opposite."

Ben has observed that "it's very easy to lower the excitement of the audience with a bad panel." And he has ideas about how to make panel discussions better. "Rule number one," he announces, "is that it's all about the moderator. Rule number two is that the moderator is not the center of attention. If the moderator talks too much, the moderator is doing a bad job. The moderator's role is to facilitate discussion among the other people, to keep things fast moving and pithy. That means that if a panelist is rambling, the moderator has to cut them off. A great moderator plays off of each of the answers so that it's a continual conversation. A great moderator adds values to the audience by asking questions that the audience actually wants to hear the answers to."

We pay automatic attention to certain sensory inputs like sights, colors, sounds, and smells, Ben says, explaining the concept of "automaticity" and how it relates to attention. "Certain kinds of sensory cues really capture our attention on an automatic level, and really matter when it comes to how we perceive an event." Color, he says, "is the number-one factor. The contrast of a color matters, as do the cultural associations we have with that color. Black, for example, is the color of sophistication in Western culture. If you're trying to do a sophisticated conference, you want to get some black, you want to get some purple, you want to get some pink. If, on the other hand, your goal is to have an exciting conference, oranges and reds and yellows are great.

"Smell matters too," Ben adds. "If you have a beautiful smell that pops a little bit, people will remember it. Also, people have automatic memory associations based on sensations. If you have an attractive smell at your venue, and they smell that a second time in a different place, they will remember your experience.

"There are more tools than ever to go and connect with people, and you could theoretically never leave your chair," Ben points out. "But deep connections are only made in person. Frankly, I think the rise of social media has *helped* events and made them more valuable, because we tend to stay home more or stay in offices more. But when you really need to meet people and build deep connections, you go to events."

WHAT WE HEARD AND LEARNED

- Embrace your expertise. People automatically listen to experts
- Violate expectations, and use disruption triggers to gain short-term attention
- Enhance participation to gain long-term attention
- Let "automaticity" be your aid

DR. WAYNE PERNELL

EXPONENTIAL SUCCESS COACH WITH A DOCTORATE IN CLINICAL PSYCHOLOGY APPLIES PRINCIPLES OF COUPLES THERAPY TO GET BIG BUSINESS RESULTS

"As long as the conversation is about 'you and me,' it will always be a tug-of-war. 'I'm right. No, I'm right.'"

DR. WAYNE PERNELL, COLLABORATION ARTIST

HOW MANY PEOPLE does Dr. Wayne Pernell—a high-performance success coach with a doctorate in clinical psychology and the founder and president of DynamicLeader, Inc.—need to work with to enhance collaborations? He makes it clear that it can start with just one person. He does a lot of work with leaders, which can result in dramatic changes in their organization's culture and their company's bottom line.

Known by his clients as Dr. Wayne or Dr. P, he also has stories about working primarily with two people. In fact, Dr. Wayne was introduced to working in corporate circumstances by someone for whom he had been a couples' counselor. "About 40 years ago, I got a call from a great guy who said, 'That thing you did with me and my wife—can you do that with me and my vice president?' The caller was the president of a major company. I was still fairly new to having my own practice, but I took a deep breath and replied, 'Sure.' I ended up going to their office. I created working agreements for them. We started with individual, and then, company values. We created a vision for them and integrated it into a strategic plan. I had some business background, but I was certainly learning along the way," he remembers. "A leadership lesson here, one focused on collaboration, is that co-creation is of utmost importance when building a culture. And culture begins at the top," Dr. Wayne says.

"In the first few sessions, they learned about communicating with each other and, more important, communicating with their team," Dr. Wayne continues. "We started to make some massive movement. About the fourth time I showed up, the line staff was out front applauding my arrival. I said, 'I haven't worked with you guys. How do you know about me? What's up?' They pointed to the top floor and said, '*They* are working so much better together. *They* know where they're headed. They've told us what they expect of us. You've made our jobs easier. Thank you for being here!' With that, I began doing organization development, which wasn't really a true discipline back then. I was sort of paving the way by looking at culture vs. just looking at performance."

After that, Dr. Wayne soon began working more extensively on culture, trying to connect all levels of employees so they each knew what the others were working on. "Pretty soon," he explains, "that company was in tune and on its way."

Dr. Wayne's analysis of this engagement points to a precursor for its success. "In this particular instance, the good news was that the president, by bringing me in, demonstrated a willingness to engage with his vice president. He indicated that even if he and his vice president were having troubles, he didn't want to get rid of him. 'We're in a relationship and we're having troubles, but we are both committed to coming together and reconciliation,' and they implied that this was ultimately in service to a common vision. That showed me what I needed to do. As long as the conversation is about 'you and me,' it will always be a tug-of-war. 'I'm right. No, I'm right.' My role was to keep their common end goal in front of them. I needed to get them to stop and note that it doesn't matter who's right or wrong. We needed to focus on the desired outcome, something everyone could work towards. My engagements often involve stopping people from playing tug-of-war and keeping them focused."

He notes, "I don't do therapy when I'm working with organizations. It might *feel* therapeutic, but it's never therapy." Focusing on a shared goal also sets the stage for the kind of frank, direct communications that Dr. Wayne feels are most effective in organizational settings. "If you're focused on an outcome, there are deliverables and there are dependencies. A dependency might be that this deliverable gets completed before anything else can happen. You're managing the output. Remember that 'management' comes from *manos*, the Latin word for hand. This is hands-on in terms of achieving a deliverable date. 'Here's the outcome we want. I'll be checking in with you to see how to support you best.' Beyond that, you might not care how the work gets done. 'I don't really care if you log in at four in the morning if that's your work time. I don't care if you log in later in the day and stay up till two in the morning to get it done.'"

Dr. Wayne's approach clearly works: He has worked with leading companies such as Schwab, 3Com, Whole Foods Market, Safeway, Bank of America, and many others. He shares his insights with the public via a weekly blog, *Wednesdays With Wayne*.

Dr. Wayne gives another example from early in his career of how speaking plainly, albeit inadvertently, helped a team get past a communications logjam. "I was working with one of a large company's regional executive teams as a consultant. Part of what I do is become a fly on the wall at the conference room table. I was at a big team meeting, head down, trying to be invisible. I was just tracking what's happening and taking notes. At one point, it was like I had a thought bubble about the president—but I said it out loud. I found myself blurting out, accidentally, 'Is it just me, or did all of the air just get sucked out of the room?'

"You could almost hear all the vice presidents swivel their heads," he remembers. "They looked at me, they looked back at him, they looked at me, they looked back at him. He took on a power posture, took a big breath, leaned back, looked around the room. There was a huge pause. We were all sweating.

"He leaned forward, took another breath, looked down, looked back up and asked, 'Well... *did* all of the air just get sucked out of the room?' The vice president sitting next to me, who had been looking down in a posture you'd expect from a seven-year-old rather than a huge man, answered, 'Yeah... yeah, it did.' The president said, 'Then we have some work to do,'" Dr. Wayne says. "He opened the door for communication. This is a guy who had not really been known for being a great communicator, but he took that moment. It was a turning point. I hadn't meant to be that blunt, or even to speak. But it's what came out at the moment. And it has informed my work. I teach people how to communicate in a way that they can be heard."

While Dr. Wayne believes that most people can be brought into productive alignments, he also identifies characteristics of problematic people in business and politics. "If you look at zealots, they all tend to say, 'I'm never wrong. What I believe in is the only way.' That means we can't have a conversation. We have absolutely zero ability to engage in a discussion that's going to be meaningful. If, on the other hand, they indicate, 'I could be wrong. I'll listen to new information'— that's awesome. That's why I like to start engagements by answering the question, 'What are we here for?' One of the sayings about collabo-ration is 'It's not about you.' The desired outcome is more important than any individual ego."

One stumbling block to effective collaboration can be perceptual bias on the part of one of the participants. "The whole idea of percep-tual bias is that we know what we know, and we look for things that validate it," Dr. Wayne, whose recent TEDx dove deeply into this, explains. "Depending on your worldview, this could be a very narrow box. When we have a perceptual bias—say, that certain racial or ethnic groups are a given way—we paint all of them the same. We could have a bias about certain types of drivers, and we'd say, 'Of course, it's that driver driving that badly.' We look for a bias and, sure enough, it's proven because we're looking for it. And sometimes we're not even consciously looking for it. Our reticular activating system (RAS) in the brain alerts us. Perceptual bias is a subconscious process. That's what makes it so insidious."

One way of addressing perceptual bias is to introduce what Dr. Wayne calls a parallax perspective. This is a shift from what you already know. "You have to be deliberate in stating to yourself, 'I don't have the entire picture. I know what I know, but I assume there's more,'" he says. "I'm typically anti-assumption. This is the one deviation from that rule. Assume there's more; there's always more."

Another way of combating perceptual bias involves bringing a representation of curiosity into the boardroom. "If I put a stuffed animal toy at the head of a conference room table, somebody's going to ask, 'What's with the monkey?' I'll reply, 'It's not just a monkey.' Somebody will say, 'It's George.' And I'll go, 'Correct. And it's not just George.' Someone else will pipe up, 'It's Curious George,' because the character is so well-known and loved. That opens up an important conversation, because if you're curious, you will stay out of judgment. The goal here is to establish a working agreement that if we find ourselves in judgment, that we need to start asking questions, right? Remember, when you live in curiosity, you stay out of judgment."

WHAT WE HEARD AND LEARNED

- Eliminate tug-of-war or "right fighting"
- Ask the hard questions and check your biases
- Guide by asking what kind of input is desired. Give input, not directions
- Stay in curiosity to stay out of judgment

ALLOW PEOPLE
TO FEEL...

EMPATHY

MARC FRIEDLAND

INVITING PARTICIPATION AND PUSHING THE ENVELOPE FOR STIMULATING DETAILS

"I realized we were really in the business of thoughtfulness, and how is the best way to express that even in its most authentic and simplest ways."

MARC FRIEDLAND, COLLABORATION ARTIST

MARC FRIEDLAND HAS amazing stories to tell that will arouse envy in most people involved in events. He has created and produced gatherings with seemingly unlimited budgets, for clients who encouraged him to set his imagination free. For instance, he describes an epic birthday party that happened in acts, included original art, and featured well-choreographed waiters who essentially served the different courses as theatrical acts.

The wonders built into that one night may outclass great circuses. But arguably his greatest impact on the events industry comes from how he has been able to set new standards for invitations—and even the envelopes.

In essence, Marc took the greeting card and made it into a multimillion-dollar event. "Done right," he says, "it's a mixed-media event. It touches the senses on so many different levels. I think it kind of helps define what we do. It involves storytelling. It involves the senses. It involves a certain slightly wacky sensibility sometimes. Style, social graces—all of those are the components that create a memorable experience."

In order to do this however, it requires having thoughtfulness as part of your DNA. It's not something you can fake. Marc started out making hand-painted greeting cards. Even then, he put strategic thought into his work. "When I made a hand-painted card," he remembers, "the individuality came forth, the thoughtfulness came forth. "I realized we were really in the business of thoughtfulness, and how is the best way to express that even in its most authentic and simplest ways." One of the original cards over 30 years ago had an AlkaSeltzer packet and said 'Thanks for Dinner.' It was tactile. It brought up an emotion in people. It brought up joy."

Marc believes that we are in for fundamental change in our gatherings. "We're entering into what I like to think of as the embodiment age. We're now out of the information age, and now we ask about *emotions*. 'How are we making people feel?' That is how we have to think about everything these days," he says.

"Also, we're in a transformational era," Marc continues. "The two things are linked, because if people don't get in touch with their emotions, there's never going to be transformation. It's no longer about Descartes' model of, 'I think, therefore I am.' We have a different perspective: 'I feel, therefore I think.' Many decisions are based on how someone feels: whether it's who you're voting for, the products that you buy, who you like on social media—it's all based on how you feel. That's what's triggering people's reactions. Transformation and embodiment are tied together, because you can't have one without the other."

Marc entered the world of events when somebody bought one of his artisanal cards and asked, "Could you make an invitation out of this?" His work on the aforementioned epic birthday celebration started, of course, with an exquisite invitation that set sky-high expectations. "Back in the day, the invitation was the keepsake that set the tone. I like to put invitations back on that pedestal. There's an entirely new generation of digital natives that crave the experiential. Receiving an interactive influencer box or invitation is an entirely new experience for them."

Stationery and invitations, he explains, had been "relegated to the fourth floor of the department store, next to the restrooms or the credit department. It was always ink on paper. There was never real emotion to it. We decided it doesn't have to be that way. We realized we could make it a mixed-media thing, to make it a piece of art. We call what we do luxury communications because it evokes feeling. Our invitations are meticulously handcrafted, no matter how simple or elaborate they are."

While Marc sometimes has the resources needed to make an event or gathering ever more spectacular, he is careful not to go too far over the top. "We make sure to avoid sensory overload. We shoot for just the right mix from an experiential standpoint." He says about one of his events, "Every element was an opportunity to look, to wonder, to say, 'Wow.' It wasn't so much about being extravagant; it was really more about the sensations every step of the way between the music, the visuals, the camaraderie of the guests."

After bringing new focus to the invitation, Marc went even farther and found a unique opportunity to elevate the previously lowly envelope: He basically took an envelope and made it into an experience. Marc tells the story of his work for the Oscars. "There aren't many moments that feature an envelope or a piece of stationery—except the Oscars. The two most famous phrases are 'The Oscar goes to' and 'The envelope please.' But the envelopes that were being used were like envelopes you get at Staples that have the silver liner in it. They didn't even imagine that that could even be an iconic keepsake."

Marc thinks more people and companies can benefit from this kind of thinking. "They just have to have the currency of willingness and the courage to do something different, with authenticity, thoughtfulness, and gratitude," he says.

WHAT WE HEARD AND LEARNED

- Elevate every element you can when gathering
- Have the courage to do something different
- Create sensory experiences, but avoid sensory overload
- More and more, it's about *how* we feel and *why* we feel

JOANNA STONE HERMAN
DEALMAKER BIRTHS NEW COLLABORATIONS DESTINED FOR SUCCESS

"People will often use the analogy that selling a company is like selling a house. Yes and no. Often it's like selling your house—but having to still live there with and work for the new owner."

JOANNA STONE HERMAN, COLLABORATION ARTIST

JOANNA STONE HERMAN has operated in highly competitive corporate and financial environments for many years. She's been an executive, an entrepreneur, an investor, an advisor, a board member, and more. She's now a partner, dealmaker, and co-head of the Media & Technology practice at a leading mid-market mergers and acquisition firm, Oaklins DeSilva+Phillips. In her current position, she doesn't have a role to play in helping companies work together once the deal to join them has been completed. She focuses on setting all sides of a transaction up for future success in the early stages, while the dimensions of the initial deal agreement are being established.

She is always tuned in to the differing emotional, as well as financial, needs of all parties involved. Starting with the sell-side, she notes, "Sometimes people step into the sales process and they're not really emotionally ready to sell their company. And if that's the case, it's probably going to be a challenging process."

Joanna illustrates her approach by describing some of the types of seller situations she's likely to encounter. "Often a big company will come to us and say, 'We have this division that no longer fits with us. Their business isn't of strategic importance to us anymore. We'd like your help selling it.' Or, 'We'd like your help buying companies that are of strategic importance.' That's pretty straightforward."

In contrast to that, she reports, "many of the people we work with are entrepreneurs who still run their company; they still are in control of their company. They often haven't yet sold majority interest in their company. They are selling something that they've built from the ground up. That's where I think it becomes incredibly important to be collaborative on an emotional level, too."

The emotional context tends to be different when a private equity concern has already invested in the selling entity. "Those companies were bought to be sold. The CEOs of those companies may be the original CEOs, but they have essentially become an extension of that private equity firm. They have been building the company with an eye to selling it. There are a few private equity firms that hold for the long term, but most private equity firms will be focused on exiting after a few years."

In order to ensure the eventual happy melding of the parties of a deal, Joanna first focuses on establishing the right relationship between her firm and each of the parties. She starts building for success from the first meeting. "We block at least four hours to spend with a new client and just say, 'Tell us everything about your company.' We go through a demo and learn about their technology. We're already experts on their industry, but we need to be experts on their company. We review everything detail-by-detail. It's a long meeting and we work hard, but it's also a really fun time, sitting in a room together with good food."

Joanna points out an important change that often happens in that encounter. "By the end of this meeting, we, the bankers, start saying 'we' when we talk about the company—because that's how we feel. That's where collaboration comes in. We started asking, 'What do you do here?' By the end of this meeting, we're saying, 'We have this strategy that is going to attract this buyer. We can deliver this.' That's a huge shift."

When the process works correctly, the client embraces this shift serendipitously. "The sellers welcome us as an extended member of their core team. We're all together," Joanna says. "They embrace this, because we've done a deep dive to understand and really get a feel for what it is to be part of that company and everything they do."

Joanna has deep empathy for the challenges that sellers face. "Doing a deep dive to understand how their business operates not only helps us better position them to buyers, it also helps us see how we can best support them in ensuring that their company thrives through this process. One of the trickiest things about a sale process is that a CEO's day-job requirements continue. All the management team's day-job requirements remain in place. They still have to run the business, and do all the things they were doing before. If anything, now there's even more pressure to deliver results. They cannot miss a number. Then, on top of that, they have to be involved in a sale process. So, we try to make their involvement in the sale process as easy as possible. Also, because we've been in their shoes before, we try to make the running-the-business part as easy as possible. We know what they're going through, and we can say, 'Hey, we know this is coming up, can we be helpful in thinking this through?'"

Establishing rapport with the seller can be an important precursor to an even more important phase: when the buy-side and the sell-side have to come together. She stresses that the seller is interviewing the buyer just as much as the buyer is interviewing the seller. "People will often use the analogy that selling a company is like selling a house. Yes and no. Often it's like selling your house—but having to still live there with and work for the new owner."

Of course, no deal is purely financial. Culture fit tends to be crucial. "Culture fit is something you really can figure out during the sale process," Joanna explains. "You have multiple meetings between buyer and seller and, if done right, you get a feel for whether you have the right buyer for the company. Both sides should feel like 'we've now come to a larger version of ourselves.'"

WHAT WE HEARD AND LEARNED

- Secure your relationship to all sides in a deal through emotional openness
- Tune in to emotional as well as financial factors
- Be empathetic to all sides
- Keep working on culture fit as you progress in any collaboration

RUUD JANSSEN
EVENT CANVAS ARTIST WHO ENVISIONS THE SUCCESS JOURNEY

"If you're able to design experiences which change behavior to a degree that you wouldn't expect that to happen — to me, that is the finest example of event design."

RUUD JANSSEN, COLLABORATION ARTIST

RUUD JANSSEN IS a co-creator of EventCanvas and the author of *Event Design Handbook* and *Design to Change*. He's based in Switzerland, and offers consulting about events, marketing, content strategy, training, and more around the globe. "Behavior is the only thing I'm trying to influence," he says. "That's what I want to isolate."

Ruud defines behavior as everything you can observe with a camera. "In effect, I put a camera on you, and I listen to what you say and do. That's the objective behavior I'm looking for. It's nothing more, nothing less, than that. If you're able to design experiences which change behavior to a degree that you wouldn't expect that to happen— to me, that is the finest example of event design."

Ruud speaks precisely, careful to fully define the terms he uses. "An event is an isolated period of time in which people are temporarily dislocated from their normal reality in order to change behavior faster or more effectively. When you travel, already you start to go into a different mode of thinking. You're out of your normal routine. By being in that moment, by being away from your daily reality, you're consciously thinking about what is changing in yourself and what's changing within others who are at the same table."

Ruud pays special attention to the event owner. "The event owner would be somebody who says, 'I think we need to get these people in the room.' The event owner has intents as to why they want specific groups of people to gather. There are, essentially, only four basic intentions, relating to change in attitude, learning, skills, and knowledge. The mix of those four—and how much you amp up the volume on each at what specific part in the experience journey—is really what creates the event design. Effecting behavior change through incremental steps is the goal of event design. Event design is nothing more, nothing less, than framing behavior change."

Ruud makes extensive use of a tool called the Event Canvas, which shows deep thinking about how an event could change behavior for different types of participants. "You can't think of everything all the time. If you have an event with 14 different stakeholders, it becomes very complex. There are 14 different cubicles. I start by looking at entry behavior and exit behavior, because the delta between them is what creates the value—provided it's in the direction of change for which I've designed it to go."

The Event Canvas is not a theoretical construct: It is a physical manifestation of intense planning collaboration. "One of the things we say when you design an event is to shell out one percent of the total time for event design," Ruud says. "Take your team, sit down, or stand up in front of a wall, put up a big Event Canvas in front of you. Let's say the event will involve 100 people spending eight hours together. That's 800 event hours. One percent of that would be eight hours to think carefully about what you're going to be doing."

Ruud is a proponent of empathy mapping, which informs the Event Canvas. "We go into the shoes of one stakeholder at a time and we look through their eyes, we think and feel like them, we listen to what they hear. We also articulate their pains and gains, because those are the building blocks that reveal the emotions that will drive actions. Empathy mapping is not something to ever attempt solo. It is a team process. You get four or five people to empathize, to think like a particular attendee."

Once you've done the empathy mapping, according to Ruud, you can show the map to that stakeholder as a tool for connection. "Hold it up in front of them and say, 'Four people spent 45 minutes thinking about you. We'd like you to take a look at it and point out to us the differences between what we *think* you think, and what you really think.'"

That person is *going* to help you adjust your empathy map of them, Ruud adds. "When you start finalizing the Event Canvas, what you're doing is adding constraints. The amount of time people have. The amount of money that it may cost. The expected revenue. The Event Canvas limits you—and by limiting you, it allows you to become a lot more creative. It allows you to validate whether something makes sense. Once you have all the restrictions on the table, what you do is go back to something called the 'idea quarantine,' which is a place where you dump ideas during the process. Then you hold those ideas up against your design frame. Every idea that's there may get a number of jobs done."

The Event Canvas process is complex, but Ruud's instinct is generally to simplify. That's why he wrote *The Event Design Handbook*, available for free via Creative Commons. Ruud wants to "equip the masses and democratize event design to a degree where the level of the poor events comes up significantly, just by giving design pointers and standardizing and simplifying things, to a degree.

"If we can get people to understand how to read the Event Canvas, it will become to event design what sheet music has become to music," Ruud adds.

WHAT WE HEARD AND LEARNED

- Effect behavior change through incremental steps
- Dedicate time to event design
- Make empathy mapping a core team process
- Get all the restrictions on the table

MARK JOHNSON
UNITING THE WORLD BY MAKING IT POSSIBLE FOR PEOPLE TO SING TOGETHER VIRTUALLY

"Eventually, I just get out of the way and let music do what it does so well: Help people find a way to work together."

MARK JOHNSON, COLLABORATION ARTIST

MARK JOHNSON IS a Grammy Award-winning producer and engineer as well as an award-winning film director—but his biggest contribution to the world is the astonishing Playing For Change multimedia movement that he and film producer Whitney Kroenke Silverstein co-founded. They, along with an ad-hoc team of people with cameras and recording equipment, created an innovative mobile technique for recording and filming musicians all around the world. They then edited their performances together into moving videos that showcase music's magical ability to transcend barriers and unite us.

Their video of musicians from around the globe, each contributing parts of the classic Ben E. King anthem "Stand By Me," racked up over 85 million views on YouTube. That set the stage for a CD/DVD set, *Playing For Change: Songs Around the World* that debuted at number 10 on Billboard's pop chart in April 2009. The momentum continued: Two years later, the second Playing For Change album, *PFC2: Songs Around The World*, debuted at number one on Billboard's world music charts.

Watching and listening to skillfully assembled recordings of musicians who have never met, and remain thousands of miles apart, somehow managing to collaborate on masterpieces was refreshing, inspiring, and popular. As the phenomenon grew, Mark created a documentary film, *Playing For Change: A Cinematic Discovery of Street Musicians*, which won honors at several international film festivals. This led to another award-winning film, *Playing For Change: Peace Through Music*. The media attention attracted supporters who helped the movement continue to grow.

The initial ideas behind Playing For Change came, in large measure, from Mark's life experience. "My first love of music is as a listener. I've just loved to listen to music ever since I was a kid. The first inspiration came after I graduated from the University of New Hampshire. I got a job at a big recording studio, the Hit Factory in New York City. I started out just getting food for the artists. Eventually, I got to record music. I noticed that the rappers and hip-hoppers had the same basic love of music that I had. Then I would work with a 70-piece orchestra from Broadway, and they would have the same love of the music. I thought to myself, 'They all go home to totally different worlds, but I get to see them at their happiest moments when they are making music.' If they could all see what I see, they would probably all be good friends. I just had this sense that music could connect every kind of person."

He adds, "The second inspiration happened in a subway station on my way to work one day. Two monks painted in white and wearing robes were singing. It was so mesmerizing that when the train came, no one got on. None of us knew what they're singing about, what language it was. I looked around, and I saw an elderly woman with a young girl next to her. I saw a homeless man next to a businessman. All these different kinds of people were connected through the music. I knew two things. First, when the music plays, everything that makes us different disappears. Second, the best music I heard was *on the way* to the studio, and not in the studio. I realized that rather than spend my life in the studio, I wanted to record the magic that had just happened, and I wanted to film it—because you had to see what was going on, too. I wanted to bring the studio to the streets, using the same quality equipment I used with Paul Simon. That wouldn't be easy. At the time, I would have to power it with really heavy golf-cart batteries."

For Mark, the next bit of serendipity came when he was on his way to work with Jackson Browne at his studio in Santa Monica, California. "I heard Roger Ridley singing 'Stand By Me.' I was about a block away from him, but his voice was so powerful. Earlier, when I was looking for a song to take around the world, I'd been listening to the John Lennon version of that song. But when I heard Roger sing it, it was destiny. I knew, 'That's the right song. This is the right version. This is a singer I want involved.'

"I asked him, 'If I come back in a few hours with recording equipment and cameras, can I record you and film you? Then I'm going to take it around the world and put headphones on other performers, so we have a consistent beat and ask them to join in.' He looked at me like I was crazy, but he said yes. But he was so good that I first had to ask him, 'Why are you singing on the street?' He said, 'I'm in the joy business. I come out to bring joy to the people.' That really set the tone for the entire project of Playing For Change. It's not a business. It's about the joy and it's about the music and then everything that comes out of that, whether it's building schools or making people feel more connected."

Having spent so much time around musicians, Mark has become adept at improvising. He stays open to serendipity. His vision for the song "Still Haven't Found What I'm Looking For" involved going to Hawaii to record John Cruz's distinctive voice. "When I was there, there was a girl sitting next to us. She just came to hang out, and she started singing with him in the chorus. I heard her voice and said, 'Wait a minute. John, please stop singing for a moment so we can focus on her.' Olivia Ruff has one of the most beautiful voices in the world. She sings the first lead vocal before we bring John in.

"Since I started, I've been to over 65 countries recording and filming music," he continues. "I've been to some of those places 15 to 20 times. Indigenous musicians and street musicians and famous musicians all get involved. It's not about one kind of music or one kind of musician. The concept is bigger: that music was invented to connect us around the world. One great thing about music is that the listener is just as important as the player. We share the experience. They play; we listen. Once I hear it, it's mine too. What I think is so cool is we have all these thousands of musicians playing, but now we also have over one-and-a-half billion people watching our YouTube channel—and they get to make it their own, too. Not a lot of people in the world will believe the same truth, but 8 billion people can believe the *feeling* of music."

At Playing For Change, Mark explains, "We say that 'world music is when the world plays music.' It's all the cultures playing music together. Each has a totally different way of seeing the world. They play the notes differently and on different instruments. But they make beautiful music together. With this kind of music, people play less, and they listen more; unlike the studio where people play more and often listen less. When you have so many cultures and languages, you just find a way to make it better, not just play your instrument. You become more humble. Everybody gets to understand each other."

Mark and Whitney were both focused on having everyone involved win. "As we grew, Whitney always asked, 'What could we do to give back?' I want to make it clear that we pay almost every musician. The only ones that don't get paid are the really successful ones who insist on just donating their time," notes Mark. "A big part of that is about them getting what they deserve. We also want to demonstrate that making music can be the basis of a business where you can reward the musicians. Sometimes the performers have found creative uses for the money. The Zulu choir featured on 'Stand By Me' started a micro-loan business in their township."

He adds, "Sometimes it takes us 30 or 40 hours of travel just to get to a place. It would be insufficient to say, 'Just play these 16 bars in a solo.' It's never like that. We want to make a connection. That's what's made having a foundation so important. It's how we can really connect with these cultures, give the musicians something that they can give back to their own communities." The Playing For Change Foundation addresses specific local needs often by creating schools or school-adjacent programs. "All the school classes are free. It's really about teaching them." Whitney is in charge of the foundation while Mark continues to run the Playing For Change music project; but the two co-founders still work closely together.

"Each foundation project comes out of the identity of the place. When we asked, 'What could we do to give back?' in the townships in South Africa, the response was, 'Why don't you build a school for the kids here so that instead of the next kid being a gangster, he might be the next Nelson Mandela.' In Nepal, the foundation project involves elderly women who travel the Himalayan Mountains on foot to teach the villagers through a play about how to protect their children from the sex slave trade. In West Africa, the focus was on things like getting clean water, solar power, and light in the maternity ward. The foundation school in Mali has 200 kids in the dance class. In Kathmandu, it's an orphanage."

Mark is all about amplifying the beneficial effects of music. "My hero is Bob Marley. He reached everybody in the world," he says. "The only evolution after that is having the whole world play music together to show people that the things that make us different actually make us stronger. That's the feeling that matters. If you just put music in between things, it makes them better. I'm here to connect everyone. Eventually, I just get out of the way and let music do what it does so well: help people find a way to work together."

WHAT WE HEARD AND LEARNED

- Get people to play together, even if they are far apart
- Make sure each player wins in the way they want
- Create connections, then get out of the way
- Stay open to surprises

ANDREW LACANIENTA
STRATEGICALLY DESIGNING TRANSFORMATIONS WITH AN UNDERSTANDING OF THE TYPES OF EXPERIENCES

"I think everyone, in one way or another, is an experience designer. I meet people all over the world and when they tell me what they do, in my brain I think, 'You're an experience designer for a library. Or you're an experience designer for an insurance firm."

ANDREW LACANIENTA, COLLABORATION
ARTIST

ANDREW LACANIENTA IS LIVING proof that the events and experience design industry is serious about reaping the benefits of advanced study of human interaction.

Today, he's a senior strategist at George P. Johnson in the San Francisco Bay Area. Prior to that, he was a freelance creative director and strategist at Drury Design. And prior to *that*, he was an assistant professor in the department of experience industry management at California Polytechnic State University-San Luis Obispo. He's articulate about the principles of outcome-based design, observation, curiosity, deep listening, ideation, real-time prototyping, iteration, and much more.

His academic training is evident when he defines his terms. "Experience means a ton of things, and design means a ton of things,"

Andrew says. "Experience design is the process of intentionally orchestrating experience to provide opportunities for participants to co-create or participate with one another and sustain interactions that lead to results desired by both participants and the designer. Experiences can be anything from your traditional meetings, conventions, and showrooms to brand activations, to an interaction at a bank with a teller.

"In the event space, we often think about experience, and it's always something extraordinary," he continues. "It's always a mind-blowing 'aha' moment. But if every experience was extraordinary, you'd be exhausted by 8 o'clock in the morning. At Brigham Young University, the department of experience design and management did some cutting-edge research and created a typology of experiences that goes from prosaic to transformative."

Andrew explains the types of experiences. "The first kind, 'prosaic experiences,' are autopilot-type experiences, like brushing your teeth. It's not particularly memorable. We just do it," he explains. "The second level is 'mindful experiences.' You're thinking a little bit more about what you're doing. Third is 'memorable experiences.' Once an experience becomes memorable, there is emotion involved."

The fourth level is "meaningful experiences," Andrew notes. "An experience becomes meaningful when discovery is involved, such as when you're discovering something new, you're learning something about yourself, et cetera." Finally, he adds, "Fifth, and last, is 'transformative experiences.' There's behavior change or a paradigm shift, or something's changing."

According to Andrew, once you understand the different types of experiences, you can intentionally design for them. Perhaps a gathering starts with a prosaic experience—then the next experience could be memorable. After that, a meaningful experience follows. While not all experiences can be extraordinary, you can intentionally design those different touches in a way that meets the desired outcomes and goals, Andrew explains.

"Academic research also resulted in the theory of structured experience," he continues. "A key characteristic of a structured experience is that it has a distinct beginning and ending, whether it lasts for seconds or hours. Within this theory of structured experiences, there are three types of experience: immersion, absorption, and engagement. Immersion activities are experiences that require a balance of challenge and skill, or action and reaction, Chess or fencing are good examples."

Andrew continues, "An absorption experience is a sensory experience of relaxation and pleasure. Getting a massage or doing a wine tasting would be an absorption experience. Engagement experiences are any type of experience that follows an unfolding narrative or story. It could be following a sporting event, or watching a theatrical play, or reading a book." The types are not mutually exclusive, Andrew adds. "Some experiences are both immersion and engagement, or so on. As part of this theory, there are propositions about the levers you can use to intensify the experience.

"With immersion experiences, there are two things that you can toggle on the mixing board," he continues. "The first thing is self-relevance. As an experience becomes more self-relevant, it's easier to become immersed. Second is the balance of challenge and skill. It's not so hard that it's making you anxious, but it's not so easy that it's making you bored. If you can balance challenge and skill and also make the experience self-relevant, then immersion will increase.

"With absorption, those sensory relaxation-type experiences, one lever is facilitating a focus on the present moment. When there is mindfulness, absorption will increase," Andrew notes. "If you can build anticipation for the experience, that will increase absorption. Facilitating some type of behavioral or social expression of positive emotion will lead to a more absorbing experience."

Finally, Andrew explains, "With engagement experiences, those that follow a narrative, there are three propositions. First is that as coherence of the story increases, engagement will also increase. Think of a story arc with a distinct beginning, middle, and end as well as with a climax and a resolution. Second is provocation. How can we effectively provoke our participants in a way that's positive? Perhaps make them kind of challenge their beliefs, or think twice about what it is that we're teaching. Third is self-relevance. Can we make this experience relevant to them and to the things that they believe and to their values and to their self? Using these three propositions, we can design the experience to be more engaging."

Andrew sees the theory as helping meet emerging demands and as having widespread relevance. "The theory can really help experience designers and event planners say, 'OK, what is this experience? What are we really trying to do here? Are we trying to elicit an experience that's relaxing and pleasurable? Are we trying to tell a story or are we trying to facilitate a challenge for our participants?' People are starting to become hungry for this. Passive entertainment, passive learning, passive in general is going out the door. We've got this giant technology bit happening where everyone's hyper-connected and everything is at your fingertips all the time. But I think we're going to see an increase in disconnection because people are hungry for human interaction."

Andrew sees beauty in the idea that everything is an experience, "Training in a corporation, or teaching students in a university setting, are just experiences," he says. "Doctors create patient experiences. If they create horrible patient experiences, they won't have very many patients. But they could intentionally design prosaic experiences and maybe a couple meaningful or memorable or transformative ones. I think everyone, in one way or another, is an experience designer. I meet people all over the world, and when they tell me what they do, in my brain I think, 'You're an experience designer for a library. Or you're an experience designer for an insurance firm.'"

WHAT WE HEARD AND LEARNED

- Provide all types of experiences, from prosaic to transformative
- Give structured experiences a distinct beginning and ending
- Consider experience type: immersion, absorption, and/or engagement.
- Employ type-specific levers to intensify experiences

J. B. MILLER

GO-TO RESOURCE FOR NEXT LEVEL COLLABORATIONS WITH GREATER IMPACT

"Experiences are what's left."

J. B. MILLER, COLLABORATION ARTIST

J. B. Miller, president and CEO of Empire Entertainment, came to the event industry after a stint in television and concert production. He brought to his work in events a sense of the importance of the narrative and the need to carefully map out the journey that audience members will experience.

J. B. is careful to note that the event experience starts *before* people gather, explaining that an event narrative begins with the invitation. That's the first taste of the experience palette, and when the messaging first lands on you. J. B. believes that from the very first moment, every element should tie back to the purpose of the gathering.

"Some events are held to inspire people," he says. "Some are meant for them to simply enjoy. Some are meant to make them think or do something. In all instances, the first impression can be a strong framing for the experience to come."

J. B. emphasizes the importance of going beyond one-dimensional experiences. "When my colleagues and I map out an event narrative," he notes, "we consider at least two different threads. One is the emotional narrative. How does the event inspire you? Outrage you? How does it make you happy? How does it make you desire something? This is the emotional path. The other path focuses on logic for the other side of the brain. How do we build a rational argument that also complements the emotional journey? And the real artistry comes in how we use both of those paths to tell a more effective singular narrative."

For J. B., a successful gathering is always an exercise in empathy. "I think it's helpful to put yourself in the shoes of the attendee—because if you don't, you're going to miss understanding what's important to them. It's also important to consider more than one person's perspective. You want to do the best event for somebody who's a jaded native of New York City, but also the best event for somebody who's just relocated from the West coast and brings different preconceptions. They may have very different experiences."

Of course, no event can perfectly delight everyone. "I think a great event," he says, "works something like a Venn diagram. There's something for everyone, but not everybody's going to resonate with every aspect. A certain percentage of people will respond strongly to one aspect, while others, not so much. We program so that the majority of the event hits the right notes for the majority of the attendees, while still feeling new and different to all."

Ultimately, the goal of a collaborative convening is to get people to do something—to engage in a target behavior. J. B. gives an example: "A purchase could be one action. Adopting a certain viewpoint or position is another, or even inspiring people to become an advocate, influencer, or a promoter of that product could be another," he says. "The purpose of our work for not-for-profits or NGOs is to compel people to adopt the sustainable development goals. Events are a great way to drive this outcome.

"With each goal there's a different call to action, and there's a different definition of what that action looks like," he continues. "We use a lot of different devices. Ultimately, you want to move the participant to the point where they, as an independent human being acting under their own agency, feel inspired to act in a certain way."

J. B. adds, "We've discovered that the best approach is often to educate and to allow attendees to reach their own conclusions, rather than dictating outcomes to them. We use event narratives to help audiences understand things on their own terms, to conclude that our outcomes are important to them, and to allow them the freedom to choose action in their own way. Because some people are activists, some are doers, and some are followers. We need to create space where different kinds of people can be motivated to act in different ways."

J. B. has a sense of stewardship and responsibility about the work he does. "This is experiential propaganda in many instances, so we are careful to not take on projects whose end goals we don't believe in ourselves. But let's be honest about it, we are trying to manipulate people. The best projects, of course, are the ones where you're manipulating people to do something that they would have done anyway. You're just prompting them to do it a little bit more efficiently."

Lastly, J. B. makes a powerful case for events as a lasting, essential human need. "There's never been a more exciting time to be in experiential or events. I think people are discovering that the efficacy of putting people together in physical and virtual spaces, carefully crafting and controlling the dimensional narrative around them and encouraging them to become an active part of the narrative through their presence is an incredibly potent form of storytelling. And, as the human population moves up Maslow's hierarchy from basic, lower-level needs—like food, shelter, water, and so on—to the higher-level needs like self-actualization, and as disposable incomes become larger, things lose their excitement for us. And experiences are what's left."

WHAT WE HEARD AND LEARNED

- Begin the tone, meaning, and story of a gathering with the invitation
- Empathy, empathy, empathy. Put yourself in the various journeys of others
- Use both an emotional and a rational thread in gatherings
- Map all elements from invitation onward

BARRY ROSS RINEHART
LEVERAGE EMOTIONS FOR IMPACT

"All of the emotions matter ... It's important to mix them up. That's the art of events."

BARRY ROSS RINEHART, COLLABORATION ARTIST

BARRY ROSS RINEHART is an award-winning public speaker, executive speaker coach, speechwriter, communications and presentations expert, and leader of corporate and private brainstorming workshops. He expresses his role more simply, calling himself a "professional memory maker."

He helps leaders, organizations, and causes achieve their goals through the dynamic communication of intelligent, multi-sensory, and emotional stories and unforgettable experiences. He does this in his role as global creative director at the New York-headquartered professional service firm Genpact. Barry is also an executive coach with a focus on business storytelling, executive presence, personal brand, and crafting unforgettable experiences.

Barry cites the poet Maya Angelou as a guidepost for thinking about experiences: "I've learned that people will forget what you said, people will forget what you did, but people will never forget how you made them feel," he says, quoting Angelou.

He believes events should run on emotions. And much like a poem, a piece of music, or a film, it's important to design the emotions of an event as a progression of moods and feelings. He cites a creative parallel in something Stanley Kubrick said. "A film is—or should be—more like music than like fiction. It should be a progression of moods and feelings. The theme, what's behind the meaning—all that comes later."

Barry stresses emotions because he sees them as key to what he believes is the true, ultimate goal of a live event: fostering a mutually beneficial relationship. That sounds a lot like collaboration, the two-way exchange of emotion and information.

"Emotions really are just a chemical reaction that we feel," he says. "That's why we call them feelings. These chemicals are released when our neurons are activated in our brains, our guts, our hearts, and, yes, even our genitals. Imagine a stadium full of people. Now imagine all the individual hairs on their heads. That's how many neurons we all have in us. It's about 86+ billion neurons. So, when our sensory radar system detects something unique, it sends a charge through our neurons, down these long arms called axons, that branch off on these hairs called dendrites, and, at the end, are these little receptors called synapses."

He continues, "Then there's a spark that releases a cocktail mix of chemicals (some hormones, but mostly neurotransmitters) that jump from one synapse to another … making a little bridge. We call those synaptic connections. And those are where our memories come from. The more unique the sensory input, the bigger release of neurotransmitters (a.k.a., emotions), the longer that connection will last in us."

Barry points out that many of us are already familiar with several of the over 100 known neurotransmitters, including serotonin, which is involved with happiness and well-being; adrenaline (epinephrine), which responds to high-stress; norepinephrine, a form of adrenaline that focuses attention and gets the body ready for action; dopamine, which corresponds with pleasure and satisfaction; glutamate, which sharpens cognitive function and memory; acetylcholine, which strengthens thought, learning and memory; GABA, which brings calmness; endorphins, which escort in euphoria; and oxytocin, sometimes called the "cuddle neurotransmitter," which helps us feel a sense of bonding and intimacy.

However, knowing that not everyone is as science-oriented, Barry simplifies it all with his list of 12 emotions appropriate to elicit at events. Each is identified by the sound a person might make. He calls them "the flirty dozen" because he thinks it's important to flirt with your audience a little to make them feel different things:

1. Ah!
2. Huh?
3. Ah-ha!
4. Ha ha!
5. Uh . . .
6. Unh-un.
7. OH!
8. Yah!
9. Awww.
10. Hmmm!
11. Aaaa! (Think, angelic light)
12. Ahhh . . .

At first sight, the list looks a bit like captions from cartoons—but when Barry explains them, his system makes intuitive sense. We recognize the sounds and the moments they refer to, and we've probably made those sounds and had those experiences ourselves.

The first emotion is "Ah!"—the sound you hear when you surprise your audience, when you startle them to get their attention.

"Huh?" is what you hear when you create a little mystery. "When you create some confusion," Barry explains, "the brains in the audience start asking, 'What's happening here? I want to understand what's happening here.' The audience starts paying attention even more. Then you could pay that off."

Meanwhile, "Ah-ha!" indicates that you have paid off one of the mysteries you created. It's a cry of revelation that happens when endorphins are released inside of you when you've just discovered something, Barry explains.

He takes us through the others, like "Ha ha!" Everyone knows humor helps speakers. Why? Because it also creates dopamine in the system, and it makes people feel good. (And it usually is very connected to an "Ah-ha!" because there's often tension and release in a joke.)

"Uh …" is an interesting emotion, Barry adds. "It indicates worry. It asks, 'What's about to happen here?' Circuses have made a living on "Uh …!" with acrobats and with all the lion tamers and things like that," he explains. "It's a great emotion to stir up in your audience."

"Unh-un," meanwhile, is a sign of anger. Getting your audience angry can be really powerful and positive, especially if you're talking about an issue of social consciousness or social good, he notes. But it is effective for business issues, too. Let's say your stock price has plummeted—you might want to get your audience angry, so they'll be riled up to do something.

"OH!" is the shocked sound you might make in conscious or unconscious sympathy while watching someone get hurt, seeing someone taking a hit in a sports contest, or hearing a story where someone had a very difficult time. This moment stirs up shock, but then empathy.

As for "Yah!"—"The sports industry has made billions of dollars on 'Yah!' because it's that exhilarating moment where something successful has happened," says Barry.

"Awww"—"This is the voluntary or involuntary expression you hear when you have touched someone's heart," he continues. "It's another emotion that you can use in your cocktail mix."

"Hmmm!" indicates arousal. This isn't just sexual arousal; it's appealing to the senses. "It could be food. It could be the promise of a treasure or a reward," says Barry.

"Aaaa!" breaks the pattern a little bit. It's less a sound a participant might make than it is the sound that a participant might hear in their mind, heralding an inspiration. If possible, inspire your audience.

And "Ahhh …" is the sound that you hope to hear at the end of an event. "You want your audience to have had a sense of satisfaction," he says.

The art of collaborative events is weaving all these emotional registers together, Barry explains. "As event professionals, we need to become master mixologists, knowledgeable and artful in how we mix these chemicals up in our audience. All of the emotions matter; it's important not just to do the same chemical all the time. It's important to mix them up. That's the art of events."

Including all the emotions is a start. But Barry has some tips on how to intensify the emotional moments you create as well. First, he reminds us to appeal to all the different senses. "When you do that, it activates different parts of your brain—so more of these neuronal connections and synaptic connections can take place, and there's more likelihood that they're going to be remembered," he says. "When someone listens to someone on stage, the language comprehension and language processing parts of the brain are activated, but only those two parts. However, when you tell a compelling story that stirs emotions, more different parts of the brain light up."

Barry doesn't regard his emotion-focused approach as an innovation that's all his own. As proof of that, he says to look no further than founding father and collaboration artist Benjamin Franklin, who said, "Tell me, and I forget. Teach me, and I will remember. Involve me, and I will learn."

WHAT WE HEARD AND LEARNED

- Always remember: "People will never forget how you made them feel"
- In any experience, create a progression of moods and feelings
- Use "the flirty dozen" to create an experience that moves emotionally
- Intensify those emotions by appealing to all senses

BRIAN SOLIS
GLOBAL INNOVATION EVANGELIST COMBINES DIGITAL AND REAL-WORLD EXPERIENCES TO REACH MORE PEOPLE

We have to design for feeling, for emotional connectivity. Empathy and digital empathy are how we can connect the dots between a larger, richer set of individuals.

BRIAN SOLIS, COLLABORATION ARTIST

"I APPROACH things not just as an experience designer, but also as an introvert. And the idea of connecting and collaborating isn't intuitive," Brian Solis begins. "In fact, it's frightening—and I don't like it. The only reason I do it is it's a mechanism to get certain ideas shared and acted on at a broader level."

Ironically, despite all this hesitancy about collaboration, Brian is radically changing the state of the art of collaboration—both through his former role as Salesforce's global innovation evangelist, and his current career as a digital futurist and analyst, author, and international keynote speaker. Before joining Salesforce, Brian established himself as a thought leader and futurist. Now, he's gone, "from thinking, writing, and studying innovation to being able to practice it at scale," he says.

Brian's not kidding about being an introvert. "Connecting with other people has been a forced behavior my whole career. Never has it grown on me. If I slip, I have to catch myself by saying, 'If you don't go to this, you're not going to be part of this conversation.' It's a constant emotional battle that doesn't go away."

While he may not be personally inclined toward collaborative experiences, Brian makes himself participate. He sees collaboration as an element of wellness that's essential to having a balanced life, and this drives him to think about how to make things more inclusive. He wants to understand and include "the voices that don't always come to the table." Everyone deserves opportunities to collaborate," Brian says, but that collaboration has to be exercised, and the more you do it, the better you get at it.

"Inclusive collaboration models benefit from greater diversity," he adds. "They make an organization stronger. Collaborative organizations will be more flexible, responsive, and valuable than autocratic ones."

Brian sees great hope in how evolving uses of technology can involve more people and improve how we work together. "You can connect the extroverts and the introverts and those in between through online and real-world collaboration in ways that are intuitive and productive. Most of these things that we traditionally have done were designed for extroverts, or at least introvert/extroverts. But now, digital and COVID have accelerated what I call 'digital introversion,' where you can be more in control of the stuff behind the screens. It's self-empowerment for connecting more and doing more."

He sees the emerging challenge as how to reimagine what the experience is supposed to be, taking advantage of the platform itself so you're not adapting the physical world to the virtual world. "You're creating an entirely new experience that enhances what it is that you do in the real world. It's a different mindset." Putting this thought into context, he says, "Especially in the trade show and convention worlds, many people are just taking what they do in the real world and putting it in a virtual space. That just doesn't work. You need to think about experiences from the perspective of game design. How can you create more immersion and personalization?"

Brian regards empathy as one of the most important tools he has. He speaks about taking into consideration the feelings of someone else, and keeping in mind that not all ideas can be extracted from one individual the same exact way. He extends the concept of empathy to what he calls "Digital Empathy."

"I call digital empathy a love language," he says. "Look at millennials and centennials, or Gen Y and Gen Z. They are digital-first, or digital-native, communities. The better you integrate technology into a real-world setting, the better it is for them. You're essentially designing for a native platform with the electricity of both digital and physical engagement. You're not using digital to be digital. You use digital as a means of engaging both brain and the biology. You bring the best of physicality and digital together so that everybody's operating optimally."

Brian is frank about the challenges involved in getting people to do things they aren't initially inclined to do. "As an experience designer, it's your job to design for a specific experience and outcomes. But you can't assume that these are the outcomes people want to have. You have to work to align people around some shared objectives, outcomes that people can work towards. You need to bring people together around a purpose, a series of missions."

He illustrates this idea with a story about Muhammad Ali. "Ali said, 'I don't like working out, but I do visualize what being a champion looks and feels like.' Collaborating is a form of exercise, but you're doing it in a way that visualizes what the shared desired outcome is for everyone."

Ultimately, the best way to get a sense of the power and sophistication of Brian's approach is to listen to him describe it in use. "We were working on an experiment around networking. The question was, 'How do you get people to network when not everybody is a networker?' The premise was that you want to foster the type of engagement that takes advantage of why people are there: There's usually a shared set of interests.

"The solution involved designing this really cool quiz to get everyone to participate," he continues. "People got the quiz before the event. Whether you were extroverted or introverted, you felt it was in your safe space, so you answered these questions. They were designed psychologically to bring out what was going to set the stage for the right types of networking. We built-in a confirmation stage where people who had taken the quiz got a report before they came so they could verify what they would like and the things that they said they were interested in."

The quiz allowed the team to skip things like icebreakers, which, Brian says, "different people react differently to. It fed a custom database where we used soft-level AI to match people with shared interests and complementary modalities.

"Then we created a geolocation button that we put into the event badges so we could connect people on visual maps or through sound as they got closer to people that were interested in the same things. As you got closer to people, it would either beep in a certain way or you would see visually that you were next to someone you had a shared interest with."

Brian describes it as "strategic serendipity." "It stripped out the awkwardness of 'What do you do?' or 'Who are you?' And it prompted connection between people who were already likeminded. It broke down the barriers."

In closing, Brian returns to the importance of designing for emotion and empathy. "There are only two kinds of experiences that people remember: the ones that suck and the ones that are amazing," he says. "Everything in between is just transactional. Too often, collaboration has been thought of as work that's largely absent of emotionality. We have to design for feeling, for emotional connectivity. That's where empathy is going to become a real big deal. Empathy and digital empathy are how we can connect the dots between a larger, richer set of individuals."

WHAT WE HEARD AND LEARNED

- The moment is right for redefining events and collaboration … this is its "iPhone moment"
- Realize that you and those on your team aren't reflective of the audience or the total prospective audience
- Have empathy for all potential participants

- Practice digital empathy, especially if you are not Gen Y, Gen Z, or Gen A
- Align people around shared interests
- Design against the best, most innovative experiences outside of your industry

CAITLIN WALKER

PIONEER OF USING CLEAN QUESTIONS MOVEMENT FOR MORE EFFECTIVE COLLABORATIONS

"A good metaphor stays in our system."

CAITLIN WALKER, COLLABORATION ARTIST

CAITLIN WALKER HAS a questioning approach that can get even the most guarded, resistant individuals to open up and get curious about themselves and others. Although she originally developed it with aggressive teenagers outside of the school systems, she has refined her proven methodology to use it in almost any scenario imaginable. Developing collective trust in international corporations, helping healthcare givers support their patients during childbirth, forging bridges across charities with clashing ideologies—even repairing long-standing hurt and damaging patterns in her own extended family.

The best news is that her methodology is essentially shareware, and she's eager to have you adapt it and use it for your own purposes. That's appropriate, because Caitlin's work has, at its core, the clean language of David Grove, a New Zealand psychotherapist who noticed that even the supposedly neutral, person-centered psychologists let their own agendas creep into questions they asked. In response, he came up with the idea of "clean questions"—questions free of the assumptions and bias of the questioner that might dissuade or inhibit an individual from revealing their inner truth. The clean questions lead the respondent to uncover the way their system and thinking is organized and their invisible architecture, and in response, they supply metaphors that often help them reveal things they have trouble articulating otherwise.

In essence, clean questions ask about:

Location

Attributes

Sequence forward

Sequence back

Metaphor

Caitlin believes that metaphors can be a potent tool for both self-understanding and for indicating where gaps need to be bridged. "They're sticky, they're natural," she says. "We talk in metaphors all the time. They make sense to us. There's something about the cohesion of a metaphor that protects you from judgment. A good metaphor stays in our system."

She draws the practice, and importance of metaphor in straightforward communication, with a simple example. "If you tell me that when you are working at your best, you are like a post office sorter; you have a box for everything, you work very fast and fill predetermined boxes—and I tell you when I'm working at my best, I'm like a fisherman relaxing in the sun and just waiting for the right moment to get the right pike—we can look at those two metaphors and know we're going to have to do a little bit of mediation so that we understand where each of us is coming from. We are not necessarily natural fits for one another."

To get people to open up, the way the questions are asked is strictly non-judgmental. That way, the answerer doesn't feel they need to conform to the questioner's tacit assumptions. This liberates tremendous personal energy and can lead to deep, personal revelations.

The way in which the questioner reacts to the responses is carefully controlled. "In a 'normal' conversation," Caitlin explains, "what you say has to stretch between two people. When there's a power imbalance, the person with less power has to fit the framework of the person with more power. Everything is a little bit warped. In this model, you take what's said and you accept it and extend it, with minimal deleting, distorting, or generalizing. That way the thing has its own voice."

A lot of Caitlin's work has focused on how to teach people to use these questions and on how they can be used to facilitate group collaboration. Caitlin is committed to knowledge-transfer so that groups can learn to progress without her facilitation. She sees this as essential to our transition from a command-and control model to becoming a mediated society—a transition for which we need new skills. "I've looked at the question of, 'How can a system of diverse individuals get curious about how we do things differently, and from that become immensely more intelligent?' I call the overall methodology Systemic Modeling. Done right, it generates a self-modeling, self-organizing system. Individuals within a self-modeling group build models of what is happening and these also create space for creativity and spontaneous learning."

Caitlin's methods are simple enough to use in primary schools with children as young as seven years. A teacher may ask, "When you're learning really well, you are like what?" "One kid might say, 'I'm like a magpie; I fly around quickly collecting everything, bring it back to my nest, then throw out all the bits I don't need. And another might say, 'I'm a slow snail; it takes me a long time to learn things but I always remember them afterwards cause there's a shining trail.' Once armed with these explanatory images and the related self-knowledge, the students are told, 'Get yourself into groups of six. Go with somebody who doesn't learn like you. Find out some different things you can do because of your different styles.' The snail and the magpie can appreciate one another's learning styles and easily see that they are likely to go about learning in different ways," she explains.

"These groups then explore the question, 'If this classroom was to be just the way we'd like it to be, so each of us could learn at our best, we'd like our classroom to be like what?'" she continues. "And then from here children can work out, 'What do we need to do and to put in place so that we have that classroom?' From a very young age, they learn to advocate for their needs, and also to advocate for the group's needs."

Caitlin finds that teenagers are also very good at picking up these skills, "Because they're quite tribal," she says. "It's a great time to teach them how to understand one another and build a sense of how they 'do things around here.' They love being able to understand communication and see through other people's drama with better ideas for working stuff out."

Core to teaching a group to be able to do this without her expert help is teaching the group to code or categorize their contributions to the group and their reactions to one another. For example, is someone speaking about a problem or an outcome? Are they talking about an example, or are they giving you a metaphor? Are they speaking in evidence, what you can see/hear, or in inference, what they are making up about what they have seen and heard.

These simple codes help members of the group notice what is happening around them, and inside them, without reacting to it. The codes give them time to respond more mindfully. "If someone in the group says 'I'm feeling stuck, the outcome of this project isn't clear enough,' the self-modeling group will notice they are speaking about a problem, they are giving the metaphor of being stuck and while they say the project outcome isn't clear enough, this is an inference, and the listeners don't know what would make the outcome clearer. The self-modeling group might ask: What would you like to have happen? To shift from a problem to an outcome. Or they might ask 'When you're stuck, you're stuck like what?' to get the problem into a metaphor and better understand it. Or they could ask 'What would you like to see or hear to make the outcome clearer?'"

Systemic Modeling supports the group to collaborate by helping them move agilely between problems to outcomes, misunderstanding to understanding, issues to actions, and then supporting them to reflect on whether the actions are getting them what they want and need to be at their best together.

The Clean Questions guide your inquiry. They get you to sequence and metaphor. The process can be used very effectively in start-ups and creating new shared ideas but it can also be used to address issues in teams that are used to traditional ways of doing things.

Caitlin provides an example of how the methodology could help address a governmental budget challenge. "We worked with a governmental department that had to take five million pounds off its budget. Under their umbrella they had lots of division heads who would normally be inclined to be territorial and perhaps even oppositional, embattled, and competitive about who got what budget.

"In a case like this, one first thing I can do is an exercise to make sure they all understand how to listen to what's being said, code it, and ask an inquiring 'clean' question," she notes. "I make this exercise non-work-related at all. I might say, 'Let's notice what we think and do one-tenth of a second after someone speaks. I'll give you an instruction, you answer it, and we will compare our answers. 'See an elephant.' I'll pause and then ask them, 'What kind of elephant is it? Where is it?' As they realize they are all different, I can then go to the next level and get them to see that when someone says 'It's a circus elephant, I'm sitting on it to have my photo taken.'"

Caitlin asks the rest of the group to notice what is happening in-the-moment."What are you inferring about that circus elephant?' One person says, 'I think the elephant is sad and it makes me feel judgmental.' Another says, 'I imagine it is brightly colored and the children are having fun.' The group learns to accept that we are always making things up all of the time; that this is natural and human. From here it is easier to work with a group to uncover unconscious bias and get people to notice and then reduce their assumptions."

After a training exercise like See an Elephant, Caitlin can take any theme the group needs to explore, such as feedback. She might get the group to explore times when they received feedback and it was really useful. The group will get models for good feedback, and then Caitlin can shift the group's attention to, "What was it about that feedback that made it so useful?"—and from here, it is a short step for the group to consider, "What feedback processes can we adopt in this team so that more of us are getting and giving useful feedback more of the time?"

Caitlin highlights how cross-bordered the methodology is by

describing her work for a corporation. "I worked with their senior managers because they wanted to develop collective trust as it had broken down," she says. "I asked them to develop metaphor models for working at their best, making decisions, organizing time, and working together as a team. The themes are different but the methodology is the same. Through this process, the group noticed patterns of misunderstanding that were coming from their different invisible architecture—how they organized time, etc. From here, they understood where each of them were likely to be coming from, and like the slow snail and the quick magpie, they were able to make small adaptations to work more effectively together.

"This situation was different from, say, my work with charities addressing female genital circumcision—but the underlying methodology was the same. Here I asked the charity leaders, 'If there was no longer a need for your charity to exist in the world, what would you be seeing or hearing?'—getting them to describe their long term outcome in evidence. Then I asked them, 'When your charity is working at its best, it's like what? What's working well, what isn't working so well, what could you do with some help on?' All the time, teaching the groups to notice their contributions and turn problems into inquiries then outcomes and into shared actions. This keeps them away from sticking points such as whether they call it cutting or mutilation and whether they speak for victims or societies. While these are important points they were not supporting the diverse groups to get their shared outcomes."

As well as in work and education, Caitlin has been able to use her knowledge and skills to get past differences at an extended family gathering. "We had an anti-vaxxer and a pro-vaxxer at a dinner a couple of weeks ago. I had asked myself, 'What's the question I can ask this table so that we can actually talk about important things, instead of arguing about the same embedded point?' The trick in systemic modeling is to go where the problem isn't. I said, 'What's your idea of a great way to approach whole community health?' That was something that they could all talk about."

With each piece of work, Caitlin says she is always thinking about how this group can use this work when she isn't there. This emphasis on creating sustainability comes from working with teenagers where Caitlin wanted them to be able to use these skills with peers, schools, their first bosses, etc., not just in a training room. She has brought these values into the workplace, and insists that any intervention has enough time and enough internal champions to keep going once she's gone.

Caitlin still finds her work challenging. "Working at this level of facilitation requires a level of adult development that a lot of us don't have—or even if we've got it in some areas of our life, we don't have it in all areas of our life," she points out. "I might do really well 90% of the time when I'm working, but I still have days I assume spite and evil, say, if a driver tailgates me or a participant in the workspace keeps taking a phone call when someone is speaking. I lean into my colleagues to share my bias or my contempt and to regain my sense of inquiry."

Systemic Modeling requires you to agree to the constructivist paradigm that one stimulus can produce lots of responses, and that reality is constructed according to our experiences. "That goes against all kinds of fundamentalism," she continues. "It goes against all kinds of religious teaching, and it goes against all kinds of teaching that we receive in schools that there's a right answer. We are systematically taught that there's right and wrong and there's good and bad. And to maintain a state of ambiguity and still be able to collaborate is not something that we're taught.

"That's what these facilitation tools do," Caitlin explains. "They democratize—and, therefore, they promote mediation rather than power games."

WHAT WE HEARD AND LEARNED

- Use a small set of unbiased questions to inquire into individual experience
- Separate what you're seeing and hearing from what you're making up
- Code what you are hearing into problems, outcomes, actions, metaphor, etc.

- Develop metaphors to humanize and make experiences translatable and relatable
- Remember that making assumptions is normal, and do all of this with a sense of fun and accepting failure
- Model out metaphor landscapes to understand how the whole system work for individuals and for the group

GOING FORWARD: COLLABORATION IS CONTAGIOUS

Again and again in our lives, we've found that when we experience positive collaboration in one area, we become more likely to collaborate in other ways. For us, collaboration has been infectious and inspiring.

We'd like to leave you with a look back at the past, and at one last collaboration artist: Benjamin Franklin. Franklin left a lot of very clear writing about his approach to collaboration, and established a legacy of collaboration with the Junto Club. Franklin and his friends set down the rules for the original Junto Club—which was also called the Leather Apron Club—in 1727.

Over the course of 38 collaborative years, this group came up with proposals that led to many of the pillars of our modern society, including lending libraries, a fire response company, a state university, a state hospital, and more. To this day, there are small Junto Clubs modeled on the original one. They often contribute to the welfare and wellness of their communities in amazing ways.

Of course, the Junto Club is just one format for coming together to make change—and the art of collaboration is rapidly evolving. Technology is opening up new possibilities. Science is providing new insights. And in this book, you've had the opportunity to get to know a sampling of the collaboration artists at the forefront of this evolution.

People who are always ready to turn to the person beside them and say, *"Let's ... "*

People like you.

Where will we go next? What will we do, make, and achieve?

Let's go find out ... together.

ABOUT THE AUTHORS

David Adler is a business and social entrepreneur who founded the event media company BizBash and the society magazine *Washington Dossier*. He has also been a senior executive for major media companies Macmillan Inc. and PRIMEDIA. He is a sought-after speaker and facilitator, with particular expertise in hosting Jeffersonian dinners.

James Cornehlsen's career includes being CEO of a Hispanic media company and being a partner at a global executive search firm. For the last 20 years, he has worked with leadership teams to foster open, honest communications as a base for collaboration and higher productivity. He has also been a board advisor. Jim is a frequent speaker on the need to pivot 21st-century leadership, and facilitates discussion among cross-functional, cultural, and cross-industry groups.

Andrew Frothingham, a member of the Authors Guild, has built a career around helping people determine what to say in all sorts of circumstances. Through working at countless events, he developed a zeal for audience advocacy. He has written numerous books, mainly light reference resources as well as humor.

OUR COLLABORATORS

1. Alexander, Jason — Emmy and Tony winner, actor, comedian, film director, and theater director. IMDB, Twitter (@IJasonAlexander), Instagram (@jalexander1959)
2. Attias, Richard — Renowned producer and executive chairman at Richard Attias & Associates. LinkedIn (richard-attias-09139915a)
3. Axelrod, Felice — Corporate philanthropy executive and special projects consultant to Bloomberg Philanthropies and Bloomberg LP. LinkedIn (felice-axelrod)
4. Banks, Bernie — Associate dean for leadership development and inclusion at Northwestern University's Kellogg School of Management. LinkedIn (bernard-bernie-banks-ph-d-4458003)
5. Belzberg, Lisa — Founder of PENCIL and adjunct professor of education. LinkedIn (lisa-belzberg-08876bb8), Twitter (@LisaBelzberg)
6. Boeke, Erica — Founder & CEO of Liberty & Company and XP Land, author, and speaker. LinkedIn (erica-boeke), Twitter (@ejboeke)
7. Boone, Mary — Owner of Boone Associates. maryboone.com LinkedIn (maryboone), Twitter (@maryboone)
8. Brown, Sarah — Activist, podcast host, chair at Theirworld, and executive chair at the Global Business Coalition for Education. Wife of former British Prime Minister Gordon Brown. LinkedIn (sarah-brown-530729a2), Twitter (@SarahBrownUK), Instagram (@sarahbrownuk)
9. Bulencea, Paul — Co-founder of the College of Extraordinary Experiences, author, and speaker. LinkedIn (paulbulencea), Twitter (@PaulBulencea)
10. Buonocore-Guthrie, Taylor — Founder, facilitator, speaker, leader of Born Free Africa, and co-creator of convers(ate). taylorbuonocoreguthrie.com, LinkedIn (taylorbuonocore), Twitter (@taylorbuonocore)
11. Cecchetto, Cheryl — Hollywood event producer, founder and CEO of Sequoia Productions. LinkedIn (cheryl-cecchetto-a000495)
12. Cirino, Michael — Experience creator, founder of House of Attention, founder of A Razor, A Shiny Knife. LinkedIn (mjcirino)
13. Clemons, Steve — Founding editor at large at Semafor and host of "The Bottom Line." LinkedIn (steve-clemons-1381801), Twitter (@SCClemons), Instagram (@scclemons)
14. Coopersmith, Esther — UNESCO Goodwill Ambassador. Linkedin (connie-coopersmith-2a287013)
15. Cowie, Colin — CEO of Thrive Hospitality and chairman & CEO of Colin Cowie Lifestyle. colincowie.com, LinkedIn (colincowie), Twitter (@colincowie), Instagram (@colincowie)
16. Drury, Chris — President, founder, and CCO of Drury Design. LinkedIn (cdrury), Twitter (@chrisdrurydesgn)
17. Drury, Jill Taub — Founder and CEO of Drury Design. LinkedIn (jilltaubdrury)
18. Endean, Tahira — Event designer, facilitator, speaker, connector, and author.

LinkedIn (tahira-endean-citp-cmp-ced-918a868), Twitter (@TahiraCreates), Instagram (@tahiracreates)

19. Fraser, Edie — CEO of Women Business Collaborative. LinkedIn (edie-fraser-38b4466), Twitter (@EdieWBC)

20. Friedland, Marc — creative director of Marc Friedland Couture Communications. LinkedIn (marc-friedland), Twitter (@Marc_Friedland), Instagram (@marcfriedland-couture)

21. Gaudini, Gianna - Head of events at Airtable, strategic corporate event leader, story-teller, and author. giannagaudini.com, LinkedIn (giannagaudini), Twitter (@Gaudini-Gianna), Instagram (@giannagaudini)

22. Goldblatt, Joe — Emeritus professor, author, speaker, consultant, and advocate for planned Events. jogoldblatt.scot, LinkedIn (professor-joe-goldblatt-1b82b53), Twitter (@drjgoldblatt), Instagram (@joejeffgoldblatt)

23. Gottlieb, Steve — Serial entrepreneur, founder & CEO at Shindig, and founder at TVT Records. LinkedIn (steve-m-gottlieb), Twitter (@SteveMGottleib)

24. Hallahan, Natalie Jones — Executive vice president at Meridian International Center. LinkedIn (nataliejonesdc)

25. Herman, Joanna Stone — Partner at Oaklins DeSilva+Phillip, executive, entrepreneur, investor, and advisor. LinkedIn (joannastone), Twitter (@joannaherman)

26. Husseini, Mo — Chief design officer at Gen City Labs. mohusseini.com, LinkedIn (mohusseini), Twitter (@mo_husseini), Instagram (@mohu)

27. Isaacs, David — President of Clearing Communications, co-originator of the World Café. theworldcafe.com

28. Janssen, Ruud — Strategic advisor, co-creator of EventCanvas, and author. LinkedIn (ruudjanssen), Twitter (@RuudWJanssen)

29. Johnson, Mark — Grammy Award-winning producer and engineer, award-winning film director, co-creator of Playing for Change. LinkedIn (mark-johnson-40429b70)

30. Kemper, Coach Kathy — Tennis coach, founder and CEO of Institute for Education, writer, connector, and convener. LinkedIn (coach-kathy-kemper-45930239), Twitter (@taecvd), Instagram (@coachkemps)

31. Khine, Mollie — Director of coaching at Flatiron School, business leader, facilitator, and co-creator of convers(ate). LinkedIn (molliekhine), Twitter (@mollierae_k)

32. Kotkin, Lauren — Senior director of education for Exponent Philanthropy, artist. LinkedIn (lauren-kotkin-276435b9)

33. Lacanienta, Andrew — Senior strategist, George P. Johnson Experience Marketing. LinkedIn (andrew-lac), Twitter (@Drew_Lac)

34. Ma, Amanda — Founder and chief experience officer at Innovate Marketing Group. amandaslavin.com, LinkedIn (amandamaimg), Twitter (@AmandaMa89)

35. Marsalis, Wynton — Musician, composer, educator, leading advocate of American culture, and managing and artistic director of Jazz at Lincoln Center. wynton-marsalis.org, Twitter (@wyntonmarsalis), Instagram (@wyntonmarsalis)

36. Marshall, Capricia — President and CEO of Global Engagement Strategies and Ambassador in Residence at the Atlantic Council, former Chief of Protocol and White House Social Secretary. LinkedIn (capricia-penavic-marshall-99b7381ab), Twitter (@AmbassadorCPM), Instagram (@capriciapenavicmarshall)

37. McBride, Anita — Executive in residence, Center for Congressional and Presidential

Studies at American University. LinkedIn (anita-b-mcbride-6154114a), Twitter (@AnitaBMcBride)

38. McGuirk, Leslie — Astrologer, writer, and product designer. lesliemcguirk.com, LinkedIn (leslie-mcguirk-750b728), Twitter (@luckystarleslie), Instagram (@lesliemcguirk)

39. Miller, J.B. — President & CEO at Empire Entertainment. LinkedIn (j-b-miller-b47b441), IMDB

40. Moulton, Seth — Marine veteran and Congressman. sethmoulton.com, LinkedIn (seth-moulton-for-america), Twitter (@sethmoulton), Instagram (@repmoulton)

41. Mufraggi, Xavier— CEO of YPO Global. LinkedIn (xaviermufraggi), Twitter (@xaviermufraggi)

42. Nierenberg, Roger — Symphony conductor and creator of The Music Paradigm. LinkedIn (rogernierenberg), Twitter (@rogernierenberg)

43. Núñez, Francisco J. — Founder and artistic director at Young People's Chorus of New York City. franciscojnunez.com, LinkedIn (francisco-nunez-b27a9931), Twitter (@Fjnunez), Instagram (@franciscojnunez)

44. Palmer, Charlie — Chef, CEO of Charlie Palmer Collective, and author. LinkedIn (charlierpalmer1), Twitter (@CharliePalmer), Instagram (@chefcharliepalmer)

45. Parr, Ben — Journalist-turned-founder, entrepreneur, author, and AI navigator. benparr.com, LinkedIn (benparr), Twitter (@benparr), Instagram (@benparr)

46. Pearson, Arthur — President & CEO at Thompson Island Outward Bound, former interim executive director of Outward Bound USA, founding director of the Outward Bound Professional Learning Lab. LinkedIn (arthurnpearson)

47. Pernell, Dr. Wayne — Exponential success coach, speaker, writer, and president at DynamicLeader. waynepernell.com, LinkedIn (waynepernell), Twitter (@WaynePernell), Instagram (@dr_wayne_pernell)

48. Peterson, Holly — Author and journalist. hollypeterson.com, Twitter (@HollyPetersonNY), Instagram (@hollypetersonny)

49. Raasted, Claus — Director of the College of Extraordinary Experiences and speaker. clausraasted.com, LinkedIn (clausraasted)

50. Rafanelli, Bryan — Founder and chief creative officer of Rafanelli Events, author. LinkedIn (bryan-rafanelli-433a843), Twitter (@bryanrafanelli), Instagram (@bryanrafanelli)

51. Rinehart, Barry Ross — Professional memory maker, global creative director, and storytelling and executive presence trainer. LinkedIn (barry-ross-rinehart-3408122), Twitter (@barryrinehart)

52. Safi, Sandy — Entrepreneur, international events producer, and co-founder of Diner en Blanc International. LinkedIn (sandy-safi-8050785), Twitter (@SandySafi), Instagram (@sandysafi_deb)

53. Sakellariadis, Nick — Principal owner of the Dayton Dragons.

54. Scalpello, Angela — Strategy activator, communications consultant, and owner of The Scalpello Group. angelascalpello.com, LinkedIn (angela-scalpello), Twitter (@HRchitect)

55. Sedky, Hervé — President, CEO, and director at Emerald (EEX). LinkedIn (hervesedky)

56. Segar, Adrian — Founder of Conferences That Work, conference designer and facilita-

tor, and author. LinkedIn (adriansegar), Twitter (@ASegar)

57. Shewey, Sarah — Founder & CEO at Happily. sarahshewey.com, LinkedIn (sarahshewey), Twitter (@pinkcloud)

58. Slavin, Amanda — Co-founder and CEO of CatalystCreativ and author. LinkedIn (amslavin), Twitter (@AJSlavin), Instagram (@ajslavin)

59. Solis, Brian — Digital futurist, world-renowned digital analyst, author of eight bestselling books, and international keynote speaker. briansolis.com, LinkedIn (briansolis), Twitter (@briansolis), Instagram (@briansolis)

60. Stark, David — New York-based event producer, designer, author, and founder and chief creative officer of David Stark Design and Production. LinkedIn (david-stark-a507bab), Twitter (@davidstarkinc), Instagram (@david_stark_design)

61. Steffert, Jonathan — Storyteller and cultural attaché for Public Diplomacy and Public Affairs at New Zealand's Ministry of Foreign Affairs & Trade. LinkedIn (jonathansteffert), Twitter (@KowhaiCreative)

62. Sullivan, Andrea — Organizational psychologist, speaker, trainer, consultant, coach, and adjunct faculty at Temple University. Twitter (@BrainStrength)

63. Szeky, Deborah — American activist, philanthropist, writer, founder of health spa's Rancho La Puerta and The Golden Door. rancholapuerta.com

64. Walker, Caitlin — Co-founder of Training Attention. LinkedIn (caitlin-walker-phd-6a11a8b), Twitter (@caitlinwalkerTA)

65. Woo, John — Senior vice president of creative and strategy at Spiro. LinkedIn (johnwoo-8010bb2), Twitter (@yjohnwoo)

66. Ziskan, Ian — President of EXec EXcel Group, HR leader, entrepreneur, teacher, speaker, and author. LinkedIn (ian-ziskin-bb1504), Twitter (@IanZiskin)